The Power of Professional Learning Networks

Traversing the present; transforming the future

Graham Handscomb
and Chris Brown

First published 2022

by John Catt Educational Ltd,
15 Riduna Park, Station Road,
Melton, Woodbridge IP12 1QT

Tel: +44 (0) 1394 389850
Fax: +44 (0) 1394 386893
Email: enquiries@johncatt.com
Website: www.johncatt.com

ISBN: 978 1 915261 27 4

Set and designed by John Catt Educational Limited

Contents

Acknowledgements   7

About the contributors   9

Networks make a difference   17
Graham Handscomb and Chris Brown

Part one: Insights, structures and systems   25

The role of networks in supporting school improvement   27
David Hopkins

Fostering collaboration across schools around the world:
insights from TALIS   43
Pablo Fraser and Gabor Fulop

Change, adaptation and transformation: peer review and
collaborative improvement during the pandemic   59
Anne Cameron and Maggie Farrar

Networking small rural schools in the pandemic   75
Toby Greany and Andy Wolfe

A new paradigm for professional development and performance
management   91
John Baumber

Reframing teacher development in uncertain times: new spaces,
new collaborations, new purposes   111
Jane Jones

Big Education: collaboration for change 127
Liz Robinson, Ellie Lister, Joe Pardoe and Rosie Clayton

Disrupters, innovators, changemakers: the global WomenEd
network 151
Vivienne Porritt with Lisa Hannay and Liz Free

A digital asset: understanding your value and new possibilities in a
pandemic/post-pandemic world 169
Kate Bancroft

Dynamic, urban professional learning networks 179
David Woods

Part two: Flourishing practice **191**

Creative collaboration: professional learning in and through
the arts 193
Steven Berryman

Discovering professional identities: a networked theatre in
education approach to support early career teachers 203
Chris Bolton

Covid-19 driven emergence of an informal network to support
vulnerable students 219
Dana Braunberger and Sarah Hamilton

Scottish Island Schools Network: bringing the remote rural voice
to networked professional development 233
Suzie Dick and Stephanie Peat

Global networking for sustainable futures: collegiality and
intellectualism as network norms 249
Alexander Gardner-McTaggart and Paul Armstrong

Creating a virtual staffroom: dynamic and organic CPD
conversations with colleagues, at a distance 265
Haili Hughes

Grassroots professional learning networks 277
Richard Holme

Teacher research groups: enhancing teacher professionalism during the
pandemic   289
Daniel Langley

Networking inside and out: using student voice to improve
professional practice   303
Marcella McCarthy

Professional learning in adult education: crucial roles and future
actions of networks and networking   315
Sandy Youmans, Lorraine Godden and Hanne Nielsen Hamlin

**Concluding reflection: What next for professional learning
networks?**   **325**

Collaborative caldrons   327
Graham Handscomb and Chris Brown

Index   331

Acknowledgements

We would like to thank our contributors for accepting the challenge and delivering their fantastic chapters. We have learned a lot and we know the readers of this book will too. What this compilation shows is that professional learning networks have the potential to radically improve how teachers learn, connect and professionalise, as well what is needed for professional learning networks to endure and flourish in the long term. Hopefully this understanding will now provide the catalyst for educators and system leaders to embrace and support professional learning networks to grow into an intrinsic part of the educational ecosystem. We look forward to seeing how this process unfolds.

About the contributors

Paul Armstrong is a senior lecturer in Education at the Manchester Institute of Education, University of Manchester. He has over 15 years of experience in educational research exploring contemporary forms of educational leadership and management, in particular the means by which schools and school networks are managed and resourced. His most recent publication is *School-to-school collaboration in England: A configurative review of the empirical evidence* with Chris Brown and Chris Chapman. He is also editor-in-chief of the journal *Management in Education*.

Dr Kate Bancroft is a senior lecturer at Carnegie School of Education and has been a course director for several postgraduate and undergraduate courses in education and the study of childhood. Kate is also an external examiner for the University of Newcastle and the University of Greenwich, examining both universities postgraduate provision in education-related subject areas. Kate's research focuses on the study of sex and gender; she is currently researching domestic abuse in England and its impact on adult female victims and their children. Kate led two online voluntary networking events during the peak of the pandemic in summer 2019, which had over 300 attendees at both.

John Baumber has enjoyed over 35 years of school leadership, including an executive head position in three Bolton high schools before moving to lead schools in Sweden and the US. John is, at present, director of the International Centre for Educational Leadership and School Improvement at the University of Bolton. He retains his responsibility for supporting the network of 75 Kunskapsskolan-inspired schools in the UK linked to the global network of schools sharing a goal-driven, personalised pedagogy that ensures students take agency and ownership of their learning.

Dr Steven Berryman is Director of Arts, Culture and Community for Odyssey Trust for Education, UK. He is also a visiting research fellow at King's College London. His research and teaching focuses on arts and cultural education, in and beyond school settings, and the professional development of teachers and leaders.

Dr Chris Bolton is a senior lecturer in drama education at Birmingham City University and is the Route Leader for PGCE Secondary Drama in Initial Teacher Education. He is also the Research Coordinator for the Secondary and Post-Compulsory Adult Education department. Before this role, he worked in secondary schools in Birmingham as a drama Advanced Skills Teacher. He has a keen interest in how drama can create spaces for meaningful dialogic learning by using artful approaches to pedagogy and the impact of collaborative networking to develop professional teacher identity/identities.

Dana Braunberger is a university instructor and co-leads research in a K-12 school. She brings over two decades of experience in K-12 schools as a teacher, school principal, and chief performance officer. Her research interests include professional learning networks, research practice partnerships, professional learning, innovation, learning differences, and self-regulation.

Anne Cameron is SPP Programme Lead for Education Development Trust's Schools Partnership Programme (SPP), providing operational leadership and driving end-to-end delivery and development. She works closely with a highly experienced team of associates to ensure the quality, impact, authenticity and sustainability of the programme and its positive contribution to the sector.

Rosie Clayton is Project Manager at Rethinking Assessment, UK, where she coordinates the movement, which is being incubated by Big Education. The movement brings together state and independent schools, universities, researchers, employers, policymakers and education experts who are seeking to make our assessment system more equitable and fit for purpose. Rosie started her career in education setting up Studio Schools and UTCs, and has recently worked on system scale projects for the RSA, Ashoka and the World Innovation Summit for Education.

Suzie Dick was the deputy headteacher at the only secondary school on the Isle of Arran, Scotland, and is now a lecturer in Education at Queen Margaret University, Edinburgh. She is the instigator of the Scottish Island Schools Network and current vice chair of International Professional Development Association Scotland with her key research interests including outdoor learning, rural education and practitioner enquiry.

Maggie Farrar was the director of Leadership Development and Research at the National College of School Leadership. She is an associate of Education Development Trust involved in the design and development of the Schools Partnership Peer Review Programme. She works internationally on the development of school-led, collaborative, self-improving systems.

Pablo Fraser is an Educational Policy Analyst working in the Teaching and Learning International Survey (TALIS) at the OECD Directorate for Education and Skills since 2018. He has been involved in comparative and international research concerning teacher professional development, teaching practices, and teacher wellbeing.

Liz Free is a Global Strategic Leader of WomenEd. Liz was the founding director of the British School in Netherlands Leadership Academy and is CEO and Director of International School, Rheintal. Liz is a global board member of TES and has chapters in *10% Braver: Inspiring Women to Lead Education and Being 10% Braver.*

Gabor Fulop has been working as a statistician and analyst at the Teaching and Learning International Survey (TALIS) of the OECD Directorate for Education and Skills since 2018. His area of expertise concerns large-scale database analysis and advanced data modelling.

Alexander Gardner-McTaggart works at Manchester Institute of Education, School of Environment, Education and Development, University of Manchester. He is Programme Director Educational Leadership in Practice, Convenor Comparative and International Educational Leadership Research Interest Group (British Educational Leadership and Administration Society), and visiting professor at

Franz Kepler University Linz, Austria. His research interests include educational leadership and global crises of climate, inequity and knowledge generation and international schools' leadership.

Lorraine Godden is an instructor at Carleton University where she teaches career development and employability skills courses. Her research is rooted in understanding how educators interpret policy and curriculum to make sense of career development and employability, work-integrated learning, adult education, and other educational multidisciplinary and public policies.

Professor Toby Greany is convener of the Centre for Research in Education Leadership and Management (CRELM) at the University of Nottingham. His research focuses on how policy and practice interact to shape educational opportunities and outcomes, in particular across local systems and through networks, and the role of leadership in these processes.

Sarah Hamilton is a doctoral student at the University of Calgary and a research lead at Calgary Academy, a K-12 independent school in Alberta. She brings over 17 years of experience working in K-12 education across Canada to her work. Sarah's research interests include mathematics education, self-regulation and executive functions, research partnerships, collective knowledge building and professional learning, including PLNs.

Lisa Hannay is a Global Strategic Leader of WomenEd and a senior leader in a high school in Calgary, Canada. Lisa is also a chapter author in *Being 10% Braver*.

Richard Holme is a lecturer in education at the University of Dundee, Scotland. He researches informal, teacher-initiated, grassroots professional development and learning. He is a qualified teacher with experience in primary, secondary and adult education sectors.

Professor Emeritus David Hopkins is chair of Educational Leadership at the University of Bolton. He completed his school improvement trilogy with the publication of *Exploding the Myths of School Reform*;

the previous books being *School Improvement for Real* and *Every School a Great School*. He was recently ranked as the 16th most influential educator in the world by the American-based Global Gurus organisation.

Haili Hughes was an English teacher and now works as Head of Education at IRIS Connect and as a senior lecturer on Sunderland University's PGCE English programme. Her research interests are mentoring, retaining experienced teachers and English teacher's professional development through subject knowledge and collaboration. She has published three books and has two forthcoming.

Jane Jones is Head of Modern Foreign Languages Teacher Education at Kings College London (KCL). She has published internationally on topics including assessment, language teaching, EAL, wellbeing, school leadership and teacher development. Jane supports teachers to develop as socially-aware teacher-researchers and critically reflective practitioners through diverse teacher learning opportunities

Daniel Langley is an assistant headteacher with responsibility for teaching and learning and professional development. He is an EdD candidate at UCL Institute of Education. His research has been published by the Chartered College of Teaching, the Foundation for Educational Development and in the Journal of Eton College.

Ellie Lister is Programme Lead at Big Education, UK, where she heads up Big Education's leadership development offer. She has a background in training and adult learning within education and is passionate about the need for a different type of leadership within schools – one that both challenges the status quo and creates psychologically safe environments to do so.

Dr Marcella McCarthy, author of *The Spider Strategy: Six Steps to Outstanding* and *Coaching and Mentoring,* has worked in schools ranging from special measures to outstanding, and is a former headteacher and university lecturer. Her current research interests include metacognition, staff wellbeing and empowering student voice.

Hanne Nielsen is a retired superintendent of education with the Simcoe County District School Board (SCDSB) in Ontario, Canada. Portfolio responsibilities included adult and continuing education, partnerships, and eLearning strategic development. Hanne's professional focus was on measuring the collective impact of programmes and services and meeting strategic priorities.

Joe Pardoe is Strategic Content Creator at Big Education, UK. Joe began his education journey by teaching in Japan and China before moving to Hull as a teacher with Teach First. He later moved to School21 to become head of humanities, head of project-based learning and later had a wider curriculum role. Joe now works for Big Education helping to spread the learning from our schools into the system.

Stephanie Peat is a Scottish primary teacher and Lead Specialist Of Professional Learning and Leadership at Education Scotland, supporting the professional learning and development of educators at a national level across the Scottish system. Stephanie currently leads the Teacher Leadership Programme, a developmental programme that supports teachers to explore what leadership means at classroom level and can look like in practice. Stephanie is also a doctoral student at the University of Strathclyde, her key research interest is teacher identity.

Vivienne Porritt is a leadership consultant supporting professional learning, impact evaluation, strategy, and women's leadership. She is vice president of the Chartered College of Teaching and a Global Strategic Leader of WomenEd, an organisation that empowers and connects women leaders. She is the co-editor of *10% Braver: Inspiring Women to Lead Education* and *Being 10% Braver*.

Liz Robinson is co-director and co-founder at Big Education, UK where she works with schools and leaders across the country to inspire change, design new approaches and grow an engaged network. A former headteacher and now system leader, Liz's passion is holistic approaches to education and leadership, as well as being a proud mum to Ella and Alys.

Andy Wolfe is the Executive Director of Education for the Church of England. This involves leading the national education work with around 4700 schools and overseeing the Church of England Foundation for Educational Leadership, which provides programmes and networks, including the Peer Support Network, which has grown to around 1500 schools.

Professor David Woods CBE has been a teacher and senior leader in schools, a teacher trainer in higher education and a local authority adviser in two LAs. He was Chief Education Adviser for the City of Birmingham before joining the Department for Education in England as Senior Education Adviser, working closely with ministers to develop educational policy and, subsequently, becoming head of the department's advisory service. He joined the London Challenge programme from the beginning as the lead adviser and then became the chief adviser for London schools and the London Challenge. He has the unique distinction of having been the Chief Education Adviser for England's two biggest cities, Birmingham and London. From 2011 to 2018, he chaired the London Leadership Strategy as an Education Trust. He has written and spoken extensively on educational leadership.

Dr Sandy Youmans is an adjunct professor at the Faculty of Education, Queen's University. She has co-led multiple CESBA funded studies of adult and continuing education in Ontario. Dr Youmans documented the work of the Eastern Regional Partnership for Adult Education during their implementation of the Adult Education Strategy (2016–2019).

Networks make a difference

Graham Handscomb and Chris Brown

The power of networking

Networking has long been an important and often crucial feature in education. This is because what can be learned by individuals is necessarily enabled or constrained by the networks within which we are immersed, with networks also determining with whom we will collaborate (Castells 2010). As they enable us to learn and engage, the more general aims of education networks typically include:

- **Facilitating a more willing distribution of professional knowledge** (Hargreaves 2010; 2012; Muijs 2015). In other words, networks can be used to foster knowledge sharing, collaboration and practice development. This can be especially useful in plugging 'structural holes' through access to expertise that is not available to individual teachers or in individual schools (Huxham and Vangen 2005; Muijs 2015).

- **The development of context-specific strategies for improvement** (Hargreaves 2010; 2012; Howland 2015). For instance, networks might have a focus on addressing challenging circumstances and/ or persistent issues of inequity and underperformance, i.e. ensuring all students, irrespective of background, gain the minimum skills necessary to function in today's society (Arkhipenka et al 2018; Armstrong et al 2021; Brown 2020; Muijs et al 2010).

- **Facilitating schools and others to share resources** more efficiently than they might previously have done, or to achieve economies of scale and reductions in risk from resource pooling (Azorín 2018; Ehren and Godfrey 2017; Gilbert 2017; Hargreaves 2010; 2012; Howland 2015).

- **Fostering of *esprit de corps*, wellbeing and mutuality.** One of the interesting features of recent crises like the pandemic, which have enforced separation, has been the drive to reconnect and develop new ways whereby teachers and schools can engage together. Networks, particularly using online technology, enable the creation of new spaces where teachers can connect and develop a common purpose and, indeed, a sense of belonging. Such fora can provide a new meeting 'place' not only for the exchange/sharing of knowledge but also to bolster a sense of identity, self-efficacy and worth (Trust et al 2016; Riley 2022).

- **Facilitating new ways of being a profession.** As the landscape of school organisation has changed, with the demise of third-tier local authority models of governance, schools and teachers have sought to carve out other means to connect as a profession (Matthews et al 2011; Wilkins 2015). Creating new, often online, networks have provided alternative means for the expression of professionalisation.

Traditionally, networks were facilitated through top-down initiatives, for instance, London Challenge, or those put in place by the Tower Hamlets Local Education Authority, as they sort to improve educational outcomes for the most disadvantaged (Ainscow 2014; Woods et al 2013). However, we are now witnessing an increasing emergence of bottom-up practice, self-directed by practitioners and schools. We can trace this shift to recent changes to educational structures, where there has been a dismantling of previous ways of working and the introduction of new approaches with an individualised focus. Although this is occurring in education systems worldwide (e.g. see Hargreaves and Shirley 2012), England, which has experienced a recent and sharp decline in the support role offered to schools from government, provides an exemplar case of such trends (Armstrong et al 2021; Greany 2017; Handscomb 2018). We only need to travel back 12 years in the past to the publication of 'The importance of teaching' white paper to encounter the coalition government's newly-discovered faith in inter-school collaborative networks. This was set very much within the context of portraying schools as needing to address the creative tension between the notions of autonomy, diversity and collaboration (Mourshed et al 2010; Handscomb 2013).

At the same time, it is recognised that the realisation of the kind of 'self-improvement' envisaged in 'The importance of teaching' typically emerges from establishing a 'culture of professional reflection, enquiry and learning within and across schools, [centred] on teaching and student learning' (Gilbert 2017:6). It is no surprise, therefore, that increasing numbers of school leaders and policymakers are now turning their attention to professional learning networks (PLNs) as a way of improving education in schools and across school systems (Armstrong et al 2021). The principle focus of any PLNs is on the core educational concerns of driving improvements to teaching, learning and student outcomes. As such, the aims of any given PLN can range from exploring and seeking to improve specific teaching practices, to engaging in a critical examination of the purpose and the aims of the curriculum. PLNs can vary in composition, nature and focus: they may consist of teachers and school leaders from different schools, educators and local or national policymakers, educators and other stakeholders as well as numerous other potential combinations. Often networks will also form in partnership or involve joint work with academic researchers. Ultimately, however, irrespective of composition or focus, the priority aim of PLNs is to build capacity, which is defined as 'the power to... sustain [the] learning of all people at all levels of the educational system' (Stoll 2010:470).

Dynamic professional learning networks

Now more than ever, however, it seems that the age of professional learning networks has well and truly arrived. The rise and proliferation of digital communication, coupled with the circumstances enforced during the pandemic experience, has led to a dynamic re-imagining of PLNs.

This is explored across the rich range of experiences, testimonies and thinking provided in this book, with chapters exploring:

- the professional learning vistas opened up through **digital opportunities**;
- the sense of **new ownership, voices and partnerships** at the heart of networks, bubbling up from groups of practitioners;
- the consequent **transformation in the form and structure of professional learning networks**;
- how they have become **vehicles for radically different forms of professional development and learning**;
- a focus upon **enhancing teachers' identity and sense of wellbeing**;
- new openings for the **expressions of professionalisation and of the profession speaking to itself**; and
- fundamental implications for **professional learning network designers and leadership**.

The impact of online developments is considerable. There is a sense of a dramatic shift from the hitherto collaborative contribution of traditional learning networks to what Bancroft describes as becoming a digital asset to others and, indeed, to oneself. In networking from one's home, it is argued that there may be greater freedom and transparency. Similarly, Dick and Peat describe how the emergence of a digital community of practice helped to empower and connect rural Scottish island communities. Often the pandemic experience precipitated a sudden transitioning to remote learning and – as Youmans et al explain – provided powerful mitigation to the challenges they faced as adult educators. Indeed, within the pages of this book, we gain a nuanced picture of how professional learning networks of schools drew on their established collaborative cultures, systems and processes to move towards online engagements. As Cameron and Farrar testify in their experience of virtual peer review, it led to 'greater system-wide agility, adaptability and innovation'.

Perhaps one of the most significant developments in the nature of networking has been the movement away from top-down models of PLNs towards the emergence of bottom-up approaches. So, for instance, Holme explores the role of grassroots professional learning groups and informal networks in contrast to top-down control and Porritt et al report on the phenomenal expansion of WomenEd networks across the world, concluding that 'this networking liberates women'. Hopkins spotlights how 'autonomous schools who are free to work collaboratively together can spur innovation and sustain the drive to innovate, as well as enhancing student achievement'.

Such autonomy enabled Robinson and her colleagues, within the space of a year, to build a hub of learning, which was a site filled with blogs, events and resources, and to 'generate tangible improvements in education on the ground'. For some, the experience of the pandemic proved to be a great leveller where, as Jones describes in her chapter, teachers took the initiative and 'provided spaces for a diversity of learning formats, in groups, networks, on social media platforms, individualised research, across subjects as well as within subject'. She identified the benefits of online formats of networking as not only enabling more extensive professional learning within and between schools but also free and extensive access to global learning communities.

This burgeoning of grassroots network activity has, in turn, led to radical challenges to the structure, coordination and orientation of PLNs. Woods describes how networks within urban communities created a new organisational sense of place and shared purpose. They helped address common concerns and challenges facing teachers and schools, such as working with disadvantaged and vulnerable groups. The WomenEd networks confronted organisational and systemic bias through the spontaneous sharing of women's lived experiences and new collaborative mechanisms such as coaching and 'unconferencing'. McCarthy highlights how the relatively neglected network of student voice was developed to fuel significant curriculum and pastoral change. Meanwhile, Hopkins sees PLNs having the potential for 're-inventing' the 'middle tier' of school governance 'by promoting the focus on learning, linkages, and multi-functional partnerships'. This is echoed in Greany and Wolfe's declaration that 'there is an important role for networks alongside formal professional development programmes in England's fragmented school system'.

At the heart of such alternative structural forms of networking are particular values that, in turn, promote distinctive purposes and practices. Gardner-McTaggart and Armstrong observe that there is an emphasis on collegiality rather than competition, which builds 'mutual understanding, respect and recognition, providing a powerful space that facilitates professional growth'. Similarly, Braunberger and Hamilton describe how teachers reached beyond their schools to self-organise into a dynamic informal professional learning network. Baumber is adamant that the pandemic, and the accompanying emergence of new modes of connection and networking, have questioned the status quo and challenged what has not been working. In particular, he argues that teacher wellbeing has become a critical imperative in schools and calls for professional development programmes adopting a personalised approach, facilitated through networking.

This focus on wellbeing, personalisation and identity is taken up by a number of contributors as they explore the *raison d'etre* of networking. In the context of arts education, Berryman explains that teachers' sense of identity working within this field will drive the nature of their professional learning activities and the characteristics of the networks such educators join or create. Bolton reflects that the pandemic has provided time and space to deepen our critical understanding of what being a teacher means. He contends that this 'exploration of new teacher identity and pedagogy [...] is intentionally in marked contrast to the quick-fix-disco-finger techniques' promoted by some educationalists! In their detailed OECD analysis of networking, Fraser and Fulop examine the relationship between teachers' engagement in collaborative activities and self-efficacy and job satisfaction, as well as how school environments support these engagements.

Linked to this view of networks promoting self-efficacy is their potential to provide a vehicle for expressions of professionalisation. Cameron and Farrar emphasise the importance of how professional agency, solidarity and continuous learning in networks all hang together. This creative interplay is also evident in Hughes' description of how a YouTube channel for English teachers from across the country facilitated informal professional conversations that were both dynamic and organic. Likewise, Langley suggests that the collaborative learning that took place through the networking of his teacher research groups 'provided teachers with opportunities to enhance their own sense of professionalism'.

The dynamic nature of learning networks and the potential they offer has significant implications for leadership. Jones records how the hiatus of the pandemic led to teachers rising to the challenge in undertaking instructional leadership roles. Greany and Wolfe found in their evaluation of two regional networks developed by the Church of England Foundation for Educational Leadership that, as well as the sharing of resources and building relationships with other school leaders, the networks enabled strategic reflection on the nature of leadership itself. Along with other chapter contributors, they identified core skills for network designers and facilitators.

We hope you find this book provides a stimulating insight into the current experience of professional learning networks and the transformative difference they are poised to make in future educational development. Join the debates on these and any areas you think we may have missed using the hashtag #PLNs.

References

Ainscow, M. (2014) *Towards Self-improving School Systems Lessons from a City Challenge.* London: Routledge.

Arkhipenka, V., Dawson, S., Fitriyah, S. Goldrick, S., Howes, A. and Palacios, N. (2018) 'Practice and performance: changing perspectives of teachers through collaborative enquiry', *Educational Research*, 60(1), pp. 97–112.

Armstrong, P., Brown, C. and Chapman, C. (2021) 'School to school collaboration in England: A configurative review of the empirical evidence', *Review of Education*, 9(1), pp. 319–351.

Azorín, C. (2018) Networking in Education: Lessons from Southampton. Presented at the European Conference on Educational Research annual meeting, Bolzano, Italy), 4 to 7 September 2018.

Brown, C. (2020) *The Networked School Leader: How to improve teaching and student outcomes using learning networks.* London: Emerald.

Castells, M. (2010) *The Rise of the Network Society.* Chichester: Wiley-Blackwell.

Ehren, M. and Godfrey, D. (2017) 'External accountability of collaborative arrangements; a case study of a Multi Academy Trust in England', *Education Assessment Evaluation and Accountability*, 29, pp. 339–362.

Gilbert, C. (2017) Optimism of the will: the development of local area-based education partnerships. A think-piece. London: London Centre for Leadership in Learning.

Greany, T. (2017) Karmel Oration: Leading schools and school systems in times of change – a paradox and a quest. Presented at Australian Council for Educational Research (ACER) Research Conference. 28–29 August, 2017. Melbourne.

Handscomb, G. (2013) Linking Educational Organisations, Organisational Partnership and Educational Networks. Module for online masters in educational leadership and management programme. Nottingham: University of Nottingham.

Handscomb, G. (2018) Improving the System, *Professional Development Today*, 19(3/4), p. 4.

Hargreaves, D. (2010) Creating a Self-improving School System. Nottingham: National College for Teaching and Leadership.

Hargreaves, D. (2012) A self-improving school system: towards maturity. Nottingham: National College for Teaching and Leadership.

Hargreaves, A. and Shirley, D. (2012) *The Fourth Way: The Inspiring Future for Educational Change*. Thousand Oaks, CA: Corwin Press.

Howland, G. (2015) Structural reform: The experience of ten schools driving the development of an all-age hard federation across a market town in northern England, *Management in Education*, 29(1), pp. 25–30.

Huxham, C. and Vangen, S. (2005) *Managing to Collaborate: The Theory and Practice of Collaborative Advantage*. Abingdon: Routledge.

Mourshed, M., Chijioke, C. and Barber, M. (2010) How the world's most improved school systems keep getting better [Report]. McKinsey & Company.

Muijs, D. (2015) Improving schools through collaboration: a mixed methods study of school-to-school partnerships in the primary sector, *Oxford Review of Education*, 41(5), pp. 563–586.

Muijs, D., West, M. and Ainscow, M. (2010) Why network? Theoretical perspectives on networking, *School effectiveness and School Improvement*, 21(1), pp. 5–26.

Riley, K. (2022) *Compassionate Leadership for School Belonging*. London: UCL Press.

Stoll, L. (2010) Connecting learning communities: Capacity building for systemic change. In A. Hargreaves, A. Lieberman, M. Fullan & D. Hopkins (Eds.) *Second International Handbook of Educational Change*. Dordrecht: Springer, pp. 469–484.

Trust, T., Krutka, D. G. and Carpenter, J. P. (2016) '"Together we are better": Professional learning networks for teachers, *Computers and Education*, 102, pp. 15–34.

Wilkins, R. (2015) Rethinking Professional Development and Professionalisation, *Professional Development Today*, 17(3), pp. 18–25.

Woods, D., Husbands, C. and Brown, C. (2013) Transforming Education for All: the Tower Hamlets Story. London: Mayor of Tower Hamlets.

Part one:

Insights, structures and systems

The role of networks in supporting school improvement

David Hopkins

Overview

The international evidence is clear that autonomous schools that are free to work collaboratively together can spur innovation and sustain the drive to innovate, as well as enhance student achievement. However, when educational policies, as in England, focus on autonomy, hierarchies and marketisation then both excellence and equity at the system level are compromised. The forms of networking and collaboration described in this chapter that focus on learning at a range of levels, provide a means of facilitating school improvement, as well as contributing to large-scale reform. They also offer the potential for 'reinventing' the 'middle tier' in terms of school governance, by promoting the focus on learning, linkages, and multi-functional partnerships.

Keywords
Autonomy
Networks
Professional development
School improvement
System reform
Teaching and learning

The provenance of networks

In reflecting on what's next for professional learning networks, it is important to remember that the construct has a distinguished provenance in education. Over the years, there has been much international interest in the role of networks in supporting school improvement (Wohlstetter et al 2003). Unfortunately, there are also various misconceptions of the network concept, particularly in terms of how policy can affect practice. Although networks bring together those with like-minded interests, they are more than just opportunities to share 'good practice'. The following definition of networks emerged from my early analysis of effective networks for the OECD (Hopkins 2003):

> 'Networks are purposeful social entities characterised by a commitment to quality, rigour, and a focus on outcomes. They are also an effective means of supporting innovation in times of change. In education, networks promote the dissemination of good practice, enhance the professional development of teachers, support capacity building in schools, mediate between centralised and decentralised structures, and assist in the process of re-structuring and re-culturing educational organisations and systems.'

In looking to the future of networks in professional learning and school improvement, this definition still holds much validity. Its implications will be discussed in more detail as the chapter progresses. In doing so and in developing the argument of the chapter, we will:

- review the international evidence on successful systemic educational reform in terms of policies for autonomy and networking.
- situate the discussion of networks in their contemporary context in England.
- present three cameos of successful networking initiatives.
- propose criteria for effective networking for school improvement.

The global evidence on autonomy and networking

The educational policy direction in many developed countries has changed quite dramatically in the recent past. There has been a rapid shift away from the government managed educational changes of the 1990s and 2000s to far more decentralised systems based on the principle of 'autonomy'. This is not to say that reforms and strategies of that period have not worked, indeed, in retrospect, they have been extremely successful in raising standards and decreasing the variation of performance in the system. As it became apparent in England, there is a limit to the impact that can be achieved by top-down reforms and another way has to be sought (Hopkins 2007).

In many jurisdictions, this other way is called 'autonomy' and is often driven by reasons and forces other than those educational. The most influential driver recently was the meltdown in global economic systems since 2008 that was coupled with an ideological desire from many governments for the 'small state'. These irresistible forces were at times also coupled with a genuine belief that there is a need to unleash the power of the profession that has previously been harnessed by too much control. There are some arguments to support such a policy direction, but there are also some caveats to be entered too. It is foolish to think that simply adopting a policy of autonomy that dismantles existing system structures and gives unfettered freedoms to schools will work by itself.

Andreas Schleicher (2018:114) in his authoritative text on *World Class* school systems, comments on the findings of recent OECD research:

> 'But all (these systems) flourished because governance and oversight arrangements gave them the freedom to create spaces for experimentation.'

> 'A (recent OECD) study also underscored the risk of autonomy leading to the "atomisation" of schools. Working with others can spur innovation and sustain the drive to innovate.' 'However, school autonomy will be self-defeating if it is interpreted as functioning in isolation. Instead, autonomy should take the form of freedom and flexibility to work with many partners.'

Schleicher (2018:117) further adds:

> 'But more than that might be needed. PISA data show that in school systems where knowledge is shared among teachers, autonomy is a positive advantage; but in school systems without a culture of peer

learning and accountability, autonomy might actually adversely affect student performance. There needs to be enough knowledge mobilisation and sharing and checks and balances to make sure academies are using their independence effectively – and wisely.'

It is evidence like this that led me to develop a framework for 'networked autonomy' (Hopkins 2013). Autonomous networked schools:

- put in place substantive collaborative arrangements.
- understand they are as strong as the weakest link. Schools that are failing and/or underperforming can expect to receive unconditional support from all network schools, as well as from commissioned external agencies.
- support and accept significantly enhanced funding for students most at risk.
- operate within a 2rationalised system of national and local agency functions and roles that allow a higher degree of coordination for this increasingly devolved system.

Such a set of principles allow schools to use 'networked autonomy' to:

- more fully express their moral purpose of enabling every student to reach their potential.
- ensure that every teacher has the maximum time to teach and to develop their professional competence.
- maximise resource allocation to ensure that this happens.
- explore the full potential of the 'inside-out' school development strategy.
- enable leadership to work more effectively with the system both within and outside the school and generate sustainable networks that deepen the impact on student learning.
- move from external to professional forms of accountability.

The contemporary context in England

The discussion in the previous section focused on what we know about effective networking and the apparent tension with policies that emphasise autonomy. In reflecting on the policy situation in England

and informed by the PISA data, Schleicher (2018:116) is sceptical about how 'granting greater school autonomy (would) actually lead to better school performance'. He continues:

'The academies show how important it is to combine professional autonomy with a collaborative culture, both among teachers and among schools. The challenge for an academy-style system is to find a way to share knowledge among schools. Knowledge in the field of education is very sticky; it does not spread easily.'

In their extensive and well-grounded research *Hierarchy, Markets and Networks*, Toby Greany and Rob Higham (2018:10) analyse the 'self-improving school-led system' agenda in England and examine the implications for schools. They describe their research as follows:

'This report analyses how schools in England have interpreted and begun to respond to the government's "self-improving school-led system" (SISS) policy agenda. While largely undefined in official texts, the SISS agenda has become an overarching narrative for schools' policy since 2010, encompassing an ensemble of reforms on academies, the promotion of multi-academy trusts (MATs), the roll back of local authorities (LAs) from school oversight, and the development of new school-to-school support models, such as teaching school alliances (TSAs).'

The SISS concept was originally and elegantly outlined by David Hargreaves (2010; 2011; 2012) in three highly influential monographs. In commenting on the new model of national teaching schools in England, as part of his vision of the self-improving school system, Hargreaves (2011:5) says:

The new teaching schools, based on the concept of the teaching hospital, are to be a critical element in a more self-improving school system. They will:

- train new entrants to the profession with other partners, including universities.

- lead peer-to-peer learning and professional development, including the designation and deployment of the new specialist leaders of education (SLEs).

- identify and nurture leadership potential.
- lead an alliance of other schools and partners to improve the quality of teaching and learning.
- form a national network to support the schools in innovation and knowledge transfer.
- be at the heart of a different strategy of school improvement that puts responsibility on the profession and schools.

To Hargreaves, the SISS was designed to be genuinely transformative, empower schools and lead to enhanced equity in student performance. In this respect, his proposals echoed Schleicher's analysis that is already referred to. The irony is that the Department for Education also claimed that their policies introduced using the SISS rhetoric would also lead to a lessening of centralised control and enhanced autonomy. The reality is that it has done nothing of the sort as these following quotations from Greany and Higham's (2018:12–16) book demonstrate:

- With academisation, powers of school oversight are moving from local to national government. This process has been uneven and often fraught. […] The picture that emerges is of chaotic centralisation, characterised by competing claims to authority and legitimacy but diminishing local knowledge about schools. (Ibid:12)
- That new local and regional markets in improvement services are particularly incentivising a focus on the types of knowledge and expertise that can most easily be codified and commoditised (as 'best practices') rather than on the joint-practice development and learning processes advocated by Hargreaves (2012) as essential for a SISS. (Ibid:14)
- MATs are commonly referred to as a form of partnership, but we argue that this is inappropriate given a common definition of partnerships as 'legally autonomous organisations that work together'. […] We argue MATs are best understood in terms of 'mergers and acquisitions', with prescribed models of governance and leadership largely derived from the private and, to a lesser extent, voluntary sectors. (Ibid:15)
- MATs have been encouraged to grow or merge by the DfE, in search of efficiencies and 'economies of scale'. However, our statistical

analysis of MAT impact on pupil attainment and progress shows there is no positive impact from MAT status for pupils in either primary or secondary academies when compared to pupils in similar standalone academies (Ibid:15).

- We conclude that rather than 'moving control to the frontline', the SISS agenda has intensified hierarchical governance and the state's powers of intervention, further constraining the professionalism of school staff and steering the system through a model we term 'coercive autonomy' (Ibid:16).

- Our findings are unambiguous in illustrating the importance of Ofsted and the wider accountability framework in influencing the behaviour of schools, suggesting that hierarchical governance is more influential than market or network coordination in England (Ibid:16).

These quotes do not do justice to the richness and complexity of Greany and Higham's research and analysis, but they do give a clear understanding of their key conclusions. Their findings are also in line with the conclusions of Schleicher and the aspirations of Hargreaves. So let us try to summarise the argument so far about the role of networking in supporting school improvement. To this point two conclusions can be drawn:

- The evidence from PISA is that forms of collaboration and knowledge transfer are a critical factor in raising standards of student performance in the most successful educational systems.

Yet

- The policy framework in England with the emphasis both on establishing hierarchies and developing the market militate against this.

The chapter concludes by suggesting policy advice and strategies for realigning policy in England that would enable our schools, leaders and students to emulate the standards and practices of the high-performing PISA systems. Before we do this, however, let us look at three practices that have been developed in England that have a proven track record of maximising the gains that can be made when utilising network practices authentically.

Networking cameos

If we are to achieve the form of collaboration alluded to in Schleicher's analysis of the PISA data that is consistent with high levels of systemic student achievement, we need to be far more precise about the practices involved. Schleicher set the scene and my definition of networked autonomy gave the construct more shape. This, despite government rhetoric, is not the contemporary practice in England where on current performance student achievement still stagnates (Perry and Hopkins 2017). Before proposing further policy recommendations, let us look briefly at three cameos of collaborative practice that fit with our definition of networked autonomy.

In his monograph, *The Education Epidemic*, David Hargreaves (2003) not only described the various forms of capital as they applied to schools, but also outlines an agenda for educational transformation based on innovation and networking. The essential task, Hargreaves argues, is to create a climate in which it is possible for teachers to actively engage in innovation and to transfer validated innovations rapidly within their school and into other schools. This does not mean a return to 'letting a thousand flowers bloom' but a disciplined approach to innovation.

If leading-edge schools – by definition a minority – take the lead in knowledge creation he asks, what happens to innovation in the rest of the system? Hargreaves responds that transformation is achieved in two ways:

- by moving the best schools (or departments/key stages within them) further ahead. That is, through frontline innovation conducted by leading-edge institutions which develop new ideas into original practices; and,
- by closing the gap between the least and most effective schools (or subject departments) – transferred innovation.

Transformation thus combines 'moving ahead' with 'levelling up'. To achieve such a 'lateral strategy' for transferred innovation requires the following strategic components:

- It must become clear what is meant by 'good' and 'best' practice among teachers.
- There needs to be a method of locating good practice and sound innovations.

- Innovations must be ones that bring real advantages to teachers.
- Methods of transferring innovation effectively have to be devised.

Schools that have adopted such an approach to collaboration are enthusiastic about the benefits such an approach generates. They agree with David Hargreaves that networks are the foundations for an innovative system of education.

The Networked Learning Communities (NLC) programme in England was a large-scale development and enquiry initiative involving 137 networks (1500 schools) between 2002 and 2006. It was a programme of the National College for School Leadership (NCSL) and was specifically designed to provide policy and system learning (as well as practical evidence) about network design and implementation. Their work also focused on network size and type, facilitation and leadership, formation processes and growth states, brokerage, system support and incentivisation. It was charged with generating evidence about how and under what conditions networks can make a contribution to raising student achievement, about the leadership practices that prove to hold most potential for school-to-school learning and about the new relationships emerging between networks as a unit of engagement and their local authority or MAT partners (Jackson and Temperley 2006).

The crucial point about the NLC programme is in the name. Their purpose was explicitly about 'learning' and by that token student achievement, and networked learning between schools rather than professional learning communities in schools, hence their potential systemic impact. There were six strands to the basic framework of the networked learning communities design (NLC n.d.):

- Pupil learning – a pedagogic focus.
- Adult learning – professional learning communities a key aspiration.
- Leadership learning – at all levels.
- Organisational learning – new organisational learning norms.
- School-to-school learning – networked learning.
- Network-to-network learning – lateral system learning.

Each network additionally elected to have at least one external partner, usually a higher education institution or local authority/MAT – or both. Finally, there were also four non-negotiable principles (NLC n.d.):

- Moral purpose – a commitment to success for all children ('raising the bar and closing the gap' is a social justice representation of the same theme).
- Shared leadership (for example, co-leadership).
- Enquiry-based practice (evidence and data-driven learning).
- Adherence to a model of learning.

In summary, successful networked learning activity in NLCs had the following characteristics (Jackson and Temperley 2006):

- Focused upon shared learning objectives, locally owned by groups of schools.
- Exhibited the characteristics of the learning design previously outlined.
- Comprised participants drawn from different schools, learning on behalf of colleagues within their own and other schools in the network,
- or comprised of participants within the same schools, learning on behalf of colleagues within their own and other schools in the network.
- Designed to enable individuals to learn from, with and on behalf of others.
- Purposefully designed and facilitated to change professional knowledge and practice in order to improve student learning.
- Housed within its design opportunities for leadership learning.
- Potentially transformative – for participants and for students – owing to its orientation towards changes in practice.

Although the focus of the NLC programme tended to be more on process than outcome, there is reliable assessment data to support its positive influence on student achievement (cited in Jackson and Temperley 2006). For example:

- Key Stage 4 data for 2005 shows that NLC schools had risen more than non-NLC schools the percentage of pupils achieving five or more A* to C grades between 2004 and 2005. In terms of average point scores across all grades, the results again show that NLC schools had risen more than non-NLC schools.

- When comparing Key Stage 4 for 2005 with the results from 2003, it can again be seen that NLC schools had risen more than non-NLC schools in the percentage of pupils achieving five or more A* to C grades.

In concluding their ICSEI paper, Jackson and Temperley (2006) claim, with some justification, that by *aligning* networked learning processes for adults and pupils and having leadership that promotes and supports that learning, there is evidence that networks succeed in their twin objectives of fostering learning communities and raising pupil achievement.

In my 'Unleashing Greatness' paper (Hopkins 2020), I argue that if a school's improvement journey is to be sustained over the long term, the developments have to be integrated into the very fabric of the system pedagogy. Mourshead, Chijioke and Barber (2010) identified three ways that improving systems do this:

- Establishing collaborative practices
- Developing a mediating layer between the schools and the centre
- Architecting tomorrow's leadership

The key point here, which also relates to Schleicher's PISA analysis, is the need for some 'mediating level' within the system to connect the centre to schools and schools to each other. The most effective networks have assumed this role and have developed productive ways of learning from their best, for collaborating purposefully and for the sharing of outstanding practice. In England, currently, the most common middle tier organisation are MATs (Hopkins 2016). In outstanding MATs, capacity is built at the local level to ensure that all those in a trust's family of schools' progress as rapidly as possible towards excellence. Figure 1 illustrates how this works:

- Central to local capacity building is the regional director or executive principal who provides leadership, develops the narrative and acts as the trust's champion in that geographic area.

- One of their key tasks is to build local capacity by training a group of lead practitioners in a MAT's ways of working, materials and strategies.
- The training design used to develop trainers is Joyce and Showers' peer coaching model (Joyce and Showers 1995, Joyce and Calhoun 2010).
- These trainers then work with the school improvement teams in each school to build within-school capacity and consistency.
- Inter-school networking allows for authentic innovation and the transfer of outstanding practice, thus building the capacity of the network as a whole.

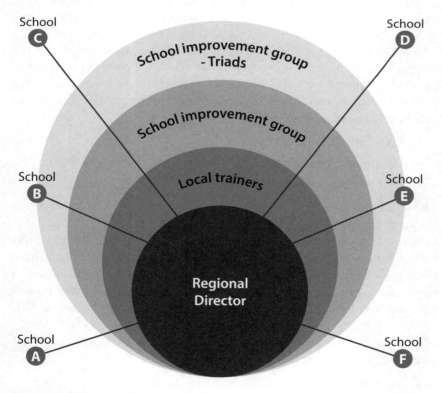

Figure 1 Building capacity

In my experience, the three key components of this strategy – school improvement teams, staff development processes and networking – should provide the focus for much of the training for executive principals or equivalent within the MAT, as they play their critical role in systemic improvement. In moving to scale, it is clear from international benchmarking studies of school performance that (Hopkins 2013):

- decentralisation by itself increases variation and reduces overall system performance. There is a consequent need for some 'mediating level' within the system to connect the centre to schools and schools to each other – networks and MATs can provide this function.
- leadership is the crucial factor both in school transformation and system renewal, so investment particularly in head/principal and leadership training is essential, hence the use of frameworks such as the 'Unleashing Greatness' school improvement strategy to guide action.
- the quality of teaching is the best determinant of student performance, so that any reform framework must address the professional repertoires of teachers and other adults in the classroom, thus the focus by high-performing trusts and networks on the progress of learners and the development of teachers.
- outstanding educational systems find ways of learning from its best and strategically uses the diversity within the system to good advantage – this is why capacity needs to be built not only within trusts and networks, but also between them at the system level.

Moving forward

To summarise, networks have the potential to support educational innovation and change and enhance student learning by:

- keeping the focus on the core purposes of schooling, in particular the focus on student learning.
- enhancing the skill of teachers, leaders and other educators in change agent skills, managing the change process and creating and sustaining a discourse on teaching and learning.

- providing a focal point for the dissemination of good practice, the generalisability of innovation and the creation of 'action-oriented' knowledge about effective educational practices.
- building capacity for continuous improvement at a local level and, in particular, in creating professional learning networks within and between schools.
- ensuring that systems of pressure and support are integrated not segmented, for example, professional learning networks incorporate pressure and support in a seamless way.
- acting as a link between the centralised and decentralised schism resulting from many contemporary policy initiatives, in particular, in contributing to policy coherence horizontally and vertically.

The analysis of the conditions required for effective networking, and the contribution of networks to innovation and change, demonstrate that networks can operate at a number of different levels. In the context of supporting innovation, one can discern an evolving typology of network types. At the basic level networks facilitate the sharing of good practice, at the highest level they can act as agents of system renewal.

1. At its most basic level, a network could be regarded as simply groups of teachers joining together for a common curriculum purpose and for the sharing of good practice.
2. At a more ambitious level, networks could involve groups of teachers and schools joining together for the purposes of school improvement with the explicit aim of not just sharing practice but of enhancing teaching and learning throughout a school or groups of schools.
3. Over and above this, networks could also not just serve the purpose of knowledge transfer and school improvement, but also involve groups of stakeholders joining together for the implementation of specific policies locally and possibly nationally.
4. A further extension of this way of working is found when groups of networks (within and outside education) link together for system improvement in terms of social justice and inclusion.
5. Finally, there is the possibility of groups of networks working together not just on a social justice agenda, but also to act explicitly as an agency for system renewal and transformation.

In looking to the future of networking, based on the evidence and argument of this chapter, one can confidently make two final points:

1. First, governments and policymakers should embrace networks not only as a strategy to assist in the implementation of a reform agenda, but also as the key means of achieving school improvement. Without some form of networking, it is highly unlikely that the aspirations for governmental programmes of educational reform, particularly in decentralised systems, will be realised.

2. Second, if one issue is certain it is that the future of schooling requires a systemic perspective, which implies a high degree of consistency across the policy spectrum and an unrelenting focus on student achievement and learning. Networks, as a natural infrastructure for both innovation and the informing of government policy, provide a means for doing just that.

References

Greany, T. and Higham, R. (2018) *Hierarchy, Markets and Networks*. London: UCL Institute of Education Press.

Hargreaves, D. H. (2003) *Educational Epidemic*. London: DEMOS.

Hargreaves, D. H. (2010) *Creating a Self-improving School System*. Nottingham: National College for School Leadership.

Hargreaves, D. H. (2011) *Leading a self-improving school system*. Nottingham: National College for School Leadership.

Hargreaves, D. H. (2012) *A Self-improving School System: Towards maturity*. Nottingham: National College for School Leadership.

Hopkins, D. (2003) Understanding Networks for Innovation in Policy and Practice in OECD, *Networks of Innovation: Towards New Models for Managing Schools and Systems*. Schooling for Tomorrow. Paris: OECD Publishing.

Hopkins, D. (2007) *Every School a Great School*. Open University Press. Berkshire: McGraw Hill Education.

Hopkins, D. (2013) *Exploding the Myths of School Reform*. Open University Press. Berkshire: McGraw Hill Education.

Hopkins, D. (2016) Building Capacity for School Improvement in Multi-Academy Trusts – from the inside out, *SSAT Journal 07*, pp. 19–29.

Hopkins, D. (2020) Unleashing Greatness – A Strategy for School Improvement, *Australian Educational Leader*, 42(3), pp. 8–17.

Jackson, D. and Temperley, J. (2006) 'From Professional Learning Community to Networked Learning Community'. Paper presented at the International Congress for School Effectiveness and Improvement (ICSEI) Conference, January 3–6, Fort Lauderdale, USA.

Joyce, B. and Showers, B. (1995) *Student achievement through staff development* (2nd ed). New York: Longman.

Joyce, B. and Calhoun, E. (2010) *Models of Professional Development*. Thousand Oaks, CA: Corwin Press.

Mourshead, M., Chijioke, C. and Barber, M. (2010) *Education: How the world's most improved school systems keep getting better*. London: McKinsey & Company.

Networked Learning Communities (n.d.) *Learning about Learning Networks*. Nottingham: National College for School Leadership.

Perry, J. and Hopkins, D. (2017) The relationship between policies effecting secondary school education in English secondary schools and student outcomes. [Unpublished paper]. Nottingham: School of Education, University of Nottingham.

Schleicher, A. (2018) World Class: How to Build a 21st-Century School System. Paris: OECD Publishing.

Wohlstetter, P., Malloy, C. L., Chau, D. and Polhemus, J. (2003) 'Improving schools through networks: A new approach to urban school reform', *Educational Policy*, 17(4), pp. 399–430.

Fostering collaboration across schools around the world

insights from TALIS

Pablo Fraser and Gabor Fulop

Overview

Recent publications in the field of education have called for filling the knowledge gaps regarding collaboration in education along with the role of school environments in shaping, leading and promoting these collaborative practices. Our chapter aims at filling part of these gaps by exploiting reports from the 2018 OECD Teaching and Learning International Survey (TALIS) (OECD 2020), the global barometer of teachers, teaching and learning. The last cycle of the survey in 2018 collected data from around 260,000 teachers and school leaders in about 50 countries and economies around the world. Using rich data from TALIS 2018, the chapter will first describe the frequency and the type of collaborative practices teachers in lower secondary engage in. It then analyses how school environments relate to teachers' engagement in collaborative activities. Finally, the chapter examines the relationships between teachers' engagement in collaborative activities and self-efficacy and job satisfaction.

Results from TALIS 2018 indicate that participation in collaborative practices is relatively common and varied. TALIS findings show that teachers who report that their school are characterised by a supportive environment also tend to engage in collaborative activities more frequently in most countries and economies participating in TALIS. Teachers who take part in the more interdependent forms of collaboration also tend to report using cognitive activation practice more frequently for teaching as well as reporting higher levels of job satisfaction. Our contribution will conclude with a reflection on the implication of these findings.

Keywords
TALIS
Teachers
Professional collaboration
Collaborative practices
School climate
Comparative and international studies

Collaboration in a time of flux

The Covid-19 pandemic has been a massive shock to the operations of the education system and its implication may have not been fully grasped to this date. Indeed, as many educational systems around the world are opening their doors back again, school leaders, teachers and students are faced with novel configurations of their working and learning environment. For example, hybrid learning strategies mixing both face-to-face instructions with distance learning supported through the use of digital technology has been a common response used by OECD countries to respond to the Covid-19 crisis (OECD 2021).

Given this potential new configuration of teachers' work, it is also highly relevant to ask ourselves to what extent teachers' collaboration and peer work might be impacted. The type, quality and frequency of teachers' collaboration has become a pillar of teachers' professional practices due to its correlation with teachers' professional learning as well to its potential impact on student learning (OECD 2020). As such, educational policy at the system, the local and the school levels has tried to install initiatives that promotes collaborative practices among teachers (Schleicher 2018). At the school level, special attention has been paid to the role of school leadership and how instructional and distributed leadership could foster a collaborative environment.

Although we may not have evidence at this moment of how these practices were transformed, looking at the data just prior to the crisis would provide an idea of what were the base level on the levels of teachers' collaboration around the world before the eruption of the pandemic. The 2018 Teaching and Learning International Survey (TALIS) (OECD

2020), the global barometer of teachers, can provide an international perspective on the spread and key features professional prior to the crisis. It can also provide insights on the association between encouraging school environments and professional collaboration, as well as what would be some of the outcomes of these types of practices. Concretely, this chapter will present descriptive and correlational data of TALIS to address the following three research questions:

Q1: What is the frequency and the type of collaborative practices engage by teachers in lower secondary?

Q2: What elements of school condition are linked with teachers' collaborative activities?

Q3: To what extent is professional collaboration linked with teachers' job satisfaction and teaching practices such as cognitive-activation practices?

What do we currently know

In the realm of the teaching profession, collaborative activities are understood as practices based on interactions between teachers with the aim of improving and reinforcing quality teaching. When collaborative activities focus on instructional changes, they can produce shared learning among teachers (Levine and Marcus 2010). For example, when teachers engage in professional learning communities (PLCs) to discuss evidence of student learning, or receive feedback based on teachers' actions after classroom observations, teachers have an opportunity to reflect on their instruction and consider specific changes (OECD 2016).

Teacher collaboration can be structured in different manners and can be seen as a continuum ranging from one-off interactions to strong and regular cooperative actions between teachers (Reeves, Pun and Chung 2017; Vangrieken et al 2015). Moreover, teachers have many opportunities to interact and work with their colleagues. Some can be formal, arising from job requirements for teachers in certain systems, but they can also be informal and voluntary interactions between colleagues that can be triggered by situations or challenges teachers collectively feel the need to address (Ainley and Carstens 2018).

TALIS categorised professional collaboration into two groups. The first group is labelled 'exchange and coordination for teaching', which consist in looser forms of informal collaboration that are not based necessarily in periodicity or a given plan. The second group is labelled 'professional collaboration', which are more complex than simple exchanges and coordination between teachers. Frequent and regular engagement in deeper forms of collaboration among teachers may be desirable for education systems in order to reap the benefits of collaboration. These activities are key opportunities for teachers to collaborate directly to improve instructional processes in the classroom and should, therefore, be leveraged by educators (Ronfeldt et al 2015).

How to boost professional collaboration? Interpersonal relationships, including mutual support, trust and solidarity, are essential building blocks of a collaborative school culture that is, in turn, integral to effective collaboration (Hargreaves and Fullan 2012; Hargreaves and O'Connor 2018). However, the relationship between collegiality and collaboration works in both directions. Through increased interactions and interdependence, frequent collaborative actions among colleagues also reinforce positive relationships, strengthen trust, and support and enhance the overall school climate (Rutter 2000; Rutter and Maughan 2002).

Teachers' collegial contact and engagement through different collaborative activities can define their everyday working conditions, which, in turn, determine satisfaction with their jobs, especially their current working environments (IBF International Consulting 2013). In addition, teachers could also view collaboration as an opportunity to consult with colleagues and engage in innovative forms of practices (IBF International Consulting 2013).

How we went about our investigation

All data is coming from the 2018 cycle of the Teaching and Learning International Survey (TALIS) developed by the Organisation for Economic Co-operation and Development (OECD). TALIS results are based exclusively on self-reports from teachers and school leaders and, therefore, represent their opinions, perceptions, beliefs and accounts of their activities. The international target population for TALIS consists of schools providing lower secondary education, as well as their principals and teachers. From the national lists of eligible schools, TALIS randomly samples 200 schools per country, and then selects school leader and randomly samples 20 teachers in each sampled school. In 2018, the survey was conducted in 48 countries and economies, 31 of them were OECD members (OECD 2019). By 'OECD average' is understood the results from the 31 OECD countries participating in TALIS1.

For the first research question (Q1) concerning the description of collaborative actives, the data reported correspond to the frequency with which teachers report engaging in collaborative activities. For the second (Q2) and third research objective (Q3), regression analyses were conducted. These analyses explore to what extent a dependent variable changes when any certain independent variable changes as well while all other independent variables are held constant.

The purpose of the second research question is to explore the association of school climate with the frequency for collaboration. For that purpose, a scale of professional collaboration was selected as the dependent variable and regress to teachers' responses on whether there teachers can rely on each other in school and collaborative school culture characterised by mutual support. The third research question consist on exploring the relation of professional collaboration with other outcomes of teachers' professionalism, in particular, job satisfaction and the implementation of cognitive practices. For that purpose, two regressions were conducted; the first regression had a dependent variable the TALIS job satisfaction scale regress to the professional collaboration scale and the second regression selected the cognitive practice scales regress to professional collaboration.

The table on the following pages (OECD 2020) presents a summary of the variables used in the analyses:

TYPE OF ANALYSES	VARIABLES	DESCRIPTION
Descriptive	Frequency to which teachers engage in collaborative practices	How often ('never'; 'once a year or less'; '2–4 times a year'; '5–10 times a year'; '1–3 times a month' or 'once a week or more') teachers do the following: 'teach jointly as a team in the same class'; 'observe other teachers' classes and provide feedback'; 'engage in joint activities across different classes and age groups'; 'take part in collaborative professional learning'; 'exchange teaching materials with colleagues'; 'engage in discussions about the learning development of specific students'; 'work with other teachers in the school to ensure common standards in evaluations for assessing student progress' and 'attend team conferences'.

TYPE OF ANALYSES	VARIABLES	DESCRIPTION
Ordinary least square regressions	Dependent variables: Professional collaboration scale	The index of professional collaboration measures teachers' engagement in deeper forms of collaboration that involve more interdependence between teachers, including teaching jointly as a team in the same class, providing feedback based on classroom observations, engaging in joint activities across different classes and age groups and participating in collaborative professional learning.
	Independent variable: collaborative school culture characterised by mutual support	Dummy variable: the reference category is to 'strongly disagree' or 'disagree' with the statement that there is a collaborative school culture which is characterised by mutual support.
	Independent variable: Teachers can rely on each other	Dummy variable: the reference category is to 'strongly disagree' or 'disagree' with the statement that teachers can rely on each other.
	Control: Female (dummy variable: reference category is male), age (number of years), years of experience as a teacher at current school (number of years), working full-time (dummy variable: the reference category is working part-time)	

TYPE OF ANALYSES	VARIABLES	DESCRIPTION
Ordinary least square regressions	Dependent variable: Job satisfaction scale	The index of job satisfaction measures teachers responses to the following statements I would like to change to another school if that were possible, I enjoy working at this school, I would recommend this school as a good place to work. All in all, I am satisfied with my job, the advantages of being a teacher clearly outweigh the disadvantages, if I could decide again, I would still choose to work as a teacher, I regret that I decided to become a teacher, I wonder whether it would have been better to choose another profession.
	Independent variable: Index of professional collaboration	
	Control: Female (dummy variable: reference category is male), age (number of years), years of experience as a teacher at current school (number of years), working full-time (dummy variable: the reference category is working part-time)	

TYPE OF ANALYSES	VARIABLES	DESCRIPTION
Ordinary least square regressions	Dependent variable: Cognitive practices scales	The index of cognitive activation practices measures the frequency with which a teacher uses cognitive activation practices in the classroom. These data are reported by teachers and refer to a randomly chosen class they currently teach from their weekly timetable. The practices are presenting tasks for which there is no obvious solution, giving tasks that require students to think critically, having students work in small groups to come up with a joint solution to a problem or task and asking students to decide on their own procedures for solving complex tasks.
	Independent variable: Index of professional collaboration	
	Control: Female (dummy variable: reference category is male), age (number of years), years of experience as a teacher at current school (number of years), working full-time (dummy variable: the reference category is working part-time)	

What we discovered

Q1

The starting point of the descriptive work is to assess how common collaborative practices are among teachers in lower secondary education across 48 educational systems across the world. Following the distinction made in the literature review we distinguished between two sets of collaborative activities: exchange and coordination for teaching (looser forms of collaboration) and professional collaboration (deeper forms of collaboration).

It is possible to observe from figure 1 that professional collaboration (team teaching, providing feedback based on classroom observations, engaging in joint activities across different classes and participating in collaborative professional learning) are less prevalent than simple exchanges and coordination between teachers (exchanging teaching materials, discussing the learning development of specific students, working with other teachers to ensure common standards in evaluations and attending team conferences).

Percentage of lower secondary teachers who report engaging in the following collaborative activities in their school with the following frequency (OECD average-31).

Figure 1 Teachers' collaboration with colleagues, source: OECD (2020), table II.4.1

Note 'at least once a month' covers the following response options: '1–3 times a month', 'once a week or more', 'less than once a month' covers the following response options: 'once a year or less', '2–4 times a year', '5–10 times a year'.

Values are grouped by type of collaborative activity and, within each group, ranked in descending order of the collaborative activities in which lower secondary teachers report to engage at least once month.

On exchange and cooperation, the most common form of collaboration among teachers is discussing the learning development of specific students: 61% of teachers, report doing so at least once a month. The results should not come as a surprise as it is to be expected that this type of discussion is part of the everyday workplace interaction of teachers. This type of common and loose interaction can be a valuable instance for teachers to learn from their peers and adapt their classes to the needs of their students.

Another important source of peer learning is exchanging teaching materials with colleagues however, on average across the OECD, only 47% of teachers report that they frequently ('at least once a month') engage in this form of collaboration. This might be due to the fact that the exchange of material required somewhat more planning and organisation than just having a conversation and thus a lesser percentage of teacher find the time to engage in this activity.

In comparison those activities labelled as 'professional collaboration' are much less frequent as a smaller share of teachers state they engage in these activities at least once a month: 'teach jointly as a team in the same class' (28%); 'participate in collaborative professional learning' (21%); 'engage in joint activities across different classes and age groups' (12%); and 'observe other teachers' classes and provide feedback' (9%). Moreover, large proportions of teachers report that they never engage in these forms of collaboration: 39% of teachers report never teaching jointly, 16% of teachers report never participating in collaborative professional learning, 20% of teachers report never engaging in joint activities across different classes and age groups, and 41% of teachers report never observing other teachers' classes and providing feedback.

Q2

How to promote teacher collaboration? Teacher collaboration is more likely to flourish and stabilise if there are proper school conditions able to create supportive environment stimulating the development of these relationships. As indicators of these good working conditions, two variables were selected; the perception of collaborative school culture characterised by mutual support and the possibility of teachers relying on each other. Teachers' engagement in professional collaboration is regressed on these two variables. The results showed that, in all countries and economies participating in TALIS, teachers who agree that 'there is a collaborative school culture characterised by mutual support' also tend to engage more often in professional collaboration (figure 2). Regarding the factor if teachers' can rely on each other, in around two-thirds of the countries and economies participating in TALIS, there is a significant positive relationship between teachers' reliance on each other and teachers' engagement in professional collaboration after controlling for collaborative school culture characterised by mutual support. These results hold even after controlling for teacher characteristics (gender, age, work experience as a teacher at current school and working full-time).

Results of linear regression based on responses of lower secondary teacher:

Results of linear regression based on responses of lower secondary teachers

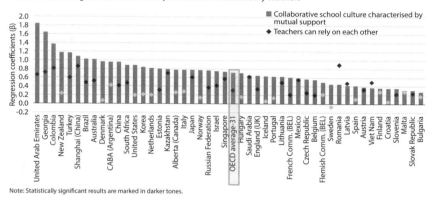

Note: Statistically significant results are marked in darker tones.

Figure 2 Relationship between professional collaboration activities and supportive school environments, source: OECD (2020), table II.4.31

Q3

Based on regression analyses, in all countries and economies participating in TALIS with available data, except Malta, teachers who report engaging in professional collaboration with their peers more often tend to report higher levels of job satisfaction, after controlling for teacher characteristics (gender, age, work experience as a teacher at current school and working full-time). Job satisfaction is a crucial factor related with teacher motivation and retention, thus professional collaboration can be a cost-effective manner to boost teachers' sense of satisfaction with their work (Klassen and Chiu 2010).

Results of linear regression based on responses of lower secondary teachers:

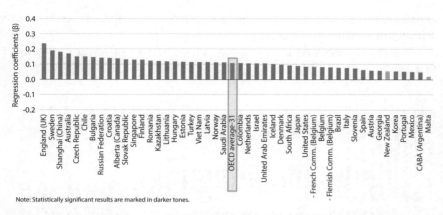

Note: Statistically significant results are marked in darker tones.

Figure 3 Relationship between job satisfaction and professional collaboration activities, source: OECD (2020), table II.4.13

TALIS also finds a significant positive association between teacher collaboration and the use of cognitive activation practices the classroom. By cognitive activation, the study refers to practices that allow students to evaluate, integrate and apply knowledge within the context of problem solving (Lipowsky et al 2009). In all countries and economies participating in TALIS with available data, regression analysis shows that, irrespective of teacher characteristics (such as gender, age, work experience as a teacher at current school and working full-time), teachers who report engaging more often in deeper forms of collaboration also tend to report using cognitive activation practices more frequently, implying better instructional quality and innovation in the practices of these teachers.

Results of linear regression based on responses of lower secondary teachers:

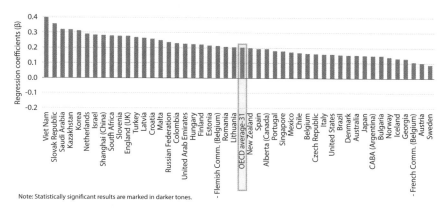

Note: Statistically significant results are marked in darker tones.

Figure 4 Relationship between cognitive activation practices and professional collaboration activities, OECD (2020), table II.4.17

The issues raised

A core pillar of professionalism in any profession is the degree to which practitioners collaborate regularly. In teaching, such professional collaboration can take the form of team teaching and participating in collaboration-based professional development. Teachers in OECD countries and economies in TALIS are quite likely to employ basic collaborative practices like discussing the development of specific students. However, far fewer teachers engage in the deeper forms of professional collaboration, which involve more interdependence. Such low instances of professional collaboration may be worrisome, considering the impact collaboration can have on promoting 21st century teaching: teachers who regularly collaborate with peers in this way also tend to report using cognitive activation. Professional collaboration is also associated with higher job satisfaction, which can be crucial factor for teacher retention.

Professional learning networks (PLNs) of teachers within and across schools, can be an instrumental form of collaborative professional development, as they are collective goal-driven professional development activities. PLNs support incremental change and positively affecting instructional quality and student achievement. While the role of school leaders is key, education systems could encourage and facilitate this process by providing all schools with earmarked funding to spend on collaborative professional development activities, and training providers could also review and restructure existing continuous professional development programmes to allow for greater collaboration between colleagues.

Moving forward

A further question that unfortunately TALIS is not able to address in the moment is to what extent the Covid-19 pandemic has disrupted the frequency of these collaborative practices or even severed the link with those factors that promote it. The school closing and the required distance learning and instruction that followed remove the physical environment of teachers. Were these collaborative practices able to survive in the digital sphere? If that is the case, what shape did collaboration take under these conditions? We can think that an advantage could be the potential extension of a professional network and reaching to colleagues from different context, which would not have been possible if collaboration was only limited to face-to-face interactions. However, do screen-to-screen interactions create the environment for deep conversations and reflection? In other words, does collaboration based in digital tools allows for the deep forms of collaboration that this article sought to emphasise?

Future iterations of the TALIS cycles should tackle these questions by capturing novel and creative forms of collaboration that move beyond daily face-to-face interaction, while exploring what implication these novel forms of collaboration have for teachers' development, practices and student achievement. These questions should guide the future of research collaboration for the next years.

References

Ainley, J. and R. Carstens (2018) 'Teaching and Learning International Survey (TALIS) 2018 Conceptual Framework', OECD Education Working Papers, No. 187. Paris: OECD Publishing.

Hargreaves, A. and M. Fullan (2012) *Professional capital: Transforming teaching in every school.* New York: Teachers College Press.

Hargreaves, A. and O'Connor, M. T. (2018) Leading collaborative professionalism. East Melbourne: Centre for Strategic Education.

IBF International Consulting (2013) Study on Policy Measures to Improve the Attractiveness of the Teaching Profession in Europe: Volume 2 – Final Report. Luxembourg: Publications Office of the European Union.

Klassen, R. and Chiu, M. (2010) 'Effects on teachers' self-efficacy and job satisfaction: Teacher gender, years of experience, and job stress', *Journal of Educational Psychology*, 102(3), pp. 741–756.

Levine, T. and Marcus, A. (2010) 'How the structure and focus of teachers' collaborative activities facilitate and constrain teacher learning', *Teaching and Teacher Education*, 26(3), pp. 389–398.

Lipowsky, F., Rakoczy, K., Pauli, C., Drollinger-Vetter, B., Klieme, E. and Reusser, K. (2009) 'Quality of geometry instruction and its short-term impact on students' understanding of the Pythagorean Theorem', *Learning and Instruction*, 19(6), pp. 527–537.

OECD (2016) School leadership for learning: insights from TALIS 2013. Paris: OECD Publishing.

OECD (2019) TALIS 2018 Technical Report. Paris: OECD Publishing.

OECD (2020) TALIS 2018 Results (Volume II): Teachers and School Leaders as Valued Professionals, TALIS. Paris: OECD Publishing.

OECD (2021) The State of Global Education: 18 Months into the Pandemic. Paris: OECD Publishing.

Reeves, P., Pun, W. and Chung, K. (2017) 'Influence of teacher collaboration on job satisfaction and student achievement', *Teaching and Teacher Education*, 67, pp. 227–236.

Ronfeldt, M., Owens Farmer, S., McQueen, K. and Grisson, J. A. (2015) 'Teacher collaboration in instructional teams and student achievement', *American Educational Research Journal*, 52(3), pp. 475–514.

Rutter, M. (2000) 'School effects on pupil progress: Research findings and policy implication' in P. Smith and A. Pellegrini (eds.) *Psychology of Education: Major Themes*. London: Falmer Press.

Rutter, M. and Maughan, B. (2002) 'School effectiveness findings 1979-2002', *Journal of School Psychology*, 40(6), pp. 451–475.

Schleicher, A. (2018) Valuing our Teachers and Raising their Status: How Communities Can Help, International Summit on the Teaching Profession. Paris: OECD Publishing.

Vangrieken, K., Dochy, F., Raes, E. and Kyndt, E. (2015) 'Teacher collaboration: A systematic review', *Educational Research Review*, 15, pp. 17–40.

Change, adaptation and transformation

peer review and collaborative improvement during the pandemic

Anne Cameron and Maggie Farrar

Overview

This chapter will draw on the work of Education Development Trust, an international educational charity working with almost 2000 schools in England to strengthen collaborative school improvement through the practice of peer review. It will examine the specific incremental changes and adaptive approaches to peer review and collaborative improvement during the time of Covid-19. This will focus specifically on how the networks of schools drew on their established collaborative cultures, systems and processes to lead their schools and communities collaboratively and effectively through the pandemic. Given that the authors believe that peer review exists to help schools address the most pressing challenges that cannot be addressed alone, it will also examine the adaptive virtual peer review model that was introduced during the period of social distancing and lockdown, and the interesting lessons that were learned around the use of technology and the opportunities that arise when physical and geographical boundaries no longer exist.

The chapter will then look at lessons for a 'bold new world'. It will examine what we have learned about networked systems and their ability to be more resilient and better able to withstand shock and disruption at times of significant change and uncertainty. It will explore the importance of professional agency, solidarity and continuous learning in networks, providing the opportunity for greater system-wide agility, adaptability and innovation. Finally, it will explore how the current accountability system has been exposed as fundamentally flawed and unable to function during the period of the pandemic. It will outline how high-quality peer review, practised in networks that simultaneously build cultures of continuous scrutiny, support and improvement, can enable the emergence of stronger, lateral and trust-based models of accountability.

Keywords
Improvement
Networks
Collaboration
Resilience

Our education system in England is increasingly more networked with almost all schools in some form of collaborative partnership. However, the quality of learning that takes place through this collaborative activity can be patchy and the overall impact is sometimes variable. Nevertheless, collaboration remains an essential part of our system. This conclusion, drawn by the Hay Group (2006) in their report on 'Decisive Collaboration and the Rise of Networked Professionalism' ('organisations cannot afford to avoid collaboration but also, that organisations cannot afford collaboration without purpose and efficiency') emphasises this need to be collaborative, but do it well.

In this chapter, we look at the practice of peer review as a vehicle to enable mature collaboration and why, through the cultivation of 'trust-based accountability' and networked resilience, it is an essential part of a reimagined education system post-Covid-19.

The power and potential of peer review

Through our work on the Schools Partnership Programme (SPP), we have seen that well-designed, well-managed, rigorous peer review that involves senior leaders, middle leaders and teachers is one of the most valuable and impactful activities that schools in a mature, sector-led system can undertake.

Adopting this approach helps build a culture of trust-based accountability, backed up by a focus on tangible improvement and a commitment to school-to-school support. Michael Fullan and Steve Munby (2016), in writing about the emergence of a new 'middle tier' in education, note that one of the critical success factors for effective, system-wide school collaboration is 'a commitment to, and capacity for, effective peer review [that] forms the engine that drives improvement'.

Peer review done well ensures that no school is isolated. It enables schools to systematically review and address weakness and share effective practice within and between schools. As the most effective peer review is embedded in a process of support and improvement, it produces the data and evidence on which effective school-to-school support and shared professional learning opportunities can be cultivated.

> 'SPP is conducted with "trust" in the real sense of the word at the heart of the process, allowing you to reveal your school, "warts and all", in the safe knowledge that the group genuinely wants to help you solve those really trying problems.' – Ann Davey, CEO Pathfinder Schools SPP Case Study 2019

Peer review cannot be imposed on a group of schools; it must come from their deep desire to be responsible for their own collective improvement and a commitment to put in the time required to achieve this.

The Schools Partnership Programme – an overview

SPP aims to do two things:

- Build the skills and expertise required to engage in great peer review.
- Build the culture change needed for this to be truly transformational and sustainable.

It is an integrated model of review and improvement:

- It is an enquiry and evidence-based learning process, focused on improving not proving.
- At its core is a belief in school, leader and teacher agency.

Our structured approach to peer review is underpinned by a rigorous three-stage cycle of continuous improvement.

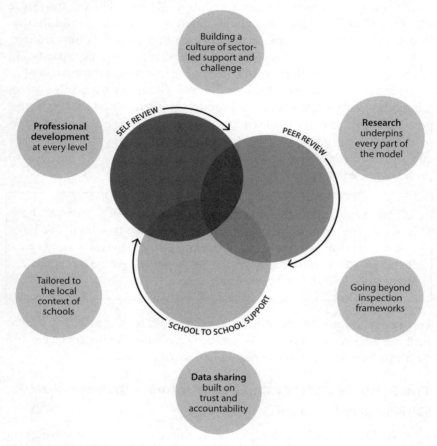

Figure 1 SPP cyclical model of learning and improvement

Stage 1: self-review

Effective peer review starts with how well the school knows itself using an enquiry-based framework. As the school being reviewed is in the driving seat, this initial conversation with as many staff as possible cultivates ownership and agency in the process.

Stage 2: peer review

The most effective peer reviews are based on an area of enquiry agreed by the school and finalised in conversation with the peer reviewers. Their role is to make sure that this agreed focus is evidence based and the outcome is going to be of most benefit to the school. In this initial conversation, the evidence to be collected during the peer review will be agreed upon. The review takes place over one day, or over a period of time if a virtual or blended review is to be conducted. The peer review ends with a feedback conversation where evidence is shared and initial findings agreed.

Stage 3: follow-up improvement workshop and school-to-school support

If peer review is going to be a vehicle for ongoing learning and improvement in school systems, then it must go further than the review itself. The SPP model includes a post-review improvement workshop facilitated by trained middle leaders from the partnership known as 'improvement champions,' involving members of staff agreeing actions from the peer review, taking place no more than two weeks after the review.

This model is built on a theory of change based on research and evidence from schools currently involved (see figure 2). It cultivates capacity building in collaborative school improvement, lateral trust-based accountability and effective partnership-based ways of working. It enables change to happen at partnership, leadership and teacher level. The model creates momentum for change and sustainability by supporting the partnerships to:

- commit to taking collective responsibility for improvement.
- changing individual beliefs and behaviours about how improvement happens.
- commit to long-term partnership maturity.

'Peer review for me has always been finding people that are like-minded, that are wanting to put in that work to help develop children and improve schools, wherever they might be and whatever their context.' – Gavin Booth, CEO Infinity Academies Trust SPP Case Study

SPP theory of change

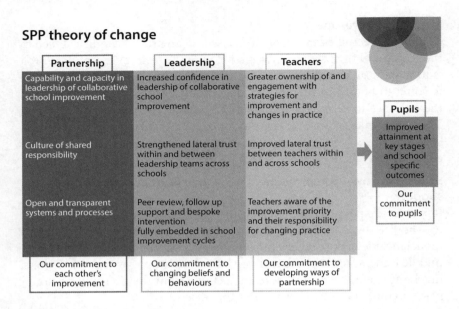

Figure 2 SPP's theory of change

We have always believed that through this commitment to 'tri-level' change, SPP can cultivate networked resilience and sustainable improvement. This has never been more necessary than during the time of Covid-19.

The next part of this chapter will explore the role that peer review has played during the pandemic and its role in supporting the reimagining of a new system of education.

Peer review at times of uncertainty, ambiguity and instability

When the pandemic hit our schools, we were curious to know whether the experience of peer review helped school leaders rapidly set up new ways of working and build strong support systems when the country started to lockdown.

Just as peer review is based on shared understanding that 'none of us are excellent until we are all excellent,' the mantra during this period has been 'none of us are safe until we are all safe'. School leaders told us that the collaborative, open and non-judgmental culture they had embedded as part of SPP helped them draw on the following:

- **Mutual support and practical help**: schools started to share key workers, staff and resources, drawing from a tight-knit partnership where, as a result of SPP, they knew each other's schools and staff well and were able to harness their collective assets for the mutual benefit of all.

- **Addressed shared challenges, sustainably**: peer review embeds an evidence and practice-based approach to problem solving, which enabled schools to resist quick-fix solutions to issues and instead employ a structured and rigorous way of viewing challenges, analysing evidence and weighing up potential solutions.

- **Support for newly appointed leaders**: some leaders were new in post and all their leadership development and preparation for headship training had not prepared them for leading in a pandemic. SPP is underpinned by the principles of coaching and this culture of mutual leadership support was of significant value to those newly appointed to leadership positions during this very demanding time.

- **Unpicking central guidance and contextualising it for the local area**: partnership-based peer review takes account of place and context. Throughout the Covid-19 period, government guidance was coming into schools regularly, was at times conflicting and didn't always address unique local contexts. Families and staff were reassured by one 'consistent voice' from local schools, which was instrumental in gaining their confidence and support.

Adapting the model to lockdown and enforced isolation

Despite the positive feedback on its value, most school leaders felt they had no choice but to pause their planned peer review cycles in the face of such unexpected disruption and restrictions. After all, how can you conduct or host a peer review when socially distancing, and what exactly would you review? However, it was also clear that the learning-oriented strategic focus that peer review is built on was in many ways welcome 'ballast' to the very operational, day-to-day approach to leading and managing through a pandemic.

School leaders also felt that the 'check, challenge and support' process that peer review modelled would help address the pervasive sense of 'self-doubt' many leaders were experiencing as they dealt with making multiple daily decisions, many of which could have significant consequences on health and wellbeing.

Our view, and the view of many schools we were working with, was 'why let a pandemic put a stop to peer review when, arguably, it's needed now more than ever?' So, we tested and put in place a model of virtual peer review that had the following core principles:

1. The **focus** of peer review would need to be sharp, especially when personal and organisational bandwidth in the shape of time and energy was limited.

2. The **value** of increased teacher agency would be even more important when much of what schools were dealing with felt out of their control.

3. The **process** would need to be based on familiar SPP methodology and core principles, even when conducted fully virtually, so that schools could pick up the guidance and use it quickly.

4. The **cycle** would need to be rapid, with a turnaround of three weeks from identification of area of focus to agreed action plan.

5. New areas of **enquiry** were emerging as a result of Covid-19 and the core SPP enquiry framework would need adapting.

Most of the review cycle was conducted virtually with the initial meeting between the headteacher and the reviewers held over an online platform. The evidence was collected virtually by the reviewers attending remote learning sessions, or visiting classrooms in school virtually. Focus groups of parents, teachers and leaders were also set up virtually. The reviews didn't happen on one day, as happens in the face-to-face approach. They were spread over a number of days to accommodate the specific evidence activity and the type of online platform required. The workshops were in the main conducted in school socially distanced and with a smaller number of people attending. The improvement champions facilitated through an online platform and a member of staff from the host school acted as a third 'in person' facilitator supporting this 'at a distance facilitation'.

What did we learn?

From this first trial and subsequent virtual peer reviews, our top line learning is that virtual peer review is much more do-able than we had originally thought. In many ways, it's an improvement on the face-to-face approach.

The very first trial of a virtual peer review in July 2020 in Yealmpstone Primary School in Plymouth found the following:

- It's easier to set up and engage online focus groups of staff, children, parents and carers, and less disruptive to the school day.
- There's more flexibility as all review activity doesn't have to be conducted on one day.
- It was much easier to keep the area of focus tight. There was less distraction for the reviewers throughout the whole process.
- The improvement workshop with remote facilitators worked well and introduced a range of online collaborative tools that the school will use again. As distance was no longer an issue, it was possible to bring in reviewers from other parts of the region and country.

Just as many partnerships are now asking themselves, 'what do we want to abandon from the pre-pandemic era and adopt and adapt from the last 18 months,' we are also asking the same question. A blended approach would seem to be the preferred future peer review model. We are now integrating virtual elements into the core programme and have introduced cross-regional peer reviews to support those partnerships that want to look 'outward' and engage in partnership-to-partnership peer reviews across the country.

The power of partnerships to withstand shock and disruption at times of change: the cultivation of network resilience and wellbeing

If partnerships were important pre-pandemic, they are even more important now. In fact, they are essential for our survival. Our conclusion from the last 18 months is that the more networked a system is, the more shock and disruption it is likely to be able to withstand. It appears that the more we reciprocally give and receive help and the more we cultivate agency to address the challenges that feel bigger than any one of us, the greater our sense of stability and wellbeing and the greater our resilience at times of crisis and complexity. Partnerships provide that sense of purpose, stability and support that we need in times of great disruption.

Michael Fullan reminds us that 'isolation is the enemy of improvement'. We also believe it is the enemy of wellbeing. As schools return to some form of 'normality', the very experience of returning to school can in itself either cultivate or erode wellbeing. Just at a time when schools may want to 'hunker down' and 'protect themselves and their staff' from any external pressure, our evidence shows that peer review has a significant role to play in strengthening wellbeing which, in turn, will stimulate learning. We have mapped the findings of a guidance document from the Mercer group (2010) on protecting the mental health needs of the workforce against our peer review core principles.

A sense of control: we need to have agency in our lives at work. Teachers and leaders at all levels have agency and control over the focus and process of SPP peer review and the actions taken as a result.

A sense of community: we need the opportunity to work with others on things that matter to us. Relationships are at the heart of SPP. A coaching culture underpins the programme and school leaders and teachers can be open and transparent.

A sense of commitment: we need to feel connected to a higher purpose in our work and why we do the job we do. SPP helps articulate a shared commitment to collective moral purpose in action.

A sense of challenge: we need to feel challenged without being overwhelmed. Challenging issues are addressed in a non-judgmental, transparent and robust manner with a commitment to a 'no blame' culture in all parts of the review.

Resilience and the ability to shape and reshape ourselves due to our individual and collective experiences will be at the heart of schools' and communities' recovery over the next 18 months. Everything we have learned during the time of Covid-19, and the reshaping of peer review, as a result, suggests to us that peer review within a highly effective partnership has a significant role to play. Ferrazzi et al (2021) identifies the following as the hallmark of a resilient team saying 'they are high in compassion and empathy. They truly care for each other and share both success and failure. For such teams, resilience is expressed in a deep commitment to "co-elevating" the team rather than seeking individual recognition of success.'

This commitment to 'co-elevation' is the practical embodiment of collective moral purpose in a partnership-based peer review where success is collective, where one school's issue becomes everyone's issue, and where learning and improvement priorities are shared and collectively explored and addressed.

Moving forward: peer review and reimagining tomorrow's education system

Effective networking, partnership and accountability

As we learn from the pandemic and begin to see this period as a 'hinge of history' where we can evolve into something better, how can our partnerships be at the heart of this journey?

One of the core elements of SPP is the cultivation of lateral trust-based accountability. If partnerships are the core building blocks of a self-improving school system, then this approach to accountability is the engine that brings it alive. Michael Fullan in his latest book *Nuance* explores accountability as 'culture', hardwired into our ways of working.

Peer review can be such hardwiring. It is never about putting on a show for each other, or hiding that which makes us vulnerable, or about 'good schools' reviewing those that need to improve, or about giving advice. It is a process underpinned by curiosity, compassion, transparency, learning and growth.

To support partnerships holding each other to account for acting on the outcomes of the peer review, the SPP process has a '90-day check-in' where a follow-up conversation takes place between the reviewers and school to check in (not check up) on progress. As a result, the insights gained and the learning experienced can be shared across the partnership.

> Peer review has enhanced our culture of collective efficacy where we work together on the things that matter to improve outcomes for all. – Helen Rowland, CEO Focus Trust

Strengthening lateral trust-based accountability is also an act of solidarity on the part of the partnership to reclaim accountability as professionals.

We have for too many years had a very narrow model of accountability in our education systems, which for many teachers means it's a dirty word and something to be feared. Partnerships allow a more multifaceted approach to accountability. In our view, there are five elements to this, all of which are at the heart of effective networking and partnership effectiveness:

1. Personal accountability to self – a commitment to learning and growth, **to know myself**.

2. Moral accountability: to students/parents/the community – **to serve**.

3. Professional accountability to colleagues **to embody a collaborative learning culture**.

4. Contractual accountability to employers/government **to commit to habits that secure continuous improvement, willing to be scrutinised**.

5. System accountability – to the wider system: **to collaborate with others** for greater impact on the lives of children and young people beyond my school or trust/alliance/local authority.

In her work on school accountability in a self-improving school system, Christine Gilbert (2012), former chief inspector of schools in England, wrote that 'if Ofsted were to take a different approach to the inspection of those schools that had undertaken a strong self-evaluation process, tested out laterally with peers, change would be dramatic'. It might seem the pandemic and its aftermath are an opportunity to test out such an assertion. However, we know only too well that organisational ways of working, cultures and habits of mind run deep. It will be all too easy to 'snap back' into familiar ways of working as we return to school in September 2021.

Just as the Covid-19 period has been called the 'great disrupter', how do we avoid the post-Covid-19 period being known as 'the greatest disappointment'? Partnerships are powerful crucibles in which our thinking and our ways of working can be 'positively disrupted'. Collectively, we can give each other permission to pause, check our assumptions, our biases and our ingrained habits. Peer review enables us to get up close and personal to each other's habits of mind and ways of working. Partnerships can provide solidarity and support to innovate and trial new ways of working. They spread the risk of failure and increase the possibility of learning and collective transformation.

The SPP peer review process is based on the asking of good questions. Engaging in the re-imagining of our education system requires us to ask those questions to which we do not have easy and ready answers. It allows us to work with unsettling questions without feeling 'unsettled'. It allows us to drop the mantle of 'expert' and sit with not knowing for longer than feels comfortable. Darren Randle (Farrar 2021) who is part of the Schools of Tomorrow (SOTO) partnership, reflects that when the questions are big enough, we have no choice but to drop the need to be an expert: 'we are all novices, everyone – everyone is part of the conversation'. The insight that we are all novices is a powerful motivator for partnership working among leaders and sets the culture for transformation.

Altruism and collective moral purpose

Given the role of leaders in leading the 're-imagining process', the next phase of peer review could well focus on 'leader to leader' peer review, providing leaders with the learning and personal professional development that can come from peer review. Particularly post-pandemic, a closer look at a leaders' role in leading transformation is a worthy focus for a peer review. On a day-to-day basis, this might look at how a leader uses her time. Caroline Skingsley (Farrar 2021) knows that it is very easy as a leader to fall back into the erosive trap of 'busy-ness' as a new term or year begins: 'Slowing down as a leader is not a failing, it's a strength – if we are frantic and overwhelmed, so will the staff and children be and we risk losing our focus on what matters, and losing this once in a lifetime chance to change and transform.'

Something has changed during Covid-19. The education system has pivoted to a shared sense of common humanity, a collective need for each other and a growing understanding of the essential benefits of collaboration. Steve Taylor shared his insights in a recent blog series, 'Learning from Lockdown' (Big Education 2020):

> The 23rd of March 2020 is a date that will forever be etched into our history. It was the date that the UK officially went into lockdown. This was a wakeup call for all schools. Prior to this, we were in a period where society in general and to be honest the education

system in particular – which was very market driven – had become unconsciously selfish. What happened from March 2020 was the flowering of a grassroots movement across the country.

Schools up and down the country began to share in a way like never before and with one core principle at its heart: helping others. It's quite a change. You see, in the past (and this is a generalisation), sharing often occurred for a variety of reasons, including to support a school because we had been asked to by government or the local authority, to get something back in return, or to look good and build a reputation. Coronavirus has changed this. It has changed what we hold dear and true and so, out of one of our country's and indeed the world's darkest hours, has come something pure and beautiful – a school system that is driven by true altruism.

This is the beauty and simplicity of peer review and partnership working – true altruism and helping others. This is the driver of partnership-based systems fired by collective moral purpose. This will be our journey out of Covid-19 through a system-wide realisation of the essential role collaboration will play, and the flowering of a radical and collective transformation of our education system.

References

Big Education (2020) Learning from Lockdown. Retrieved from: www.bit.ly/3uniy1f.

Education Development Trust (2021a) Collaborative Practice Insight 5: Resilience. Reading: Education Development Trust.

Education Development Trust (2021b) Virtual and cross-regional peer review. Retrieved from: www.bit.ly/3ixjpqE.

Farrar, M. (2021) Everything Must Change [Blog] *Schools of Tomorrow*. Retrieved from: www.bit.ly/3yYz4ch.

Ferrazzi, K., Race, M. C. and Vincent, A. (2021) 7 strategies to build a more resilient team. Harvard Business Review.

Fullan, M. and Munby, S. (2016) *Inside-out and downside-up*. Reading: Education Development Trust.

Gilbert, C. (2012) Towards a self-improving system: the role of accountability in schools. University of Nottingham, Nottingham: National College of Teaching and Leadership.

Hay Group (2006) Decisive collaboration the rise of networked professionalism. London: Hay Group.

Mercer Group (2010) Mental health and the coronavirus: A best practice guide to protecting the mental health of the workforce. Retrieved from: www.bit.ly/3L6gGRo.

Networking small rural schools in the pandemic

Toby Greany and Andy Wolfe

Overview

This chapter draws on findings from an evaluation of two regional networks developed by the Church of England Foundation for Educational Leadership to support senior leaders in small rural schools in England. The networks were launched in September 2019 with a focus on two areas: school improvement and social action by students. In March 2020, due to the pandemic, all schools in England were closed except for the children of 'key workers', with most children supported to learn at home until schools partially reopened in June 2020. The evaluation tracked the networks before and during the pandemic, enabling us to gather insights into how networking supported leaders in this challenging period. The chapter starts by reviewing existing literature on small rural school networks, setting out five evidence-informed core features for networks. It then summarises the findings from the evaluation. This shows that, while they were initially intended to enable the sharing of resources, ideas and practice and the building of relationships with other school leaders, a new core function evolved in response to the demands of lockdown – to enable theologically informed strategic reflection on leadership. This new core function helped participating leaders to sustain themselves and to refill their 'reservoirs of hope' (Flintham 2003; 2009) during the crisis. We conclude by setting out some implications for future network designers, including a proposal that network facilitators must be skilled in three areas: convening, catalysing and coaching. We argue that there is an important role for networks alongside formal professional development programmes in England's fragmented school system.

Keywords
Rural and small school leadership
Rural and small school networks
Covid-19 pandemic
Network facilitation
Professional development
Coaching

Introduction: context of the networks and the evaluation

This chapter draws on findings from an evaluation of two regional networks developed by the Church of England Foundation for Educational Leadership (the foundation) to support senior leaders in small rural schools in England. The networks were launched in September 2019 with a focus on two areas – school improvement and social action by students. Each network was supported by a separate facilitator, working part time. Both facilitators had previously been a headteacher in a Church of England primary school and one had experience of facilitating an existing network for small rural schools. Nationally, the foundation supported the facilitators, including through the provision of faith-leadership focused resources, which were used in the network meetings. Network membership was free and open to any small rural school, with recruitment supported by the two dioceses. The networks met in three ways:

- in online sessions (using Zoom), organised and run by the network facilitators.
- in face-to-face events convened by the facilitators.
- in 'hublets', i.e. sub-groups of school leaders who met together independently in self-facilitated groups.

The formative evaluation ran throughout the 2019/20 academic year and focused on the networks in two diverse rural areas, Kent and Yorkshire. The evaluation included:

- a literature review.

- observations of network meetings, 'hublet' meetings and advisory groups.
- termly interviews with network facilitators and the headteachers of six case study schools.
- an online survey of all participating schools.

In March 2020, due to the pandemic, all schools in England were closed except for the children of 'key workers', with most children supported to learn at home until schools partially reopened in June 2020. Both the networks and the evaluation were adapted to reflect the changed context, enabling us to gather insights into leaders' experiences of lockdown and how networking supported them in this challenging period.

The chapter starts by reviewing existing literature on small rural schools and networks, setting out a number of evidence-informed core features for networks. It then summarises the findings from the evaluation, showing that while they were initially designed to enable the sharing of resources, ideas and practice and the building of relationships with other school leaders, a new core function evolved in response to the demands of lockdown – to enable theologically informed strategic reflection on leadership. This new core function helped participating leaders to sustain themselves and to refill what Alan Flintham (2003:4) calls their 'reservoirs of hope' during the crisis, meaning: 'the calm centre at the heart of the individual leader from which their values and vision flow and which continues to enable effective interpersonal engagement and sustainability of personal self-belief in the face of not only day-to-day pressures but critical incidents in the life of the school'. We conclude by setting out some implications for future network designers, including a proposal that network facilitators must be skilled in three areas: convening, catalysing and coaching. We argue that there is an important role for networks alongside formal professional development programmes in England's fragmented school system.

Rural school leadership and networks

England has over 5000 rural primary, secondary and special schools, of which a third are very small (<110 pupils) and around two thirds are run by the Church of England (Church of England 2018). Rural secondary schools perform higher than their urban counterparts overall (as measured in academic outcomes at upper secondary – Key Stage 4) (DEFRA 2019). However, students living in disadvantaged rural areas perform lower than their urban peers, for example, in 2017/18, rural areas had lower achievement in English and maths GCSE for all levels of deprivation compared with urban areas (DEFRA 2020).

Rural schooling and rural school leadership have been researched extensively in different international contexts, revealing the range of ways in which rural schools can connect young people to their communities and prepare them for life, work and citizenship (Mette et al 2019; Zuckerman 2019; Schafft and Jackson 2010). However, there has been limited large-scale research into rural schools and schooling in England in the past two decades (Hargreaves 2009). There is sometimes an assumption that small rural schools will face inevitable challenges and will offer a reduced curriculum experience for children, although such pre-conceptions were partially confounded by research conducted in the 1990s and early 2000s (ibid). Nevertheless, more recent research has tended to focus on the improvement challenges that rural (and, often, coastal) schools face (The Key 2018; Ovenden-Hope and Passey 2019; Menzies 2019; Muijs 2015). These include: geographic, social and cultural isolation; limited employment opportunities; high transport costs; patchy broadband access; stretched budgets; recruitment, retention and workload issues for staff; and, in small schools, narrower curriculum options.

Research indicates that networks have become more important to all schools in England in recent years, partly in response to reduced support from Local Authorities as a result of large-scale academisation after 2010 (Greany and Higham 2018). Greany and Higham's research included a focus on rural and urban localities, revealing that the nature and focus of collaborative activity ranged from a local cluster that did little more than organise an annual inter-school sports day, through to partnerships which involved staff at multiple levels and which impacted on virtually every aspect of life and learning for adults and children within member schools. Common activities within stronger local primary clusters included: headteacher meetings, curriculum or subject leader networks, assessment and moderation groups, peer reviews, research projects and joint practice development or shared professional development for staff, and providing joint extra-curricular provision. Greany and Higham concluded that the partnership landscape in England was complex and disjointed, even within a single locality, but the overall picture was of 'winners and losers', with some schools seen to be further disadvantaged as a result of policy and market-driven changes.

Turning to research specifically on rural school networks, studies in the 1990s identified the impact of increased school autonomy and responsibility resulting from Local Management of Schools, introduced via the 1988 Education Reform Act. One early finding was that rural schools were likely to collaborate as a way of increasing capacity to respond to new government-imposed curriculum and accountability requirements. Coopers and Lybrand (1995) identified different models of cooperation, reflecting increasing degrees of closeness, from the 'shared bursar model', to the 'cluster' model, to the hard federation model, in which formerly separate schools become a single entity with a common governing body. The number of federations and executive headships grew gradually in the first decade of the new millennium, often as a way of sustaining very small schools, but these formal federations only ever encompassed a minority of rural schools (Chapman, Muijs and Macallister 2011). Meanwhile, though, other forms of partnership between rural schools have continued to develop, often with diverse aims and structural arrangements. For example, a small-scale survey (Muijs 2015) found that rural schools were collaborating in largely self-initiated networks to address school improvement concerns, to provide curriculum breadth, and to enable professional development and networking opportunities for otherwise isolated staff.

Core principles for networks

Popp et al (2014:18) explain that, 'at their base, networks consist of the structure of relationships between actors (individuals and organisations) and the meaning of the linkages that constitute those relationships'. In this chapter we adopt Provan and Kenis' definition of a 'network' as involving three or more 'legally autonomous organisations that work together to achieve not only their own goals but also a collective goal' (2008:231). In practice, as we identified in the previous section, partnerships and networks between schools take many forms, from relatively informal local clusters through to more structured arrangements, such as federations.

School to school collaboration, partnerships and networks offer significant potential for sharing learning and expertise between schools and across systems, for providing support to schools that are struggling, for ensuring 'joined up' provision that meets the needs of all children, and/or for supporting innovation (Armstrong et al 2020). However, there is relatively weak evidence on how networks and collaboration enable impact, partly because it is challenging to assess impact from more diffuse partnerships. The evidence is strongest in relation to formally brokered school-to-school support and federations, for example, where a successful school supports a lower-performing school to improve (Muijs 2015; Chapman, Muijs and Macallister 2011). Despite these potential benefits, networks are not a panacea and various observers have highlighted that they can have a 'dark' side (Bidart, Degenne and Grossetti 2020; Kamp 2013).

Based on a review of the literature,[1] we identify a number of evidence-informed core principles that help to differentiate more and less successful networks, and which informed the evaluation findings. These are summarised as follows:

- successful inter-organisational networks reflect a shared goal or interest as well as shared values, practices and attributes, including trust, all of which take time to build;
- network impact relates to the level of commitment and contribution of network members, reflecting shared ownership and benefits;
- a number of design features are important for network effectiveness, such as the availability of resources (including time);
- networks often focus on generating and diffusing knowledge, which can be assisted by the adoption of shared protocols and tools; and
- leading and managing networks requires sophisticated skills and qualities.

---

1   These findings are synthesized from the authors' own work as well as a range of wider studies: Yancovic et al 2020; Brown 2020; González, Ehren and Montecino 2020; Armstrong, Brown and Chapman 2020; Rincon-Gallardo and Fullan 2016; Ainscow 2015; Chapma 2015; Muijs 2015b; OECD 2015; Hargreaves, Parsley and Cox 2015; Suggett 2014; Muijs and Rumyantseva 2014; Kamp 2013; Muijs, West and Ainscow 2010; Hill and Matthews 2010; Hargreaves 2010; 2011; 2012a; 2012b; Jackson and Temperley 2006; Glatter 2003.

Summary findings from the evaluation

Rural schools faced distinctive Covid-related challenges

The Kent and Yorkshire networks involved around 20 school leaders each, with a smaller core of very active participants. Schools participating in the networks varied widely in terms of their size, leadership arrangements and cohorts. The smallest case study school had 42 students on roll, but the sample also included much larger, two-form entry, schools. The case study sample included one assistant head, three headteachers of single schools and two executive heads of two-school federations. These leaders described similar challenges, including geographic isolation, small staffs and limited leadership capacity.

Case study school leaders described some benefits from being a rural or small school during lockdown, for example in terms of being able to connect with parents and the community. However, they suffered the same pressures as other schools nationally during the pandemic (Thomson, Greany and Martindale 2021), in terms of the need to lead continuous change on multiple fronts, some of which were exacerbated by their small size and geographic isolation.

Every case study school was engaged in at least one existing network, such as a teaching school alliance[2] or local cluster. Although one school leader felt well supported and connected by these existing networks, the remainder did not. Issues with existing networks included being dominated by the agendas and needs of a particular academy or multi-academy trust (MAT) and a lack of 'fit' in terms of personal or school ethos. Leaders reported a mixed picture on how these existing networks operated during the lockdown, while some became more active and supportive during the crisis, others 'went quiet' as schools 'battened down the hatches'.

Two contrasting networks: one looser and more open, one tight-knit community

Turning to the foundation-run networks, participants often struggled to attend face-to-face events, due to limited capacity in school and the

---

2   Between 2010 and 2019, a school could volunteer to be designated as a teaching school by the government if it met specified performance criteria. Designation schools had a remit to provide initial teacher training (ITT), school-to-school support for schools facing challenges, and ongoing professional and leadership development for staff across a voluntary alliance of partner schools, although the precise size and nature of this network was not prescribed.

distances involved. Most, therefore, welcomed the option of meeting online in principle, although many participants struggled with this initially due to poor facilities and/or lack of confidence in using the technology.

The evaluation identified five hublets that met between two and six times over the course of the year. Participation in these hublets depended on the initiative of individual school leaders. Some leaders saw this as a place to 'focus on their own agenda' and to learn from each other, for example through visits and learning walks.

The two networks differed in their approach to membership. One facilitator focused on accessibility, for example by offering multiple slots for online and face-to-face meetings, to give participants more opportunities to engage. The other met as a more consistent group and relied more on in person meetings, with an advisory group drawn from member schools also meeting to shape the network agenda. The result was that the former network appeared looser and more open, while the latter became more of a tight-knit community. The literature indicates pros and cons to each approach (Greany and Kamp 2022; Granovetter 1973).

Network purpose evolved in response to the pandemic: 'an oasis for reflection'

The question of who should set the agenda for the networks – i.e. whether they should be organic and 'school-led', or should adhere to the requirements of the foundation or the dioceses – remained live in both networks. One example was how meeting agendas were set and facilitated. On the one hand there was pressure to include centrally developed resources aimed at developing faith leadership and to address common areas of need, such as helping schools prepare for the new SIAMS[3] inspection framework. On the other hand, school leaders wanted opportunities to reflect on their own experiences and to learn from each other, particularly during the pandemic.

In terms of network content, social action and school improvement were initially two distinct and pre-set network agendas, but both

---

3   SIAMS (Statutory Inspection of Anglican and Methodist Schools) is the inspection schedule to which Church of England schools are subject under Section 48. The schedule is based around a core question: How effective is the school's distinctive Christian vision, established and promoted by leadership at all levels, in enabling pupils and adults to flourish?

networks allowed them to merge. The impact of the pandemic meant that schools did not have the time or capacity to generate significant new projects or collaborations in these areas. Nevertheless, the networks did impact on how leaders conceptualised and approached their existing social action work across the school, leading them to focus more intentionally on developing young people's agency.

Overall, the evaluation shows that the networks were successful in securing and maintaining engagement from a core group of school leaders. The structure of the networks, in particular the use of online, face to face and 'hublet' formats, worked well for the participants who remained engaged. A key factor in this success was the use of skilled and credible facilitators. The networks provided participants with a 'safe space' in which to reflect on their personal and professional values and priorities, which was particularly valuable during lockdown. By the end of the year, the networks appeared to be developing into sustainable communities, characterised by robust peer challenge and debate and with the potential to become more self-sustaining.

The networks had two initial functions, the sharing of resources, ideas and practice in relation to faith leadership and social action, and the building of relationships with other school leaders. As they developed, however, and particularly as a result of lockdown, a wider purpose developed, which we characterise in terms of theologically informed strategic reflection on leadership, including the personal and emotional dimensions of leadership. For example, interviewees described meetings as pushing them to spend time thinking about things they were 'passionate about' but which, nonetheless, could get 'pushed to the side', and being encouraged to 'take risks' and 'be courageous' in their roles. One facilitator described their network as offering 'an oasis for reflection'.

Moving forward: implications for future networks

We argue that network designers must consider and define the desired function(s), or purpose(s), of any proposed network early on, involving network participants in this process. Clarity on purpose will enable a more meaningful discussion around the type of network that is needed and the practical steps needed to develop it, in line with the core principles for networks derived from the literature. Furthermore, it will help clarify responses to foundational questions, such as – do we want 'tight-knit' communities or more open networks? Who should set the network agenda? What is the desired balance between 'top down' and 'bottom up' priorities? Importantly, the answers to these questions may take time to emerge and may change over time: the evaluation clearly shows the value of networks remaining responsive, agile and iterative, rather than seeking to define and impose overly prescriptive aims and structures.

The evaluation indicates that without successful facilitation, networks may not emerge and/or may drift and dissipate. Three facilitator roles and skills appear to have been particularly valuable in the two networks studied: convening, catalysing and coaching. These facilitator roles/skills can be seen as one way of framing the 'sophisticated leadership qualities', highlighted in our fifth network principle. We argue that network designers should focus on how these can best be developed:

- **Convening** relates to how the facilitator can best recruit members and facilitate the development of a sustainable, 'school-led' network community over time. It is important to articulate the collective purpose or goal that unites participants and to establish shared expectations around ways of working, while leaving space for network members to feel sufficient ownership of the process in order to suggest and implement changes and to adapt the purpose over time in response to external circumstances (including pandemics!). Time and care need to be taken to listen to all participants, diagnosing their current knowledge and experience and adapting content and session design to personalise the experience so that all can benefit. These approaches should seek to foster – and periodically articulate – shared values, practices and attributes in order to build commitment and trust. Similarly, network members should be encouraged to identify and commit the resources required for network effectiveness, such as dedicated time for participating teachers.

- **Catalysing** relates to how the facilitator works to ensure that the network is successful in generating (innovation) and diffusing (exploitation) useful knowledge. This can include introducing new expertise or ideas as well as sparking the identification, codification and sharing of existing practices in ways that lead to change and improvement across member schools. Many networks do not develop clearly articulated theories of action for how knowledge is mobilised and shared, but wider evidence indicates the value of agreeing a core set of approaches backed by shared language, protocols and tools, which can then provide a platform for productive collaboration between teachers and schools (Glazer and Peurach 2015). For example, in the case of the foundation's networks, this might involve agreeing the respective role of the network events and hublets, and the kinds of learning processes, protocols and routines that can best facilitate knowledge sharing across each.

- **Coaching** relates to the facilitator's role in encouraging leaders to reflect deeply on their personal and collective purpose and practice. This contrasts heavily with the notion of delivery of a programme of study, and facilitators must be deliberate and self-aware as to their modus operandi in networks, which are frequently more about drawing knowledge and experience out of the network members, as opposed to delivery of knowledge from a programme leader to the participants. In both cases, however, we argue that the modelling, unpacking, exemplification and application of core knowledge is essential to the professional development of those involved.

In order to secure sustainability, we argue that there is merit in giving participating school leaders ownership of the networks and how they operate, even from the outset. For example, by adopting steering groups as a consistent feature and by devolving a network budget to this group.

Finally, it is important to recognise the differences between formal professional development programmes and networks, not least given the 2021 implementation across England of a more coherent national approach to the design and delivery of teacher and leadership programmes (Early Career Framework, National Professional Qualifications and Teaching School Hubs). These reforms focus professional development activity onto the achievement of individual role-specific qualifications, potentially providing value to individuals and contributing to greater coherence across the sector. However, we argue there remains an important parallel place for networks, which can provide more flexible, contextually relevant support for individual and organisational development than is possible in formal programmes. Such peer-to-peer communities can help to bridge structural holes in England's fragmented school system and can have a positive impact on leaders' development – both in terms of knowledge acquisition and application in role, and also their wider character development, wellbeing and resilience. In this sense, the thoughtful combination of formal programmes and networks can replenish leaders' 'reservoirs of hope' (Flintham 2003) and enable them to flourish together.

References

Ainscow, M. (2015) Towards self-improving school systems: Lessons from a City Challenge. London: Routledge.

Armstrong, P. W., Brown, C. and Chapman, C. (2020) 'School-to-school collaboration in England: A configurative review of the empirical evidence', *Review of Education*, 9(1), pp. 319–351.

Brown, C., (2020) The networked school leader: how to improve teaching and student outcomes using learning networks. Bingley, UK: Emerald Publishing.

Chapman, C. (2015) From one school to many: Reflections on the impact and nature of school federations and chains in England. *Educational Management Administration & Leadership*, 43(1), pp. 46–60.

Chapman, C., Muijs, D. and MacAllister, J. (2011) *A study of the impact of school federation on student outcomes*. Nottingham: National College for School Leadership.

Church of England (2018) *Embracing change: Rural and small schools*. Available from: www.bit.ly/3NgJkkB.

Coopers & Lybrand (1995) *Safety in numbers: small schools and collaborative arrangements*. Birmingham: National Association of Schoolmasters Union of Women Teachers.

Daly, A. and Chrispeels, J. (2008) 'A question of trust: Predictive conditions for adaptive and technical leadership in educational contexts', *Leadership and Policy in Schools*, 7(1), pp. 30–63.

Department for Environment, Food & Rural Affairs [DEFRA] (2019) *Rural education and childcare*. London: Department for Environment, Food & Rural Affairs. Retrieved from: www.bit.ly/3JIEsCH.

Department for Environment, Food & Rural Affairs [DEFRA] (2020) *Statistical Digest of Rural England: March 2020 Edition*. London: Department for Environment, Food & Rural Affairs.

Echazarra, A. and Radinger, T. (2018) *Learning in rural schools: Insights from PISA, TALIS and the Literature.* OECD Education Working Paper No. 196. Paris: OECD Publishing.

Ehren, M. and Perryman, J. (2017) 'Accountability of school networks: Who is accountable to whom and for what?', *Education Management, Administration and Leadership*, 46(6), pp. 942–959.

Evans, M. P. and Stone-Johnson, C. (2010) 'Internal leadership challenges of network participation', *International Journal of Leadership in Education*, 13(2), pp. 203–220.

Flintham, A. (2003) *Reservoirs of Hope: Spiritual and Moral Leadership in Headteachers.* Nottingham: National College for School Leadership.

Flintham A. (2009) *Faith, Hope and Spirituality in School Leadership.* PhD thesis. Liverpool: University of Liverpool.

Glatter, R. (2003) 'Collaboration, collaboration, collaboration: the origins and implications of a policy', *Management in Education*, 17(5), pp. 16–20.

Glazer, J. L. and Peurach, D. J. (2015) 'Occupational Control in Education: The Logic and Leverage of Epistemic Communities', *Harvard Educational Review*, 85(2), pp. 172–202.

González, A., Ehren, M. and Montecinos, C. (2020) 'Leading mandated network formation in Chile's new public education system', *School Leadership and Management*, 40(5), pp. 425–443.

Granovetter, M. (1973) 'The strength of weak ties', *American Journal of Sociology*, 78(6), pp. 1360–1380.

Greany, T. and Higham, R. (2018) *Hierarchy, markets and networks: analysing the 'self-improving school-led system' agenda in England and the implications for schools.* London: UCL Institute of Education Press.

Greany, T. and Kamp, A. (2022) *Leading Educational Networks: Theory, Policy and Practice.* London: Bloomsbury.

Hargreaves, L. (2009) 'Respect and responsibility: Review of research on small rural schools in England', *International Journal of Educational Research*, 48(2), pp. 117–128.

Hargreaves, A., Parsley, D. and Cox, E. K. (2015) 'Designing rural school improvement networks: Aspirations and actualities', *Peabody Journal of Education*, 90(2), pp. 306–321.

Hill, R. and Matthews, P. (2010) *Schools leading schools II: The growing impact of National Leaders of Education*, Nottingham: National College for School Leadership.

Jackson, D. and Temperley, J. (2006) *From professional learning community to networked learning community*, conference paper for International Congress for School Effectiveness and Improvement (ICSEI) Fort Lauderdale, USA, January 3–6.

Kamp, A. (2013) *Rethinking learning networks: Collaborative possibilities for a Deleuzian century*. Bern: Peter Lang.

Menzies, L. (2019) *Breaking the link? Attainment, poverty and rural schools*. Available from: www.bit.ly/3izTHBT.

Muijs, D. (2015a) 'Collaboration and networking among rural schools: Can it work and when? Evidence From England', *Peabody Journal of Education*, 90(2), 294–305.

Muijs, D. (2015b) 'Improving schools through collaboration: a mixed methods study of school-to-school partnerships in the primary sector', *Oxford Review of Education*, 41(5), pp. 563–586.

Muijs, D., West, M. and Ainscow, M. (2010) 'Why network? Theoretical perspectives on networking', *School Effectiveness and School Improvement*, 21(1), pp. 5–26.

Ovenden-Hope, T. and Passy, R. (2019) *Educational isolation: A challenge for schools in England*. Plymouth: University of Plymouth and Plymouth Marjon University. Available at: www.bit.ly/36J9hsv.

Perry, B. L., Pescosolido, A. and Borgatti, S. P. (2020) *Egocentric network analysis: Foundations, methods and models*. Cambridge: Cambridge University Press.

Popp, J., Milward, B., MacKean, G., Casebeer, A. and Lindstrom, R. (2014) *Inter-organizational Networks: A review of the literature to inform practice*. Washington, DC: IBM Center for the Business of Government.

Provan, K. and Kenis, P. (2008) 'Modes of network governance: structure, management, and effectiveness', *Journal of Public Administration Research and Theory*, 18(2), pp. 229–252.

Schafft, K. and Youngblood Jackson, A. (Eds) (2010) *Rural education for the twenty-first century: Identity, place, and community in a globilizing world*. Pennsylvania: The Pennsylvania State University Press.

Suggett, D. (2014) *Networking as system policy: Balancing vertical and horizontal dimensions*. Retrieved from: www.bit.ly/3Lfgv6y.

The Key (2018) *The challenges of leading a rural school*. Available from: www.bit.ly/3IyolGp.

Thomson, P., Greany, T. and Martindale, N. (2021) The trust deficit in England: emerging research evidence about school leaders and the pandemic, *Journal of Educational Administration and History*, 43(3/4), pp. 296–300.

Vangen, S. and Huxham, C. (2003) Enacting leadership for collaborative advantage: dilemmas of ideology and pragmatism in the activities of partnership managers, *British Journal of Management*, 14, pp. 61–76.

Yancovic, M. P., Torres, A. G., Figueroa, L. A. and Chapman, C. (2020) School improvement networks and collaborative enquiry: fostering systemic change in challenging contexts. Bingley, UK: Emerald Publishing.

A new paradigm for professional development and performance management

John Baumber

Overview

The pandemic has impacted many things in education. It has shone a light on some of the things we have done that does not lead to the best of outcomes. It is amazing, over a decade from the first meta-analysis by John Hattie (2012) and the system persists with the things we know have little impact. This chapter argues that the pandemic has provided an opportunity to pause and reflect. As teacher wellbeing has become a critical imperative in schools, it is a time to review how we have built our professional development programmes and take the opportunity to adopt a personalised approach. It is natural that if we do this, we should reshape our performance management procedures so it brings more compassion, and a recognition that all teachers want to be the best they can be – removing judgment and replacing it with trust and collective teacher efficacy.

Creating networks within and across schools is critical to this. The system will only transform if there is a viable alternative to the present (Fullan 2020). Networks can support but can also bring a capacity to shape and challenge the status quo in the system. It entails deploying the right drivers – not autonomy but collaboration, not external accountability but building capacity and internal skills, not fragmented approaches but systemness, and not technology, but using it to enhance pedagogy.(Fullan 2016).

Keywords
Professional development
Networking
Peer review
Performance management
Personalisation
Laboratory Schools

A critical turning point

In their recent book *The Devil is in the Detail*, Michael Fullan and Mary Gallagher (2020:5) refer to the lyrics of a song by Leonard Cohen: Ring the bells that still can ring. There is a crack, a crack in everything that's how the light gets in.

We are at a point in education (and probably also in life) where the pandemic has either driven us towards a more cautious operational risk-averse mentality or triggered an opportunity for change and transformation. There is much talk about getting back to where we were or to a new normal, but the reality is where we were was neither a preparation for the future, nor was it meeting the needs of the present. Over the last few decades many educationalists and politicians have encouraged teachers to think about 21st century skills. There are many ways that these skills can be categorised, which are very often attached to a particular letter such as the 6 Cs (Miller 2018) and the 5 Rs (Claxton 2002)[1]. The reality is that many of these skills, such as teamwork and resilience, creativity and problem solving, are skills that young people should have had in the 20th century. The rapid pace of societal change

---

[1]   In '21 lessons for 21st Century' Harari (2018) highlights the challenge of preparing young people for 2050 when we have little idea of the shape of society or the economics they will face. He thinks teaching should switch to the 4 Cs: critical thinking, communication, collaboration, creativity and playing down technical skills.
Fullan (2018) and Miller (2015) developed this further adding two more: character education and citizenship/culture. Fullan argues that students should also possess emotional intelligence, grit, perseverance, an intrinsic desire to learn, and the capacity to empathise with others.
Guy Claxton (2002) in his work on Building Learning Power approached the same issue but categorised them as being resilient, resourceful, reflective, reciprocal and responsible. Through these 5 Rs, the children will be able to have greater success and reach their full potential as learners.

and the impact of technology has simply brought these to the fore and in sharp relief.

To face this unprecedented challenge, how do we prepare our profession, and at a time when our resources are likely to be stretched? The contention here is that we need to think about professional development in a different way and link this closely to staff wellbeing and their moral purpose. And we would further contend that this mandates us to think carefully about our performance management strategies. Of course, these changes can and are being taken by individual leaders in individual institutions, but so fundamental are the challenges and the need for transformation at pace, it demands that we work together to exploit the 'crack' that has opened. Many see this moment as like the industrial revolution because the metrics have fundamentally changed.

Bringing about radical change through networking

Very often professional development is left largely to individual schools with perhaps some collaborative central input – often at the start of a year or semester – but centralised performance management is usually layered on from a national or middle tier of district or trust level. For instance, many states in the USA, have drawn on the Danielson Framework for Teaching (Danielson 2013) which draws up teaching components that can then be used to define judgments about teacher quality and impact (see figure 1 and figure 2).

DOMAIN 1:
PLANNING AND PREP

- Demonstrating knowledge of content and pedagogy
- Demonstrating knowledge of students
- Setting instructional outcomes
- Demonstrating knowledge of resources
- Designing coherent instruction
- Designing student assessments

DOMAIN 2:
CLASSROOM ENVIRONMENT

- Creating an environment of respect and rapport
- Establishing a culture for learning
- Managing classroom procedures
- Managing student behaviour
- Organising physical space

DOMAIN 3:
INSTRUCTION

- Communicating with students
- Using questioning and discussion techniques
- Engaging students in learning
- Using assessment in instruction
- Demonstrating flexibility and responsiveness

DOMAIN 4:
PROFESSIONAL RESPONSIBILITIES

- Reflecting on teaching
- Maintaining accurate records
- Communicating with families
- Participating in the professional community
- Growing and developing professionally
- Showing professionalism

States will then mandate a set of teacher evaluation procedures whereby teachers are observed and graded against a set of clearly defined rubrics.

The standards vary from country to country, but this is a common approach. Sometimes this is used formatively and in other cases it is linked to performance or merit pay.

Figure 2 shows what a school might generate from such a process that might also inform future staff development.

Figure 1 Framework for teaching domains (source: Danielson 2013)

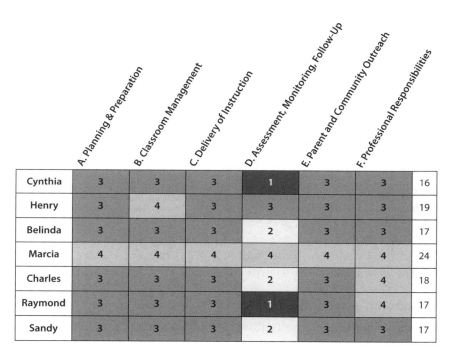

	A. Planning & Preparation	B. Classroom Management	C. Delivery of Instruction	D. Assessment, Monitoring, Follow-Up	E. Parent and Community Outreach	F. Professional Responsibilities	
Cynthia	3	3	3	1	3	3	16
Henry	3	4	3	3	3	3	19
Belinda	3	3	3	2	3	3	17
Marcia	4	4	4	4	4	4	24
Charles	3	3	3	2	3	4	18
Raymond	3	3	3	1	3	4	17
Sandy	3	3	3	2	3	3	17

Figure 2 How performance management can use the Danielson domains (source: Danielson 2013)

The question is whether this is a constructive mechanism to support the rapid response required to transform learning. If not, it could be argued that there must be either a significant political shift in policy at a national or district level, or networks of schools to determining a viable alternative that can inform the system. It is unlikely, however impressive they are, that an individual school leader can breach the statutory expectations that jurisdictions, districts or trusts set up to monitor quality, but perhaps groups of schools or networks can demonstrate an alternative approach.

Educational systems are inherently conservative, so despite the unprecedented creativity and innovation by teachers through the pandemic, there is little sign yet of any systematic change to reflect the present or future situation (Schleicher 2020). Other educationalists feel that now is the time for the profession and the networks of schools to fashion change rather than waiting for national policy shifts and that great leaders, great teachers and great schools can make a significant difference while still meeting the accountability measures but are imposed upon them. This is what Tim Brighouse (2015) described it as finding a gaps in the hedge. In fact, system change will only take place when there is a viable believable alternative (Fullan 2020).

Networks of schools (be they formal like multi-academy trusts, or informal built around a common set of values and ambitions) have the capacity to make a shift. Together they can harness a range of ideas, draw on research and take account of the essential pedagogical shifts, such as increasing the use of technology and more hybrid teaching. A network brings security and validity to changing practice, which in turn builds trust and confidence in school governance. It is very unlikely that such change will come from central government or individual schools who, at the moment, are tied up with the minutiae of operational matters. Networks foster dialogue and bring security to collaborative creative processes.

Unleashing greatness

The business guru and bestselling author Tom Peters (2003) has written much over the years about getting business and services like education to wake up to the new world in which they live, where creativity and the individual are to the fore. He believes that monolithic organisations and bureaucracies prevent us from moving things forward to reflect the world in which we now inhabit. In his book *Re- imagine!* he vociferously castigated what he perceived to be an education system that relates back to the Fordist era where employees needed to know their place and individual initiative and creativity was stultified. Sir Ken Robinson (2006) similarly accused schools as killing creativity.

The creation of the International Centre for Educational Enhancement (ICEE) at the University of Bolton focused on helping schools shift practice that brings about change that really leads to sustained improvement for learners. Through a range of school networks committed to a common moral purpose of equity, social mobility, personalisation and globalisation, ICEE positions itself between research and policy and the classroom seeking to address some of the natural conservatism at a system level. The belief is that effective networks support educational innovation and change by:

- **keeping the focus** on the core purposes of schooling.
- **enhancing the skill** of teachers, leaders and other educators.
- **providing a focal point** for dissemination of practice.
- **building capacity** for continuous improvement at a local level.
- **acting as a link** between centralised and decentralised policy initiatives.

One of the critical networks at the heart of the centre is its Laboratory School Partnership, believing that this network could provide that viable alternative. The schools commit to an improvement and change strategy entitled 'Unleashing Greatness' (Hopkins 2020). This is built on the seminal work by Professor David Hopkins. Over the years he has talked about curiosity and powerful learning (Hopkins 2015). The starting point is to ask all schools to really clarify their moral purpose and identify their non-negotiables. In any new educational paradigm, this moral purpose needs to reflect the monumental societal forces that technology, climate change and the pandemic require of us.

Figure 3 identifies the elements of practice of the Laboratory School Partnership. Critical elements are the peer-to-peer reviews where through appreciative enquiry schools work together to share their work together, building up researched practice and sharing with the wider system. Obviously, at the heart of the collaboration is the quality and effectiveness of teaching and learning set in the context of moral purpose and current relevance.

Figure 3 The core elements of Laboratory School Practice

If we take on board the much-used statement borne out of the McKinsey report that 'the quality of the education system cannot exceed the quality of teachers' (Barber and Mourshed 2007:5), then creating effective classrooms driven by a clear purpose must then guide the structure, focus and content of professional development. This requires instructional leaders the know how to shape these ideas, values and principles into effective teaching and learning in every classroom. There is no doubt that over the last 20 years the knowledge and understanding of teachers about how children learn has expanded exponentially. Research from individuals like John Hattie and organisations like the Educational Endowment Fund have provided teachers with the tools to sharpen practice and achieve more for their young people. Teachers are now sharing a new vocabulary and understanding of how learning takes place, e.g. spaced assessment, retrieval practice, cognitive load, etc. And yet the data that really proves we are making any substantial difference to outcomes is limited. Even when we try to convince ourselves that standards are rising, the reality is different (Coe 2013).

We would maintain that this is because we do not embed practice across a school allowing for significant in-school variation and faulty implementation. The 'Unleashing Greatness' framework seeks to address this as we will discuss later but, first, we might consider the effectiveness of our professional development structures in schools.

Demolishing the traditional model of professional development

Many schools in the UK rely on their five days of designated training time with a monthly schedule of directed time sessions at the end of days. In some cases, these are built into the schedule with schools finishing earlier one day every week for perhaps a two-hour session. In other international contexts, different approaches are taken. In the United States and in Sweden (particularly in the free school and charter school worlds where more potential freedoms exist) significant time is set aside before the school year begins for teachers to have two or three weeks to work together both for professional development and planning. Whereas meeting, planning and development time is at a premium in many UK schools, other settings balance teacher and student contact time differently. Finland is renowned for its significantly lower contact time with students and high levels of quality professional development (Sahlberg 2010). In these other systems, they do not rely on sessions at the end of days when teachers are likely to be more tired and less receptive.

Quality professional development is not just about finding the time; there is a bigger and more fundamental issue. We know that simply explaining the theory of how a change in practice should occur and even then, demonstrating it, will only have a limited impact and one that is probably transitory. The real change comes when teachers together practice, get feedback and then coach one another to be exceptional practitioners (Joyce and Showers 1995). The Unleashing Greatness framework asks us to recognise that substantial improvement and change can only occur when the full faculty of a school works together to a common agreed narrative that creates consistent teacher efficacy by establishing clear protocols that explicitly build teacher expertise and repertoire, followed by practice, feedback and peer coaching. This can lead to sustained change. Unless we catalogue and detail the nature of teacher techniques and tactics, it has no stickability beyond the training input and risks short-term improvement.

This is not to say there is no value in external input from speakers and consultants; it can bring validity and evidence from outside the school.

Nor does it mean that for individual teachers who might be early in their career or struggling with change or improvement, a more instructional approach is required. Instruction and demonstration alone do not build the capacity we need. This is a mindset issue and about school culture. It is about recognising that there is expertise in all our schools that can be shared and developed and refined. School improvement and, therefore, improved teaching practice is a bottom-up process where everyone sees it as their shared responsibility. Teachers need to own their professionalism and expertise.

Bringing agency

But returning to the pandemic, technology has taught us that there is a way to effectively personalise our professional development. Organisations like Creative Education and the National College in the UK, 2Revolutions in the USA, have created high quality bite-sized online resources that enable teachers to personalise their learning around a set of professional goals. It allows teachers to diagnose their development needs and then build their own professional plan at a time that suits them.

This cannot sit separate to performance management. Giving more agency to teachers to improve their practice must enable them to demonstrate that growth. Traditionally schools have built up their school improvement plan and asked teachers to establish one of their performance targets related to student outcome and then one or more centrally determined professional development goal or teaching standard.

Just as we have learned about our students, returning to any sort of normal schooling from the pandemic, the impact on each individual – teacher and student – has been very different. There's been no more important time to recognise two things about our students and our fellow professionals. Firstly, the need to personalise our response and secondly to redefine disadvantage. In the case of teachers, many will be having to re-discover their sense of purpose and wellbeing but are now realising the school they knew before has changed, students have changed, technology has changed. They will need to have personal goals to regain their professional confidence in addition to meeting the more strategic approach planned by the school.

Gavin Drake (2013) identified that it is crucial that we think about our self, our life and the world around us every day. To fulfil our potential, he argues that it is important we develop various competencies: focus, belief, responsibility, attitude, purpose, clarity emotion, empathy and influence. The core purpose of a school leader is to achieve the very best for all learners in the school, but they can only achieve this with the full support of his/her colleagues each able to give of their best. Change is messy and impacts on every teacher differently. As such, the leader needs to be adaptive and needs to understand the different mindsets and anxieties across the school. If they do not take account of these the outcomes will be lessened. They need the space to build positive thinking strategies to meet a set of personal goals. It is certain that in this climate, a centralised professional development and observational performance strategies are not sensitive enough to need. But equally powerful is for teachers to see themselves as part of something bigger and being a part of a network enables them to share their work with others without fear of internal judgment. It gives everyone access to a wider repertoire of teacher strategies.

Instructional rounds and personal goals

The instructional round is a key part to the 'Unleashing Greatness' framework. It belongs to the appreciative inquiry set of research methods and involves leaders from inside the school and from the wider network coming together to distil the expert practise of any given school. This distillation provides a set of theories of action which describe the sorts of teacher's behaviour that leads to positive student outcomes and progress (see figure 4). Recently at Beaumont Primary School in Bolton, a group of six primary heads and the network lead identified these theories. The network of school leaders not only bring their own understanding of teaching and learning but in the process learn themselves how a school effectively implements its Teaching and Learning Framework.

THEORIES OF ACTION

1 PRIOR LEARNING

When teachers systematically refer back to prior learning (e.g. last year, last week, yesterday) and uses it to scaffold current learning;

Then learners cognitive load is reduced, their learning is reinforced and they are more confident to proceed.

2 VOCABULARY AQUISITION

When all the adults in the school adopt precise and consistent approach to the acquisition of vocabulary such as subject specific and transferable vocabulary and apply to a variety of contexts;

Then learners cognitive load is reduced, their learning is reinforced and they are more confident to proceed.

3 COLLABORATION

When teachers consistently utilise paired and group work for discussion and questioning as an expected feature of most lessons;

Then learners understanding is deepened they use a range of question strategies and become more confident.

4 HIGH EXPECTATIONS AND PUPIL VOICE

When all the adults in the school have high expectations of learners they establish a culture of respect, rapport and value pupil voice;

Then learners themselves feel increasingly valued and their confidence is enhanced and learning is increased.

5 ROUTINES AND PACE

When all the adults in the school establish routines that are well understood and use this to increase the pace of learning;

Then learners have more time for learning, are increasingly secure in their own progress and work in a calm and purposeful environment.

6 BASIC SKILLS AND TEACHER MODELLING

When teachers take a consistent approach to the acquisition of basic skills through careful modelling, and making the learning steps explicit;

Then learners make more rapid progress and become increasingly confident in the application of these basic skills.

7 SCAFFOLDING

When teachers thoughtfully and explicitly use scaffolding to promote learning in a variety of curricular contexts;

Then learners become more independent in their learning, are able to access the same learning content as their peers and can also use the same scaffolding techniques to teach each other.

8 LEARNING ENVIRONMENT

When the school reflects it's high expectations for its pupils in the learning environment e.g. learning displays of writing and is consistent in it's messaging;

Then learners' learning is continually reinforced and they gain confidence through having their learning reflected back to them.

9 QUESTIONING

When teachers consistently and self consciously use questioning to probe and deepen learning to check understanding ('cold call') and are reluctant to accept the first answer;

Then learners understanding deepens and they expand their repertoire of questioning skills to use in their collaborative conversations and situations.

10 METACOGNITION

When the school and it's adults utilise the range of the theories of action above in a self conscious and consistent way then a learning culture is established that prizes metacognition;

Then learners become increasingly curious and their passion for learning is ignited.

Figure 4 Theories of action for Beaumont Primary School (Postle 2021)

This by itself, will not improve the school; they must then identify the protocols and models of practice that can be implemented. It must then be replicated and coached consistently and with confidence across all classes. But it's important to recognise that each individual teacher will be on their own journey and need to establish their own personal journey. A school will not want to work on every element at once and will select areas where all teachers can work together. That does not preclude other individual choices. But here we start to see the power of networking.

Having completed many instructional rounds it is not surprising that common theories of action and expert practice are seen across the network. For instance, it is likely that most schools will have something about higher order questioning. This is where the network can start to bring capacity; as they start to develop their protocols and models of teaching inevitably brings a wider range of ideas and repertoire. If collaborative teaching leads to better learning outcomes, why would that also not apply to teachers and their techniques.

Other networks within ICEE

Our work, like most education faculties at the university is inevitably concerned with research publications and teaching – in our case at a postgraduate level. However, we all committed to placing ourselves between this traditional role and live practice in schools. This means developing networks of schools who together can support one another and inform the system by modelling practise and creating their own action research. We work with local authorities and multi-academy trusts. We work with primary groups of schools (hubs) and special school and alternative provision groups. One example is the SAIL network (student agency in learning]. This grew out of a continuing relationship with Kunskapsskolan, who themselves have run a large group of schools in Sweden over the last 20 years, and now with partner schools around the world. The SAIL schools are inspired by the goal-driven personalisation that underpins the whole school design approach of Kunskapsskolan. This design has provided a set of values, principles, and tools which in Sweden has led to them being the most successful network of schools not just in terms of student outcomes and added value, but in the personal skills and agency that the young people can develop and demonstrate.

We will return to the Kunskapsskolan group of schools shortly but the distinguishing feature of the SAIL schools in the United Kingdom is the spirit of collaboration and trust that is facilitated by a small core team. Despite being located across the country with schools from Cornwall to Essex and from Norfolk to Wigan there is no spirit of competition but a sense of trust and willing to learn from the different contexts of the schools in all phases primary secondary and special.

We can examine this at a more micro level. Two of the tools used to build agency in students and to inspire them to set and reach their long-term and short-term goals is the use of a logbook and the individual personal coaching session for every student every week. If students are given the freedom of constructing their own schedule each week, they need to be challenged to reach those goals – it cannot be a permissive structure process. What traditionally we would have called the form teacher now becomes a coach, who every week can help the student review progress and if necessary, so they come up with alternative strategies to challenge themselves or reach back to their goals. To support this each student each week creates their personal goals creating a very visible learning journey towards long-term goals. The logbook is the personal project plan they can record and review.

The difference between the SAIL network in the UK and the group of schools in Sweden established by the company – and built from scratch – is that, in the UK, all schools existed already and are tied into the strong accountability framework that epitomises the UK system. We have borrowed the metaphor for our schools that they are ' building an aeroplane while it's flying' . As such, all have had different starting points with different year groups and at different pace. If you take the idea of the instructional core (City et al 2009) with the three points of the triangle being content, teacher and student providing the context for the tasks, then any change to anyone part of that triangle impacts on all the others (see figure 5). It's a process of whole school design. The network becomes so powerful as we share the pedagogy of one another's change process which they can see through instructional rounds , visits, and meetings. Nothing is more powerful that leaders and teachers leading professional development in other schools; they have a different sort of credibility. So they benefit from a network introducing change in a range of contexts, learning from those who went before, but also form the international partners being challenged by what happens in completely different systems and being able to ask themselves, 'why would that not work here?' Removing the system facts such as Ofsted enables schools to think more creatively about strategies and techniques.

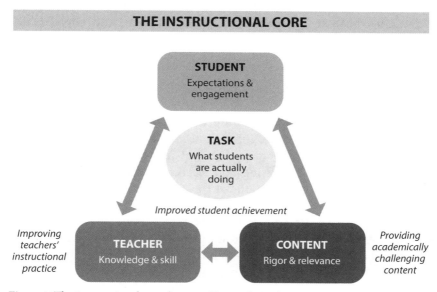

Figure 5 The instructional core (source: City et al 2009)

In Sweden, a group of schools every year conduct a detailed survey across all their schools with parents, teachers, and students to test the efficacy of each part of their model . This gives them the opportunity to benchmark and then discover from their colleagues where best practice may lay and where learning can take place. This now gives our UK schools the opportunity to test their growth against this much more unified group model.

It would be true to say that trying to provide a 15-minute coaching session for every student every week on a one-to-one basis in the UK schools is a challenge. It requires a new set of priorities for a school so they can justify a small reduction of traditional teaching time, but more importantly they can prioritise the significant use of teacher time. It would be an extreme act of faith to do this universally and at once. However, the SAIL schools I've been creative with the use of senior students acting as assistant coaches and a small group coaching model as initial steps in the journey. The core principle is to ensure that every young person has a chance to reflect every week against their goals and to feel the interest of the teacher who knows them well and always recognises whatever challenges faced them there is always a way to reach their goal.

Again, the SAIL network can actively review and support this through its instructional rounds and benchmarking surveys. The spirit of trust and freedom to share across the network has built real creativity and professional growth.

Returning to the Swedish group of schools, it would be true to say the whichever one of the 20-plus schools you visited you would recognise through the design of the building to the schedule and practice of teachers a common approach that has been tested and refined through the years. This uniformity of operational process enables the teacher to focus on the job of teaching and learning. Our English colleagues look enviously across to the Baltic at the consistency they have created. Kunskapsskolan often refer to themselves as a chain of schools and this is very different to the sort of network that we've been able to build around the ICEE. Tightly controlled chain networks present a different range of challenges, as they need to build in real self-reflection and the opportunity for creativity and ownership of their continued development and approach. The UK network of individual schools – although more challenging to manage and facilitate – have an inbuilt diversity that inevitably creates variety and options. The ICEE hope that their creativity and the hot house of change in Laboratory Schools will return the favour or enhanced practice back to our international colleagues.

Let us explore and compare this to an alternative view of the work of a district or local authority or multi-academy trust. Let us assume that at the end of the year the trust or authority leaders gather to interrogate the data from its schools and from this diagnose where they should put their energies for more improvement. Very often this could lead to intervention from the group or from an external consultant in areas or schools of concern. The group will know where problems may lie, but will they know why and what steps are needed to make that change? The system in England is littered with well-meaning examples of where short-term fixes not linked to detailed practice failed to secure long-term sustained progress.

City et al (2009) describe how building a network that then engages in repeated instructional rounds is a game changer. Here the players get into the detail of educational practice and see that student success is built out of network or system success. The rounds process, create and model a specific set of ideas so the schools and system at large can learn from their own practice, develop acute understanding of the next problem they need to solve, and take control of their own learning in ways that can lead to sustained improvement over time.

Moving forward: achieving real personalised professional development

We should think differently and in a more personalised way about how professional development could be. The context of schools now, means all staff in schools are faced with radical change and in many cases personal anxiety about the widened gap in student progress and personal wellbeing.

By way of conclusion, this checklist summarises how we might adapt and personalise our professional development and by necessity the performance management processes in a school. Above all, it identifies the power of working within a network to ensure change is both creative and sustained.

1. Build a collegial approach to the improvement of teaching and learning through appreciative enquiry identifying where in the school expert practice sits and then build protocols so it is extended into every classroom.

2. Allow space for teachers to practice and coach one another in a non-judgmental climate.

3. Take every network opportunity to build up the theories of action so we learn across schools and well as within. are building a masterful profession from the ground up

4. As we come to confirm what works and why, hone it into day-to-day practice of quality first teaching for all.

5. Ensure the networks are collaborative willing to share and benchmark their work. Encourage creativity and innovation that can be cross referenced and assessed. Establish peer to peer

partnerships across the network acting as critical appreciative friends.

6. Enable the existing online bite-sized programmes or develop your own learning 'nuggets' so teachers can take responsibility of their own professional journey.

7. Make teachers feel they are part of some bigger purpose and though their practice and action research can inform the wider system. Encourage collaboration at all levels of the network

8. Redevelop performance management. If teachers are coaching one another, are reflective and can report through a portfolio of evidence or an action research report internally and externally, then observation three times a year seems arbitrary and against the principle of teacher efficacy. There is plenty of data in schools about performance already.

9. Build a masters level profession with a University like Bolton and the ICEE so as teachers critically reflect on review, they can build evidence for master's modules.

Share at a range of levels and benchmark across the network. It's very powerful to be able to ask, 'How did you manage to do that successfully or why do you think this hasn't worked as well for us?'

Finally, we should go back to Daniel Pinks' work on motivation. There are three key aspects to building a motivate profession.

1. Purpose: I have a moral purpose and want to be part of something bigger than me and my school.

2. Mastery: I want to be the best I can be and feel that I constantly learning and shaping practice.

3. Autonomy: I take the responsibility as to how I can reach my goals even if some are set by the organisation I work with (Pink 2009).

Applying this different mindset creates a positive collaborative culture in the schools and models the best of learning to the young people within.

References

Barber, M. and Mourshed, M. (2007) How the world's best performing school systems come out on top. London: McKinsey & Company.

Brighouse, T. (2015) Seizing the Agenda: Finding the Gaps in the Hedge Whole Education Annual Conference. Retrieved from: www.bit.ly/3DeMssM.

City, E. A., Elmore, R. F., Fiarman, S. E. and Teitel, L. (2009) *Instructional rounds in education: a network approach to improving teaching and learning.* Cambridge, MA: Harvard Education Press.

Claxton, G. (2002) *Building Learning Power: Helping Young People Become Better Learners.* Bristol: TLO Ltd

Coe, R. (2013) Improving Education: A triumph of hope over experience. Inaugural Lecture, Durham University. Centre for Evaluation and Monitoring.

Danielson, C. (2013) *The Framework for Teaching.* Self-published.

Drake, G. and Jackson, J. (2013) *Mindspan: Peak Performance Manual for Your Mind.* Bookshaker.

Fullan M. (2016) *The new meaning of educational change.* London: Routledge.

Fullan M. (2020) Global Ed Talks with Anthony Mackay: An Interview with Michael Fullan. Washington, DC: National Center on Education and the Economy.

Fullan, M. and Gallagher, M. J. (2020). The devil is in the details: System solutions for equity, excellence, and student well-being. Thousand Oaks, CA: Corwin.

Harari, Y. N. (2018) *21 Lessons for the 21st Century.* London: Jonathan Cape/ Penguin Random House.

Hattie, J. (2012) *Visible learning for teachers: maximising the impact on learners.* London: Routledge.

Hopkins, D. (2020) 'Unleashing Greatness – A Strategy for School Improvement', *The Australian Educational Leader*, 42(3), 8–17.

Hopkins, D. and Craig, W. (2018) Curiosity and Powerful Learning. Sydney: ACEL, McREL McREL.

Joyce, B. and Showers, B. (1995) Student achievement through staff development (2nd ed). White Plains, NY: Longman

Miller, B. (2015) The 6 C's Squared Version of Learning Skills for the Twenty-First Century, *Flipped 4 Science* [Blog] 1 June. Retrieved from: www.bit. ly/3uSzdub.

Peters, T. (2003) *Re-Imagine Business excellence in a disruptive age.* London: Dorling Kindersley.

Pink, D. (2009) *Drive: The Surprising Truth About What Motivates Us.* London: Canongate.

Robinson, K. (2006) Do schools kill creativity?, *Open Growth* [Online] 26 February. Retrieved from: www.bit.ly/3DiS0m3.

Sahlberg, P. (2010) Key Drivers of Educational Performance in Finland. Lecture to Centre of International Mobility, USA

Schleicher, A. (2020) Global Ed Talks with Anthony Mackay: An Interview with Andreas Schleicher. Washington, DC: National Center on Education and the Economy.

Reframing teacher development in uncertain times

new spaces, new collaborations, new purposes

Jane Jones

Keywords
Critical teacher development
Collaborative teacher learning
Disruptive practice
Networking
Personal learning spaces
Socially aware professional development

Overview

Uncertain times and the recent global health crisis precipitated unparalleled changes in teaching and learning arrangements and the professional development landscape. Technological disruption propelled teachers into the need for fast upskilling in order to develop, at pace, online classrooms and learning. Teachers proved to be immensely adaptable in this endeavour, and in a mindset of 'all in it together', engaged in collaboration, peer coaching and resource-sharing like never before. Professional development transited effectively to online formats with many benefits that included more extensive collaborative learning across subjects and free access to global learning communities that were previously the preserve of elite specialist groups. The crisis proved a great leveller and provided spaces for a diversity of learning formats in groups, networks, on social media platforms, individualised research, across subjects as well as within subject.

Teachers took the initiative and undertook instructional leadership. This has led to a new hybrid paradigm of professional development, replicable in either online or face to face in schools, that reflects this diversity and fluidity. Aware of persisting social and educational disadvantage that came to light in online teaching scenarios, many teachers have aligned themselves with a socially responsible professional development agenda, designed to challenge inequalities and develop strategies to improve educational opportunity.

Professional opportunities in times of crisis

In this chapter, I analyse and reflect on the resetting of aspects of teacher professional development hastened in recent times by the Covid pandemic. My position is as a teacher educator working with teachers within university and school settings. I draw on data from two sources, an ESRC Project on Teacher Quality and Retention in which I have been involved[1] and the views of several of my former trainees with whom I have remained in professional and personal contact, referenced as P (project) and FT (former trainee) respectively. Their insightful accounts provide a rich picture of teaching, learning and professional development perspectives during the pandemic period.

The pandemic generated marked changes in the professional development landscape, changes that have endured and are becoming embedded in new personalised professional development discourses and practices. Communication in the community was extensive during this period owing to online communication accessibility and a perceived desire of all colleagues to 'keep in close contact' whilst in an isolation context. Such contact has proffered a good insight into the changes that have taken place in classroom teaching and learning, teacher collaboration and learning and the multiple challenges. The changes have required creative thinking about the scope and methods used to engage teachers in professional opportunities, a term that, for me, highlights choice and agency for teachers as opposed to 'development'

1   Research Project run by researchers at King's College London: Understanding and mitigating the impact of Covid-19 disruption on trainee and early career teachers in secondary schools to ensure teacher quality and enable retention is funded by the Economic and Social Research Council (ESRC) as part of the UK Research and Innovation's rapid response to Covid-19 [Grant Number ES/W00/1950/1].

that aligns with a notion of 'outside-of-self' developers. However, a variety of recognisable terms for what is in essence teachers' professional development are used in this chapter.

The aim of this chapter is to show how the move to online has created spaces for professional development (PD) that were hitherto restricted, spaces teachers now consider an entitlement in their personal and professional learning, spaces for teachers to interrogate, critically reflect, challenge and take a lead. The spaces are often disconcerting ones that focus on inclusion and social justice given how existing comfortable narratives were challenged by massively inequitable learning conditions that came to light with online learning. These spaces belong to what Britzman (2007) calls a teacher development world of uncertainty and the unknown to which teachers need to adapt further as they did miraculously with recent pandemic-related disruptions.

Disruption and uncertainty

Schools have long been hubs of effective technology used for a range of purposes. Teachers engage with technology effortlessly in the way that children from a very young age are technologically adept, 52% of three to four-year-olds having their own iPads according to a survey by the OECD (2019). Technology advances constantly and disrupts practice to usher in new technologies and new pedagogies. This is seen as part of a positively charged flow of technological advancement and innovation, although not without caveats as Yelland (2006) details. In the other sense of disruption, an event that prevents things going on as normal, teachers may feel insecure especially where change is abrupt and unexpected. As the literature shows (Fullan 2001; Hargreaves 2007), teachers need to be included in change processes and have personal investment to make change actionable.

Trainee teachers are, on the whole, exceptionally IT (information technology) literate because of a lifetime of everyday use of technology and proved to be adaptable to change during the pandemic as I described elsewhere (Jones 2021). Nonetheless, the unprecedented circumstances propelled all teachers into very rapid learning in the available technologies to undertake online teaching. The inspiring teacher leaders who have contributed to a wealth of teacher learning and professional opportunities in the field are of particular interest. Examples of teachers taking an instructional lead include this teacher with ten years of experience in a primary school that I visited:

> FT: *I taught some colleagues how to use Teams and Google through my own research. I signed up for some online training and found some online live videos about creative literacy then did a demo for colleagues.*

Another example from a secondary school teacher, with five years of experience, described her cascading to her subject team.

> FT: *After some whole school training, subject leaders were then asked to cascade sessions in their departments. I ran a session on Teams for my colleagues and we have created a Teams space for sharing documents.*

Teachers in many schools in my institutional school network have acknowledged the emergence of a more level playing field in teacher development need and learning. Teachers, it was suggested, benefited from whole school PD and from personalised coaching, all on a similar learning curve – learning together, sometimes by expert teachers as above, sometimes powered by bottom-up expertise from trainee teachers. Interviewed for a Teacher Quality and Retention project, one faculty leader reflected this view: *'There has been a great levelling in all this. We all had to learn how to do online together. Trainee teachers and very experienced teachers all in it together as they say. In my position, I was supposed to take a lead, but it was like the blind leading the blind. But we got there.'*

It is this 'getting there' that is significant. Teachers have resolutely focused on adapting to new ways of teaching, learning and assessing, not just reactively but with a proactivity and determination to adapt at pace with creative solutions to the disruption of the status quo. The disruption to routine served to generate a greater collaborative purpose in an increasingly diversified approach to teacher learning and development generally, opening up new spaces to accommodate personal needs, preferences and collaborative endeavours to support pupil learning that has proved inequitable and challenging. A senior teacher exemplified the challenges.

> P: [...] *not forgetting the kids who could not access a computer or only irregularly, some didn't attend, trying to keep them out of trouble,*

finding them food, big safeguarding problems in addition to their learning.

An experienced teacher mentor interviewed in the project said: *'We have been having a daily dialogue with colleagues about our teaching and problem-solving and collaboration like never before'*. It is a dialogue and collaboration that have fully used internal expertise with a shared purpose, both academic and pastoral.

Collaborative learning

Darling Hammond and McLaughlin (2011) capture the zeitgeist of uncertain times and the scope of a new collaborative professional development agenda when they assert that: 'Teachers individually cannot reconceive their practices and culture of the workplace' (2011:4). They stress the need to give teachers space to engage in 'cooperative experiences' and to share their knowledge. This is reflected, for example, in what this senior teacher said about cooperation in her school.

> P: *We had weekly meetings online and sharing what we had learned during the lockdown: oh, I found this resource, I found this website, or what shall we try this week. It was a learning process all together, it wasn't like me telling them what to do, I wanted more let's work this out together. This was especially important with the range of social issues we had to deal with on a daily basis.*

The natural but not exclusive learning group in secondary school is the subject department. This has traditionally been the case but became accentuated because of the requirement to operate within a subject 'bubble' during the global health crisis. My observations indicate a significant shift from information and organisational issues in departmental meetings to discussions and peer coaching, often on the use of technology in virtual and real classrooms but, more importantly, as a consequence, a re-thinking of practice. An experienced teacher of 20 years and mentor commented:

> FT: *We were lucky to have an excellent IT policy before the pandemic and were used to hybrid teaching and learning. What the covid crisis did was encourage us to discuss getting the best out of situations and questioning the status quo of decades of traditional modes of teaching.*

This statement resonates with the research by Van der Spoel et al (2020) with Dutch teachers who found that the crisis '[…] caused many educators to re-evaluate their methods of teaching […] and focus on the core element of the curriculum'. Having grappled with the basic training and absorbed the mechanics, teachers have engaged in a reflective re-interpretation about the teaching of their subject and, furthermore, begun a critique of online practices. Another former trainee asserted that 'CPD will need to work against being reliant on technology. Looking at how to teach zero tech lessons'.

Critical reflection on subject pedagogy has been a focal point in the context of teacher collaboration that emerges from my observations during my research activity over the last few years. A teacher in her third year commented:

> FT: *As well as top up IT training sessions as new things came up, what I found useful has been the weekly sessions run by our departmental staff on a rota on teaching strategies in the new regime. That is how I came to understand the training we had already had.*

This comment references an important point about how teachers need to understand and make sense of training provision to be able to build what Beattie calls 'competence and self-confidence and … a coherent body of pedagogical practices and professional knowledge (2000:19) A teacher in her fifth year said:

> FT: *In the department, we do a ten-minute share every two weeks with all of us on a rota on areas like resources and good practice.*

Such modest accounts of teaching and learning are valuable in developing a new repertoire of good practice and dig more deeply into the essence of trying to define not just 'what works' but in what context and how best with all pupils.

Across curriculum boundaries

Online working provided a professional development arising from teachers being enabled to cross boundaries in an enriching and time-effective way. Some teachers were able to join meetings in different subject areas and in larger groups online as described by this head of faculty in a project interview: *'Normally I would visit departmental meetings on a rota but online, I was able to go from one department to another and also to have mega, whole faculty meetings. It was great. We really enjoyed it and learned so much from each other. It is something we wish to continue.'*

This activity was not simply about attending different meetings but about learning from other subjects and developing cross-subject pedagogical knowledge. Cross-subject pedagogies were also found to be the focus in other collaborative learning opportunities in other schools such as in one school, where the MFL department discussed retrieval practice together with colleagues in maths. One of the Languages teachers commented on what she learned from her maths colleague.

FT: *He starts lessons with a retrieval activity responding to feedback from the previous lesson, including misconception. Also, he sets a quick self-assessment task towards the end and he uses the information to create the retrieval starter for the next lesson. I like how this is systematic.*

The teacher learning here was simple but effective, involving the realisation that retrieval practice could be used to both review learning and to plan forwards in a very systematic way in addition to being a spontaneous activity used by the teacher in a lesson.

An experienced mentor, with some 18 years in teaching, a former trainee, explained how professional development was experienced across a network of schools of which his school was part more regularly and enabled insightful learning from other subject areas with 'profound benefits'. A trainee teacher of mine in another school described the shared arrangements: 'We had a wwww (what worked well with) *every week from different departments and we had a shared drive on Google. We all used each other's things. We had shared spreadsheets about what worked with particular pupils where we'd share what worked for us. Back in school, the barriers were down and we hung out with others and people were always walking in and out of classrooms. It was rare to go a week without someone else observing and people often team teaching.'*

Thus, it can be seen from these examples that not only were subject barriers broken down, but the 'secret gardens' (Wilson 1989) of other subject colleagues' classrooms opened up. Gore and Rosser (2019:9) advocate for cross-grade and subject collaboration from their research and found that this type of collaboration '... *generated new insights about pedagogy that helped teachers improve their practice (intellectual change) and lifted teachers' expectations of students as well as their view of colleagues and motivation to collaborate (attitudinal change)'*. Such research shows how exploring classrooms and pedagogies in subjects other than one's own can combat misunderstanding of different subject teaching and, I would add, respect for other subjects' ways of teaching and consideration of how to contribute to a more coherent experience of learning for the pupils.

The intersection of collaborative and personal learning spaces

Collaborative professional development is indisputably fruitful but, crucially, collaboration intersects with teachers' individual styles of learning. A study by Shanks et al (2012:185) of Scottish teachers' preferences regarding professional learning and development highlighted this in their assertion that: *'Although teachers may be part of a community of practice, they are also individuals with their own experiences and perceptions of work and workplace learning'*. An experienced teacher, mentor and responsible for PD explained her school strategy in a project interview for promoting work both in subject teams and for individuals to follow their needs and interests: *'In the circumstances, we have had some essential whole staff training for all staff online such as safeguarding and technical updating and EAL but staff have been asked to work in their subject areas and also to work on issues of interest to them. I and other colleagues are here to support them.'*

A recently qualified teacher in the same school, a former trainee, mirrored how recently introduced teaching arrangements and restrictions had provided some space to explore the possibilities for self-learning: *'We have had quite a few whole staff CPDs but we are encouraged to work in our subject teams and to participate in our own areas of interest. Topics I chose included implementing languages specific online learning, the cognition-conscious classroom, retrieval practice [...] As I had noticed the children were a little anxious, I also researched the topic of understanding anxiety in education'*. Teachers all have their individual ways and preferences for learning modes, times, topics and spaces, just as the pupils do, and such an affordance gives teachers agency to reflect on and explore issues of interest or areas of their need. Such personalised learning complements the school community learning programme and provides impetus to discover a greater world of learning, connectedness and knowledge sharing, paradoxically at a time when a global health crisis imposed many restrictions.

Learning communities and networking

One consequence of the various global health 'lockdowns' was the greater connectivity, communication and networking across the globe that developed spontaneously. Networks, always seemingly a good idea, are complicated and not easy to sustain. However, Lieberman asserts that 'networks are particularly well suited to making use of new technologies and institutional arrangements. By their very nature they are flexible, borderless and innovative; they are able to create collaborative environments' (2000:221). This chimes very much with what teachers reported, of their reviving of old networks and online groups but especially of joining new networks and learning communities, in which social media played a large role. Social media with both open learning communities such as on Facebook, and closed groups as with private WhatsApp groups are now a well-established mode of teacher learning and information and strategy sharing. A former trainee, now teacher in her fifth year describes the informal learning in her subject WhatsApp group: *'We always share ideas on our WhatsApp group when we discover a new strategy to make learning more effective on Teams. One departmental collaboration we did last week was trying out new assessment for learning strategies at home with the students. We discussed using two devices, using the chat function so we can quickly scan the chat whilst sharing the screen to the students on our computer – it's been effective so far.'*

Duncan-Howell concurs that 'online communities are being increasingly used by teachers for professional support, guidance and inspiration... and able to deliver authentic and personalised opportunities for learning' (2010:324). This is also reflected by one trainee teacher who commented: *'I enjoyed the exchanges and banter in the Twitter and Facebook groups. I appreciated the time I had to do things that interested me. I did a lot of the OU courses, joined international networks and attended online conferences for free and listened to TED talks – I loved hearing researchers and authors talking about their work and not just reading it'.*

This rich account of one individual's 'connectivity' resonates with a study by Prestridge (2019) of teachers in international settings that showed that teachers use media in various ways. These ways including researching as 'info-consumers' (searching for information) and mediating as 'info-networkers' (sharing information), showing how teachers have acted as researchers and knowledge sharers. Prestridge (2019) asserts that the extensive use of social media has caused a paradigm shift in professional development and a massive sharing of materials and strategies on a large number of social media platforms. Generally, a vast amount of self-accessing material has been created and made available in the last few years, freely available and opening up a wealth of teacher learning opportunities from which individuals are able to choose. An example of this was an international conference on language learning held in Hong Kong with very eminent speakers that was enjoyed by student and practising teachers online, where they were able to engage in chat with eminent speakers and engage with research. Indeed, one trainee teacher presented on English as an alternative language (EAL) strategies at an international conference. For such an event, access would otherwise normally have been accessible only by an exclusive and regular paying group. Another 'secret garden' has been opened up.

Time for a reset!

Global health events have necessitated professional learning changes and teachers have taken firm and confident control of what the changes have meant for them and the students they teach. There has been a burgeoning collaboration and connectedness between peers, friends, colleagues, students and other professionals, in different locales and contexts as well as global connectivity via the internet. Connectedness and closeness have mattered. The changes have not been without loss or challenges: on the contrary, the ubiquitous technical complexities, fails and crashes, as well as the impoverished social and interactional dimension and wellbeing issues have been tangible. However, technology upskilling has meant using technical skills to explore a new world of learning as an accessible reality. There are important points here about equitable professional development with a more open access to a wider range of opportunities for all teachers. This has resulted in a much greater role for teachers in taking responsibility for their professional learning, serving to strengthen their professional identity and democratic rights for inclusion in their professional learning journeys.

The only silver lining from the darkness of the global health crisis was that it created spaces and time for teachers to think, explore, research, collaborate and to take agency in the self-regulation of their own learning. Time for professional development has always been an issue. It remains largely unsolved and lack of time is a factor in teacher turnover – 'No time to talk!' as Schad (2019) expresses it directly. The temporal frames for professional development will need to be reset. Teachers have, in fact, enjoyed space and time affordances as a result of a disruptive and democratic process that have been empowering and led to rich personal development, generous sharing and collaborating.

Moving forward

The changes have opened up space for institutional professional development to develop as a diverse and dynamic hybrid offer of professional opportunities. Such an offer would identify learning opportunities for all colleagues and ensure space for personalisation, spontaneity and innovation, taking on board the following:

- Professional development needs to be conceptualised as a process not an event (Harwell 2003), and a complex one at that (Guskey 2002). This would entail a fluid mapping of PD opportunities for teachers.

- Collaboration is central to teacher PD in enabling teachers to work together in a continuous dialogue. Darling Hammond and Richardson (2009:5–6) suggest a variety of strategies including peer observation, examining student data, study groups and professional learning communities, all of which need a focus on student learning and outcomes, and are both intensive and sustained.

- A rich network of peer coaching, and peer learning is empowering of colleagues and provides equity of professional development according to need. The research of Zwart et al (2007) emphasised the individual nature of coaching as teachers had different learning entry and end points in the coaching process but the process unequivocally triggered new reflection processes.

- Professional development is interpreted by individuals in their own ways. Personalised learning needs to be encouraged and negotiated, considering 'the needs, concerns and interests of individual teachers, personal and professional needs, individual learning preferences and input regarding how they will learn' as Hunzicker (2011:177) describes.

- Social media and online communities are a central plank in providing a diverse range of learning opportunities. A school professional development plan needs to acknowledge networking opportunities for learning as well as their crucial role in personal support and wellbeing – 'offering support, advice, feedback and collaboration opportunities' (Trust 2012:133).

- Reflection is crucial to all the previously mentioned points. Teachers need time and opportunities to reflect, whether in personal deliberation or in social interactions. Either way, Zeichner and Tabachnick (2001:81) state that reflection is integral to teachers' understanding of themselves their practice and their contexts, where 'the rapidly unfolding of classroom events is partly shaped by the teacher's intellectual intuitions, not merely by routinised or uncritical responses to instructional demands'. Reflection always begs the question 'reflecting on what?'.

- Continuous professional development becomes critical professional development. The question from the last point is answered by Kohli et al (2015) who assert that with a 'critical professional development [...] teachers can successfully position themselves as experts in their own social justice oriented professional growth'.

Here, teachers assume a critically reflective activist stance to their professional learning that gives it a new urgency and rationale.

Disrupted educational schedules and the considerable inequalities highlighted in learning opportunities for pupils, have led to re-thinking teaching critically – not just pedagogically but in a more socially just and diverse way. Research by Price and Valli (2005) highlighted the passion driving teachers to become agents of change precisely because of their experiences of change and enhanced socio-political awareness. Teachers having had the chance to negotiate their professional learning has proved to be an investment in the skills of confronting permanent change and uncertainty in education. This has been very visible in the evident glaring unequal opportunities for student learning that teachers came across during their online teaching, such as lack of space and equipment for some pupils and impoverished home support.

None of the suggested strategies are new per se. However, by combining Mercer and Gregerson's (2020) vision of a thoughtful professional development that seeks to grow teachers' strengths and emphasises wellbeing (a huge issue for teachers and students alike), and adopting Kohli et al's critical professional development stance something quite radical would emerge. It would respond to the new needs of socially aware schools and agentic teachers with a socially responsible critical professional development agenda. The challenge is to think how to create such a rich tapestry of teacher professional opportunities that reflects such an agenda.

References

Beattie, M. (2000) 'Narratives of Professional Learning: Becoming a Teacher and Learning to Teach', *Journal of Educational Enquiry*, 1(2), 1–23.

Britzman, D. P. (2007) 'Teacher Education as uneven development: toward a psychology of uncertainty', *International Journal of Leadership in Education*, 10(1), 1–12.

Darling Hammond, L. and McLaughlin, M. W. (2011) *Kappan: Kappanmagazine. org.* 92(6), 82–92.

Darling Hammond, L. and Richardson, N. (2009) 'Teacher Learning: What Matters?', *Association for Supervision and Curriculum Development*, 66(5), 46–53.

Duncan Howell, J. (2010) 'Teachers making connections: Online communities as a source of professional learning', *British Journal of Educational Technology*, 41(2), 324–340.

Fullan, M. (2001) *The New Meaning of Educational Change* (3rd ed). London: Routledge.

Gore, J. and Rosser, B. (2016) 'Beyond content-focused professional development: powerful professional learning through genuine learning communities across grades and subjects', *Professional Development in Education*, 48(2), 218–232.

Guskey, T. R. (2002) 'Professional Development and Change', *Teachers and Teaching: theory and practice*, 8(3/4), 381–392.

Hargreaves, A. (2007) 'Inclusive and exclusive educational change: emotional responses of teachers and implications for leadership', *School Leadership and Management*, 24(3), 287–309.

Harwell, S. (2003) Teacher Professional Development: It's Not an Event, It's a Process [White paper]. Waco, TX: Cord Communications.

Hunzicker, J. (2011) 'Effective professional development for teachers: A Checklist', *Professional Development in Education*, 37(2), 177–179.

Jones, J. (2021) 'Learning in Lockdown: New vistas for teacher development', *Teaching Times*. Retrieved from: www.bit.ly/3NAa9R3.

Kohli, R., Picower, B., Martinez, A. and Ortiz, N. (2015) 'Critical Professional Development: Centering the Social Justice needs of Teachers', *International Journal of Critical Pedagogy*, 6(2), 7–24.

Lieberman, A. (2000) 'Networks as learning communities: Shaping the future of teacher development', *Journal of Teacher Education*, 31(3), 221–227.

Mercer, S. and Gregerson, T. (2020) *Teacher Wellbeing*. Oxford: Oxford University Press.

OECD (2019) *What do we know about children and technology?* Paris: OECD Publishing.

Prestridge, S. (2019) 'Categorising teachers' use of social media for their professional learning: a self-generating professional learning paradigm', *Computers and Education*, 129, 143–158.

Price, J. N. and Valli, L. (2005) 'Preservice Teachers Becoming Agents of Change: Pedagogical Implications for Action Research', *Journal of Teacher Education*, 56, 57–72.

Schad, E. (2017) 'No time to talk! Teachers' perceptions of organizational communication: context and climate', *Educational Management Administration and Leadership*, 47(3), 421–442.

Shanks, R., Robson, D. and Gray, D. (2012) 'New teachers' individual learning dispositions: a Scottish case study', *International Journal of Training and Development*, 16(3), 183–199.

Trust, T. (2012) 'Professional learning networks designed for teacher learning', *Journal of Digital Learning in Teacher Education*, 28(4), 133–138.

Van der Spoel, I. Naroozi, N., Schuunk, E. and van Ginkel, S. (2020) 'Teachers' online teaching expectations and experiences during the Covid 19 pandemic in the Netherlands', *European Journal of Teacher Education*, 43(4), 623–638.

Wilson, E. (1989) *The Secret Garden of Teacher Education*. East Lansing, MI: National Center for Research on Teacher Education.

Yelland, N. (2006) *Shift to the future: Rethinking learning with new technologies in education*. New York: Routledge.

Zeichner, K. M. and Tabachnick, B. R. (2001) Reflections on reflective teaching in J. Soler, A. Craft and R. Burgess (eds.) *Teacher Development. Exploring our own practice.* London: Paul Chapmen Publishing.

Zwart, R. C., Wubbels, T., Bergen, T. C. M. and Bolhuis, S. (2007) 'Experienced teachers learning within the context of reciprocal peer coaching', *Teachers and Teaching: theory and practice*, 13(2), 165–187.

Big Education
collaboration for change

Liz Robinson, Ellie Lister, Joe Pardoe and Rosie Clayton

Overview

We believe that the school experience for most students, in most schools, most days, is too narrow. We have articulated a vision for a more expansive education, what we call an education of the head, heart and hand. We model this in our own schools. Our approach is to share and develop these ideas and we find that very many parents, educators and students agree. However, most feel stuck to a greater or lesser extent by the high stakes accountability of our sector. They want to take their school or classroom on this journey, but don't know where to start. We have designed a range of tools and interventions which support them, and they are all focused on networked learning.

This chapter includes case studies of three initiatives:

1. Learning from Lockdown (bigeducation.org/learning-from-lockdown)– an open source blog and insights website aiming to capture the new approaches and learnings from this period.

2. Rethinking Assessment (rethinkingassessment.com)– a significant collaborative project, using design thinking methodologies to engage a large number of interested parties and create collective influence.

3. The Big Leadership Adventure (bigeducation.org/bigthinking/be-programmes/big-leadership-adventure/) – a two-year development programme for change makers (senior leaders from across the sector)

The chapter will give an overview of the work we are doing and highlight the different approaches to networked learning through the lens of these programmes of work.

Keywords
Leadership
Network
Collaboration
Innovation
Learning

Writing this chapter has been a fantastic opportunity to reflect on aspects of our practice at Big Education and to draw out the theme of networking and collaboration in our work. For us, it is an implicit and embedded part of how we do things, and here we will explore first a little of the philosophy and mindset that means that this is such an integral part of our approach, and then describe and reflect on three distinct parts of our work to exemplify what this looks like in practice.

A bit of philosophy to get us started...

The problem of individualism rather than collectivism can be traced back to the philosopher Rene Descartes. His famous *cogito, ergo sum* (I think, therefore I am) formed the basis of Western philosophy for many centuries. His idea was that he could not trust his 'sense' data, what he saw, felt or touched. He argued he might have been tricked into seeing or feeling those things by an evil demon. The one thing he thought he could trust was his own thinking – 'I think' and that means I exist. One of the issues with Descartes' position is a problem philosophers call 'solipsism'. This simply means that his trust in his own thoughts alone has the implication that he cannot 'prove' the existence of other people. The only thing I can be sure of is my own thinking and any indication of another person could be part of the deceit of the 'evil demon'. Thinkers through time have tried to overcome this, one of the classic conundrums of the discipline.

As one of the authors of this chapter is an undergraduate studying philosophy, this just seemed mad to her. She understood the logic of the argument, but it just left her cold, and trying to logically overcome 'solipsism' did not seem a good use of one's time. So, she was delighted to go on to learn about the work of Edmund Husserl and then Martin Heidegger and those that followed. Heidegger[1] challenged the fundamental premise of Descartes' argument. He argued that our experience as humans simply *is* embodied and social. He even devised new words to describe this experience, as he felt there was not a word that properly captured this: *dasein* (Heidegger 1978), most often translated as being-in-the-world. There is no abstract 'being' in our own heads, every experience is essentially in-the-world, with other people implicitly present. He talked about a hammer, it was made by another and is meant for use on wood cut by another, in service of making things to be used by others. This notion immediately transformed my journey of learning within philosophy[2] but also provides the fundamental underpinning of my approach to leadership and life! It means integrating our connection with, and understanding of, other people into every aspect of our lives. Living is social, learning is social, being is social.

So how does this human-connected conception of the world relate to our work at Big Education?

What is Big Education?

We believe that most students, in most lessons, on most days, in this country (England) get a narrow educational experience, one that over-indexes on a certain set of learning priorities and approaches at the expense of all else. And we know that this is not ok.

It is not ok because rates of mental health problems in young people are growing at worrying rates.

It is not ok because retention rates of teachers in the first five years are poor.

It is not ok because employers increasingly see the limitations of exam results and are recruiting for a wider set of skills that school has often not developed in young people.

It is not ok because headteachers experience extreme pressures due to high stakes accountability approaches, making them less likely to innovate and try new things.

---

1   Heidegger was a controversial political figure and member of the Nazi party. Our interest in his work in no way condones his racist views.

2   There are of course, many other inroads into this whole area of the philosophy of mind and body in Western philosophy (and indeed in Eastern traditions).

It is not ok because our current norm-referenced exam system means there will always be a percentage of students who fail.

Big Education is trying to do something about all of that.

What do we do?

Big Education is a multi-academy trust (MAT) that also functions as a social enterprise. We currently run three schools, School 21 (all through) and School 360 (primary) in Newham and Surrey Square (primary) in Southwark. We have an embedded culture of innovation with a focus on an expansive educational experience; an education of the head, heart and hand. Each school has developed expertise in a range of pedagogical approaches that underpin its expanded curriculum vision – all linked back to a more ambitious vision for the ultimate purpose of schooling, to empower young people to take on the world. These approaches include a focus on oracy, real world learning, problem-based learning and activism.

The purpose of forming the trust was to bring together a focus on 'next practice' as well as 'best practice'; we have worked hard to create horizontal structures focused on peer relationships and accountability – a focus on improving rather than proving[3]. In addition, we aim to amplify and elevate approaches that support our vision. Voice 21, a charity working with over 1000 schools nationally, was formed at School 21 and is a powerful example of how we aim to scale and share insights and approaches.

We also run a range of programmes, professional development and projects that aim to have a systematic influence by inspiring, designing and growing effective approaches with an ever-expanding network of leaders, teachers, schools, MATs and organisations. We created the Big Leadership Adventure as a way to support changemakers in the sector. Our diagnostic tool, for example, is a powerful instrument to enable school teams to ask a bigger set of questions about their work and make practical steps towards a 'big' education.

---

3   This brilliant phrase comes from Education Development Trust's Schools Partnership Programme peer review approach.

Figure 1 Big Education's why, how and what

In terms of our own schools, we worked from the start to integrate collaboration and sharing into our approaches. We use peer review and support extensively as the backbone of our approach to accountability, investing heavily in relationships and a culture of openness and trust. We know this is critical in establishing the basis for sharing, learning and trying new approaches. We have adopted these principles across our programmes and projects and will now share three examples. The first is part of our 'inspire' work; 'Learning from Lockdown'. This is followed by a piece of 'design' work; Rethinking Assessment. Finally, an example of 'growth' work; our Big Leadership Adventure. These have been written by members of the team who have led on the work and this co-authorship seeks to retain the authenticity of our collaborative approach.

Case study 1: Learning from lockdown

When the pandemic hit Britain in March 2020, three powerful forces were unleashed. Firstly, there was a renewed understanding of the power of community. People came together in order to help each other to get through a crisis and there was a strong understanding of how we were much more connected than we had previously realised. Secondly, things we had always taken as fixed and immovable suddenly seemed fragile and temporary. Schools closing for the first time in living memory and exams being cancelled for the first time ever would not have factored into even the most skilled forecaster's mind in March 2019.

This breaking of precedents allowed the third force to flourish – a moment of profound reflection and rethinking. Perhaps we could learn from the experience and rebuild a better society - precisely the question asked in the timely publication Educating Tomorrow: Learning for the Post-Pandemic World (Brown and Luzmore 2021). The convergence of these three forces had a strong effect on the education system – the question now is what, if any, changes will result from this moment of great learning?

What we did

We quickly realised that we were in the midst of the biggest unplanned experiment in education in history. We wanted to capture the learning as it happened. We developed a number of design principles to guide this fast-paced work:

- As many voices and views as possible
- A range of contributions from policy experts to teachers, students and parents
- To be open to what emerged in terms of content and themes
- To capture what was happening right now
- To bring out the learnings that may be important for the future

As the pandemic progressed, it was clear that a number of key themes were developing, ranging from how to run parents' evenings, to staff and student wellbeing. We also realised that we, as an organisation, were in a position to help bring people together and share our view on some of these themes. We organised webinar discussions and used these as a platform to explore emerging themes and to listen hard to the experiences of others. The feedback was incredibly positive and so we looked to find a way to share these insights at scale. This led to the development of a series of 'playbooks',[4] a curation of ideas, examples and tools to help other leaders, in a format that they could access at their own convenience and with ready-to-use tools.

Why we did it

So, why did we do it? The first reason is simple – we wanted to capture the moment. Capture the feeling of change and the optimism that we could build a better education system in the future. Capture the voices of people experiencing the situation first hand. Capture the learning which was taking place. However, we not only wanted to document the moment, we wanted to shape it. We understood that we were in a time of great upheaval and we knew that without leadership, there was a danger that the lessons would be lost in the scramble to return to the status quo. Powerful changes can be made when there is desire from the bottom which is harnessed by leaders who can direct the momentum.[5]

What happened?

In the space of a year, we built a hub of learning – a site filled with blogs, events and resources. We were able to collect and curate more than 100 blogs all about different experiences of education in the pandemic and suggestions for how we could use this in the future. However, we did not want to be simply a resource site, we wanted to turn it into a community to generate tangible improvements in education on the ground.

---

4   These are available at bigeducation.org/bigthinking/courses-and-playbooks/
5   See *Newpower*, Timms and Heimans

We did this a number of ways. Firstly, we focused initially on targeting 'high-profile' educators (for example, those with large Twitter followings) to gain momentum on social media. We also set up a newsletter (and accompanying mailing list) that helped us to communicate with the network on a regular basis and continually drive home, that this was not just a blog site, it was a movement of changemaker leaders – they were a part of it and we wanted them to contribute. The mailing list also allowed us to track engagement, for example, we were able to see our geographical spread and the types of roles people held. This data showed that we had a range of educators join our community, from CEOs of education trusts to classroom teachers and interested parents. We found the regular newsletter, as well as pushing on social media, allowed us to sustain the community and ensure a regular stream of contributions to the site.

Using the data we gathered, the themes of the blogs, as well as the more quantitative data already mentioned, we were able to highlight areas of focus. We ran a number of webinars that brought together people from all over the world and from lots of different fields who were able to listen, share and discuss their experiences and ideas related to a particular theme we had chosen. These events were useful as a way of bringing people together, but we also wanted to ensure schools had the right resources to make changes as a result of these discussions. Therefore, we published 'playbooks', used by senior school leaders across the country to develop strategies for their school post-pandemic. Initially, we published these for free although, to get access, people needed to join our mailing list. Feedback on the playbooks was positive as it helped turn abstract ideas into concrete changes in organisations – the community supported this by sharing case studies and offering a sense of 'group safety'. We even found out that an entire school district in the US was using our resources to re-think their staff wellbeing work!

The following are some examples of the content of our playbooks:

Questions to shape school discussions

It is worth having specific discussions among both senior leaders and the whole staff body about communication.

These are some prompt questions that could shape those discussions:

 How frequently should we communicate with staff, pupils, families, stakeholders?

 How will we know this is enough?

 What are the best methods of communication?

 How do we gather detailed feedback from staff, pupils, families to gauge the mood, range of feelings, how communication is 'landing with them" ?

 How do we respond to feedback?

 How transparent should we be about how things are going/dilemmas, problems being faced?

03

3 Be open and transparent

In a crisis it is natural to turn inwards. So many of our decisions are taken by a small group of people. These are often the most senior, rather than the best informed. The decision-making process is often carried out behind closed doors.

When we communicate to others, our thinking, why we have come to this conclusion, has been lost over time - and there is no opportunity to discuss why something is happening or what its rationale is. This is a common state of affairs in most organisations.

Instead we need to be willing to open up our thinking to scrutiny as well as the conclusions, we should want to persuade people by the quality of our arguments not because we are higher up the pecking order.

Information gets out eventually. People can either find it out from you or someone else. It needs to be you. In a crisis situation rumour can replace fact very quickly. So being open from the start builds trust. And trust is your most vital commodity when asking families to come back to school during a health crisis. Being open means being clear what you don't know too. ' We don't know where this situation will lead, but I can tell you now (X)'. So make sure you know what you know and are clear what you don't know.

Example

"We have laid out our current thinking on health and safety based on the expert advice. As you know the advice has changed many times so we are trying our best to make the best decisions for our context. We have had experts audit what we are doing, all of those documents are available and I will be available for detailed questions after school today for those who remain worried about any aspect of them. Please also feedback to your line manager any specific concerns that you have."

08

How to communicate for maximum impact

These 10 principles are only as good as the way they are used and some thought needs to be given to the methods and frequency of the communication.

Here is a short checklist to use when thinking about communication with a key stakeholder group: e.g. parents, teachers, pupils

Communication	Reflection
How often do I communicate?	
In what format?	
How do I seek feedback and what evidence do I use?	
Which of the 10 techniques did I use?	
Which worked well?	
Which need refining?	
Which additional ones will I use next time?	
What time do I devote to getting this right?	

Reflection exercise

Choose a piece of recent communication - possibly to parents, or to a staff meeting and reflect on how effective it was using these first five tools.

1 Did you anchor decisions to values and key principles?

2 Did you describe the journey with key milestones?

3 Were you open and transparent?

4 Have you repeated the message so that you weren't relying on everyone hearing it just the once?

5 Were you careful about the unintended consequences of the language you used?

11

What did we learn?

Building communities is difficult and requires sustained effort, focus and leadership. We also learned that it is not inevitable that change will occur, even if there is desire to make it happen. The systems of the status quo have a strong gravitational pull, it requires a huge amount of energy to break away. We believe that people want to contribute to the development of a better system and we also know that if change is to stick, there has to be a grassroots movement as well as strong leadership. However, if people are to contribute, they may need support in order to do so. We tried to make it as simple as possible for people to get their ideas heard by, for example, having a number of writing templates to use ('Three things I have learned during the pandemic which we need to continue in the future'). However, we also learned that it is important to offer encouragement to those who are nervous about talking about their ideas. If you don't focus on these things, you will only hear from the people who are always heard anyway. Those who are confident and able to communicate with ease will continue to influence the network, while those who have great ideas but lack confidence will continue to step back. This is really important from a diversity and equality perspective.

Finally, we realised that building these networks to change the system is a marathon, not a sprint. Slowly building up data and information about the community is not glamorous, but it is of vital importance. Although we had to move quickly at the beginning of this project, our next steps are to slow down, reflect and develop a targeted strategy to develop this work to make a real difference over the long term.

Case study 2: Rethinking Assessment

Rethinking Assessment was established in 2020 during the pandemic as a response to the widespread disruption to national annual standardised assessments, with a group of school, college and MAT leaders coming together with universities, policymakers and employers to seize the opportunity to push for change. Our aim is to create a more equitable assessment system that recognises the full breadth of strengths of every child and better serves their needs, as well as those of employers, higher education institutions and wider society. To date, Rethinking Assessment has focused on making the case for change through research and thoughtful blogs, and co-designing new practical solutions that can be tested out in different education settings.

What we did

We first convened an advisory group made up of leaders from across education, including bridging the state and independent sectors, to steer the project. This group published an open letter which set out the aims and rationale, and kicked off the debate with a series of blogs covering different aspects of the need for change. At the same time, we launched a new web platform (rethinkingassessment.com) to provide a space for sharing ideas, research reports, analysis and community engagement. Secondly, we established two working groups to investigate how we can better recognise academic strengths, and how we can start to recognise those broader dispositions such as oracy, creativity, collaboration and critical thinking which are important for success in life and work. The working groups followed a design thinking working methodology which involved defining the problem/s, research and horizon scanning, analysis, and generating new ideas.

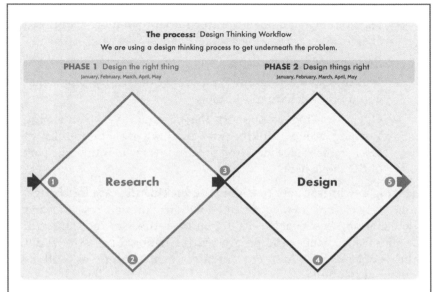

The process: Design Thinking Workflow
We are using a design thinking process to get underneath the problem.

PHASE 1 Design the right thing
January, February, March, April, May

PHASE 2 Design things right
January, February, March, April, May

Research

Design

Design principles

When launching new projects, or convening diverse groups of stakeholders who have not necessarily collaborated before, it's important to agree on ways of working from the outset and create alignment around shared principles. Our starting point was the following:

How we engage:

- Being present and participating fully
- Trust the process, and in each other's positive intent
- Listen to learn
- Having a beginner's mindset
- Being bold and taking risks
- Continuous learning

How we work:

- Actions and solutions orientated

- Facilitation and guided working rather than more traditional chairing
- Provocation and challenge from external experts
- Multimodal meetings utilising a range of creative approaches and tools – including tech tools
- Open working to support the community – connecting working group thinking into building the community of teachers, school leaders and practitioners who want to be part of the movement

Having a twin-track approach in both making the case for change, and co-designing new ideas and solutions through research and deliberation, has enabled us to build a diverse and powerful coalition for change, and progressed the national narrative about the problems with our current assessment system as well as potential solutions.

What happened

We now have a committed team of approximately 40 members of our advisory group and working groups, who have together come up with a range of critical focus areas around which we are planning to launch action research pilots. These include interdisciplinary learning, the development of new qualifications utilising multi-modal assessment methods, the evidencing of key dispositions, and the design of a new comprehensive learning record for learners. We also have a wider community of 3000 people who are interested in the aims and work of Rethinking Assessment, and have joined policy webinars and social media discussions.

What did we learn about building networks and networked learning?

It's still early days for Rethinking Assessment, but there have been a number of important learnings so far.

Including:

- Having early stage financial support from the Edge Foundation to appoint a project manager. Coordination and orchestration in some form is key. The foundation is more than just a funder, rather an embedded partner in change, actively participating in the working group process and playing a central role in connecting Rethinking Assessment into aligned initiatives and the policy community.

- Having a diverse coalition of individuals and organisations involved who are themselves well networked within their respective communities, and can both communicate within these communities and draw insight. Individuals and organisations represent different aspects of the education system, from primary to higher education, teacher training, further education and employment, academics who are specialist in neuroscience and child development

- Working in an open and facilitative way, creating and holding a space that is both challenging for participants and purposeful. As mentioned, setting and aligning on ways of working at the beginning.

- Following a design thinking process has opened up new avenues for exploration, and the organisational and working group structure has been able to flex depending on the needs of the project. For example, teams were created within working groups, and different people took on leadership roles at different points, to maximise collective skills, expertise and available capacity.

Case study 3: The Big Leadership Adventure

Given our aims as Big Education – to rethink and redesign aspects of our system – creating the leadership capacity to do this is an essential priority. We began creating the Big Leadership Adventure in 2018, and it is now established within the sector. It is a two-year learning and development programme for leaders within the sector (not just in schools) who are committed to a 'big' education and want to be part of the change. In cohorts of 30 to 40, leaders work with us and each other to explore new mindsets about leadership and developing their skills and expertise in new approaches.

Before designing the programme, we commissioned a piece of research to explore the underlying qualities needed for this different type of leadership, and this led to the development of a powerful reflection and coaching tool – our leadership wheel.

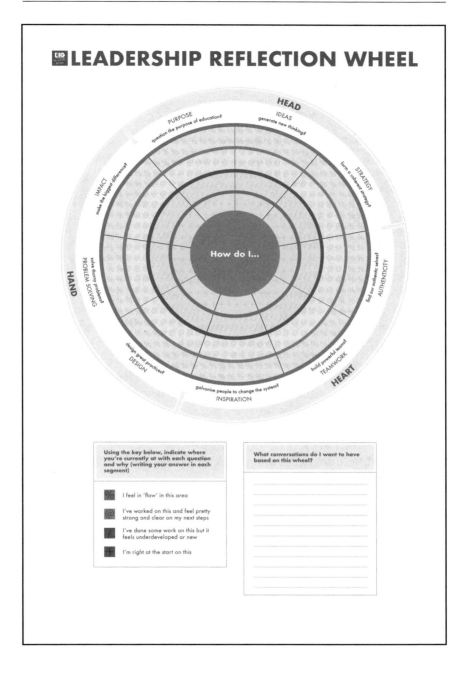

LEADERSHIP REFLECTION WHEEL

HEAD

PURPOSE
question the purpose of education?

IDEAS
generate new thinking?

STRATEGY
form a coherent strategy?

IMPACT
make the biggest difference?

AUTHENTICITY
find our authentic selves?

HAND

PROBLEM SOLVING
solve thorny problems?

How do I...

DESIGN
design great practices?

TEAMWORK
build powerful teams?

INSPIRATION
galvanise people to change the system?

HEART

Using the key below, indicate where you're currently at with each question and why (writing your answer in each segment)

% I feel in 'flow' in this area

@ I've worked on this and feel pretty strong and clear on my next steps

I've done some work on this but it feels underdeveloped or new

I'm right at the start on this

What conversations do I want to have based on this wheel?

A mindset for collaboration

This unearthed the need for leadership that values diverse perspectives regardless of hierarchy and challenges the notion that there is one way of doing things. We have also learned that this has to be underpinned by a sense of psychological safety. This leads to people:

- feeling empowered to find new solutions,
- questioning and challenging the way things are done,
- being open to learning,
- recognising that there can be new ways of doing things, and
- truly listening to others.

These ideas are underpinned by an extensive body of research and theory spanning organisational psychology to neuroscience and psychology. We are particularly interested in the conditions that leaders can create to bring the best out of those they lead as well.[6] This is underpinned by models exploring how our own self-awareness is critical to our journey as leaders, such as adult ego development[7] and constructive development theory (Lucey 2021; Lucey, Lister, Robinson and Parry 2021). This open and empowering mindset is important in relation to collaboration and networked learning[8] as it influences our ability to be open, willing to take risks and challenge our thinking.

All of this is what enables openness to new solutions, collaboration, a learning culture and most importantly, a belief that we together are more powerful, more creative and more likely to succeed in innovating, and the skills to manage the complexity of multiple viewpoints.

---

6   Leadership behaviour that brings the best out of leaders themselves and others is induced through developable behavioural resources (Cameron 2008; Cameron 2021).

7   A leader's level of self-awareness and understanding of the impact one has on others is relevant to both the direct and indirect influence leaders have on their organisations and the individuals within them (Gilbride, James and Carr 2021).

8   Connection and relational skills are key for leaders and all to optimally function (Algoe 2019; Crocker, Canevello and Brown 2017); we need to create more safe and collaborative relationships in schools (Lucey and van Nieuwerburgh 2020), and developing relatedness between colleagues to fully foster self-determination and motivation (Ryan and Deci 2000; Gagné and Deci 2005).

Collaboration in practice

Getting the right methodology that underpins our approach was critical. Too often we see very prescriptive approaches to programme design, which is both disempowering and, we believe, ineffective in developing some of the more expansive capabilities in our model. To develop this type of leadership, we have been heavily influenced by the research of Cordingley et al (2020) on what the evidence tells us about leadership of continuous professional development:

- Every context is different and we know that a 'one size fits all' approach doesn't work. We provide frameworks and tools to support leaders to navigate their contexts and ultimately empower those around them to do the same.
- We recruit leaders into a learning, rather than performative stance, which also demonstrates the culture and ethos that, we believe, should underpin a school.
- We ensure leaders have access to examples of the content they are exploring in a range of contexts, and develop networks that enable them to see their school in the wider system.

In practice, this looks like:

- Coaching triads or basecamps – subgroups where relationships are deepened and leaders provide mutual support through reflection, feedback and challenge.
- Explicitly sharing the expertise and experience in the group, empowering leaders to run sessions and model the learning with and from one another.
- 'Train the trainer' route for year 2 – explicitly empowering leaders to deepen their expertise in our tools and approaches to enable them to support others.
- Use of connective technology to enable sharing of ideas, resources and social connection,
- Publishing blogs from leaders (many of them writing for the first time) as a way to share and amplify their experiences and insights.

- Leaders receiving regular feedback from one another, even on their application to the programme.

Understanding our impact

We have partnered with CUREE (Centre for the Use of Research and Evidence in Education), who have supported us to design impact measures and map the findings against existing research literature that impacts on pupil outcomes. This has enabled us to establish a broad set of comparators for understanding the strengths and development areas of the programme.

As we gather impact stories through our formative evaluation, which will be published in early 2022, we feel both humbled and hopeful for this approach to leadership across the sector:

- 'The BLA has given me the confidence to lead and to enact change. My thinking has evolved in so many ways in the last two years. BLA has supported me in networking with so many inspiring leaders and people not just in the educational sector but more broadly. It has widened my horizons. I have learnt to read more widely and to look globally for innovation and ways that work and bring them back into my own setting. I have developed my vision of education and I have developed my purpose.' **Co-headteacher, Southwark, London.**

- 'I've grown from someone who probably used the term 'imposter syndrome' a few too many times, to someone who owns their role as an educator and the wider responsibilities that come with that. I have grown massively in my capacity to be braver, more vulnerable and accepting that I don't always have all the answers so I need to seek out those who do. There is so much I will take away from this process and feel it has been a pivotal moment in my teaching career which will help to shape my role in education for years to come.' **Middle leader, Wandsworth, London.**

- 'A course for leaders who are creative, courageous and innovative and are not afraid to challenge the status quo. The BLA enables you to do exactly that – embark on an adventure to consider your values and motivators and how these influence your practice as a leader. It gets me thinking in a way in which I can both improve as a leader and potentially improve the system in which I work.' **Executive headteacher, East London.**

If Covid-19 has taught us anything, it is that no instruction manual on leadership could have ever prepared us for handling the pandemic. We need leaders who are dynamic and agile. Leaders who are not afraid to find ways to navigate restricting accountability measures that hold back our young people. We need leaders who are empowered and empowering and we are delighted to be supporting some brilliant ones to learn with and from one another.

What are the themes from this work?
It is clear that learning with and from others is embedded into our approaches. This *connected view of learning* applies from the classroom to the wider system and has a powerful effect on the design and implementation of our work. It is all underpinned by a high trust, relational and collaborative mindset and commitment of resource to these aspects. This requires us to move beyond competition and, at times, individual ego needs and act with generosity and humility. It requires us to develop deep expertise and also to 'hold this lightly' as we continue to learn and develop our thinking. This mindset of curiosity is a critical underpinning of our approach and is outlined in Dr Neil Gilbride's study of the adult ego development (as described by Loevinger) of educational leaders (Gilbride et al 2020).

These preconditions or principles go to the heart of how we think about our roles as leaders, including how we design them. The lead author (Liz Robinson) is now in her second shared leadership role, having been in a co-headship for the latter period of her time as a head, and now as co-director at Big Education. Sharing the leadership explicitly has many powerful implications and is rooted in a high trust, relational model which acknowledges the potential of collaboration.

It is also interesting to reflect that in writing this chapter we have opted for a collaborative approach, explicitly drawing on and sharing the work of others. This explicitly embodies the values and approach of Big Education that we have adopted in the trust as a whole.

Moving forward

Our behaviour as professionals within the education sector is deeply influenced by our values as well as our own personal development. Competition, as a value, is built into our educational paradigm at all levels – from exams and qualifications, to ranking schools, to the sharp-elbowed house price hiking school place scramble. When we compete, we focus on us and ours. We keep things to ourselves. This, we believe, limits collective progress.

Furthermore, our conception of ourselves and what it means to be 'right' or have 'the answer' can also have a limiting effect on our ability to collaborate and learn together. As a sector, it is important to explore this relationship with 'expertise'. The focus on evidence-based practices can be limiting if we allow this to:

- stop us from keeping on learning – thinking we have the answers.
- relying on evidence which provides insights into a limited set of questions, because finding answers to some questions is really hard. These hard or 'wicked' problems are usually the most important!
- creating hierarchies in our relationships which disconnect us and disempower many within the sector.

A networked approach to learning is helpful as it embeds some of the necessary mindsets around humility and generosity into the work, allowing for new co-creation and learning for the benefit of the system as a whole.

References

Algoe, S. B. (2019) 'Positive interpersonal processes', *Current Directions in Psychology*, 28(2) 183–188.

Brown, C. and Luzmore, R. (2012) *Educating Tomorrow: Learning for the Post-Pandemic World*. Bingley: Emerald Publishing.

Cameron, K. (2008) *Positive Leadership: Strategies for extraordinary performance*. San Francisco: Berrett-Koehler Publishers, Inc.

Cameron, K. (2021) Why energy is so important for leaders, *SmartBrief* [Online] 5 August. Retrieved from: www.bit.ly/3EyNMrl.

Cordingley, P., Higgins, S., Greany, T., Crisp, B., Araviaki, E., Coe, R. and Johns, P. (2020) Developing Great Leadership of CPDL. CUREE, Durham University and University of Nottingham.

Crocker, J., Canevello, A. and Brown, A. A. (2017) 'Social motivation: costs and benefits of selfishness and otherishness', *Annual review of Psychology*, 68 299–325.

Descartes, R. (1641) Meditations on first philosophy.

Gagné, M. and Deci, E. L. (2005) 'Self-determination theory and work motivation', *Journal of Organizational Behavior*, 26(4), 331–362.

Gilbride, N., James, C. and Carr, S. (2020) 'School principals at different stages of adult ego development: Their sense-making capabilities and how others experience them', *Educational Management Administration and Leadership*, 49(4).

Heidegger, M. (1978) *Being and Time*. Hoboken, NJ: Wiley-Blackwell.

Lucey, C. (2021) 'Evolving The "7 tools" for leadership: a research paper exploring the "7 tools" evolvement from Paradigm A to B'.

Lucey, C., Lister, E., Robinson, L. and Parry, L. (2021) Big 8 Leadership Foundation: The Research, A development workshop pre-read. Big Education.

Lucey, C. and van Nieuwerburgh, C. (2020) '"More willing to carry on in the face of adversity": How beginner teachers facing challenging circumstances experience positive psychology coaching An interpretative phenomenological analysis', *Coaching: An International Journal of Theory, Research and Practice*, 14(1), 62–77.

Ryan, R. M. and Deci, E. L. (2000) 'Self-determination theory and the facilitation of intrinsic motivation, social development, and well-being', *American Psychologist*, 55(1), 68–78.

Disrupters, innovators, changemakers

the global WomenEd network

Vivienne Porritt with Lisa Hannay and Liz Free

Overview

The WomenEd network inspires and supports women educators and leaders to lead and to reshape education. We want a profession that is equitable, and inclusive in which women are enabled to be leaders. To achieve this, our global networks need to disrupt the systemic elements which mean that men are disproportionately represented in senior leadership roles across education. We network to hasten change and to innovate in the ways women are supported and developed. Since 2015, WomenEd has grown to 36 networks across 20+ countries with a core team of seven strategic leaders and over 160 network leaders. We continued to grow through the pandemic in terms of new networks, over 40,000 followers as well as writing our second book authored by 35 members of our global community. Ironically, the pandemic has seen women leaders being celebrated for their success whilst also 'unwinding years of painstaking progress toward gender diversity' (Thomas et al 2020).

This paradox means WomenEd has adopted a brave new world view. We share women's lived experiences, research papers and books; we organise unconferences, webinars, coaching and initiate WomenEd networks: this networking liberates women. We challenge organisational and systemic bias as the pace of change in that respect is painfully slow.

Therefore, we also challenge individual women to shake free of stereotypes and bias, to be 10% braver and to join a supportive community of women. The nature and purpose of networking by women is being changed.

Keywords
Leadership
Women
Networking
Global
Equitable
Disrupt

Connecting, supporting and empowering women leaders

The WomenEd network inspires and supports women educators and leaders to rise, to influence and to reshape education. We want a profession that is equitable, ethical, and inclusive in which every woman is enabled to achieve her aspirations and ambitions. To achieve this our global network disrupts the systemic elements which support the disproportionate representation of men in senior leadership roles across education. We network to bring about change, to innovate and to support and empower women to lead in education.

WomenEd was created in May 2015 with the intention to connect aspiring and existing women leaders and to give women a voice in education discussions on Twitter. That was our initial focus as we saw women being edged out of conversation or silenced by comments in Twitter exchanges or a preponderance of male leaders speaking at conferences. The synchronous publication of data about women leaders in education in England suggested that 1700 leaders were needed to represent the proportion of female teachers (The Future Leaders Trust 2015). Education DataLab also published data about the gender pay gap in full time teachers and leaders in 2010/11 in England. We were astonished to hear there was any gap given a clear pay framework for teachers and leaders and shocked to see the significant disparity between women and men.

Our initial aims were to give women a voice and have greater representation of women leaders on Twitter. We were welcomed by women educators and by some men. Other men mocked us, querying our desire to have an unconference, or insisting that an all-male line up at an event was acceptable in a feminised profession, as, after all, if women didn't put themselves forward, that was a deficit in women! (Brands and Fernando-Moti 2017).

Galvanised by such inequity, the original seven leaders in England organised an unconference for 200 women to highlight what we had learned and share this with more women. Our first unconference was organised via social media, particularly Twitter, and the first time the original seven organisers met in person was the night before the unconference.

We applied the unconference principles of an informal exchange of information and ideas between participants. We wanted to remove the hierarchy of more formal conferences which can lead to passive participants receiving knowledge from experts. Our aim was to enable participants to contribute as speakers and delegates or to lead discussion groups. There were no experts, simply women collaborating to see what was possible to achieve.

We had expected negative responses from men and, the night before the first unconference, we were all saddened by seeing a tweet from a group of men who thought it a joke to portray WomenEd though an image of women physically fighting each other: 'An image of two women fighting had been posted. It resonated with the female "catfight" trope used as a negative image of feminism' (Fuller 2021a:121). This representation of the stereotypical trope of cat fighting, suggesting women cannot get along with other women, was called out by our growing community suggesting to us that some women were already becoming more confident in the Twitter space: the tweet was then deleted. However, some women were silenced temporarily: 'I hadn't blogged for ages because I'd had sort of criticisms from some of the male voices again [laughs] on Twitter. And you do listen to these voices whether you want to or not (co-founder E)' (Fuller 2021a:121).

Many women at our initial unconference commented on the joy of responding to so many women facilitators and the nature of the conversations between women throughout the day. It was clear there was an appetite for us to go further and we shared ideas to grow networks across England. Alongside this clear desire of women, the small male backlash also had a positive outcome in that it pushed us to articulate what WomenEd was now about: 'We had to very quickly really drill down to, 'Who are we? What do we stand for? What is our why?" (Fuller 2021a:121). From this, WomenEd's values were created. Our eight values have underpinned and driven our networks and impact since.

- Clarity
- Communication
- Connection
- Confidence
- Collaboration
- Community
- Challenge
- Change

Following what became our first national conference in England, and drawing on social network theory, we began to:

- structure our networks for learning and relationships.
- create virtual and physical links within and between networks.
- agree the functions that network activities serve.

We were encouraged by the description of such networks as 'sites of participation, sharing, inquiring and discovering where peer-cultures can flourish, interests can develop and expertise can be shared' (Van der Baan et al 2014:5).

As a network of volunteers, we wanted a decentralised community in which members would feel empowered and decisions could be made quickly. We also wanted to create a learning community in which new knowledge gained would result in experimentation, subsequent reflection and then action. Such action would change behaviour, both for our individual members and their organisations. We worked on a balance between:

- Similarity of purpose and passion – to connect, support and empower women leaders.
- Exchange of varied experiences and ideas – through online discourse and events.
- Reciprocity – mutual, shared values and a desire for impact for women leaders in education.

The grassroots approach of a volunteer network of women enabled us 'to develop a counter-discourse to the dominant leadership discourse in education' (Fuller 2021a:129). We could discuss social justice, authenticity, sexism, feminism, racism, and intersectionality openly and be clear that we wanted women to 'have the confidence and belief in their ability to lead as a woman' (Porritt 2017). We reduced hierarchies and crossed boundaries enabled by social media and its speed and agility: our platform on Twitter brought about significant growth.

The growth of the WomenEd community

Europe

Whilst we were clear on our initial purpose and values, it is true that our early growth was organic and dependent on responses by individual women who self-selected to join us, one of those being Liz Free. Liz is now CEO and Director of International School Rheintal, Switzerland, and supports our European networks as one of the current core team of seven global strategic leaders.

WomenEd travels. It is a network that lives and breathes with the community. With its origin in the UK, and a mission and vision that resonates with our #GlobalProfession, it continues to spread throughout the world.

I initially became involved with WomenEd in the winter of 2016, subsequently launching @WomendNL in the Netherlands on International Women's Day 2017 with two other leaders from my school group. An enthusiastic group of international leaders, we took the approach of bringing together people we knew, and people they knew, to have a launch network event. We judged that it was a resounding success with new and old connections. We raised the profile of women in education leadership and began to address concerns, key issues, and positive approaches for this self-selecting community in the Netherlands. However, we used the medium of English and connections had a bias to one specific sector, the international school community.

The idea of self-selection is a key fundamental principle of a grassroots movement. People choose to engage. We drew on the words attributed to Mary Mead, 'Never doubt that a small group of thoughtful, committed citizens can change the world; indeed, it's the only thing that ever has.' This is the approach we took and set up several people to become regional network leaders. Like the founding members of WomenEd, it was a small group of people wanting to effect a change. However, this presented critical challenges that we have subsequently learned from and are still unpicking today.

We currently have four campaigns for WomenEd, two of which are focused around increasing representation and diversity of women in education leadership. Our founding @WomenEdNL network leads, whilst well intentioned, inadvertently set up an exclusive network. The network was visibly and metaphorically dominated by white women working predominantly in the English-medium and the international sector. Whilst the core network team had representatives from the UK and the Netherlands, it certainly was not diverse and language dominance in the non-domestic language excluded the community the network was intended to represent. This led to some challenging conversations, reflection, and introspection as we sought to address the very lack of representation we had created and had intended to challenge. The network continues to develop and has engaged with a wider representation. However, it is a different dynamic and level of engagement when you invite someone to a party that has already started rather than inviting them to plan the party together, beginning with equity.

We wanted to learn from this and implement practices that are inclusive and representative of the communities of women that our networks serve. As new leaders wanted to set up networks in countries across Europe, we started to think very carefully, intentionally and deliberately about equity and representation. We took our experiences from the existing country networks in the UK and Europe and put in place written protocols that now underpin the development of all our global networks. Our internal commitments of network leaders document says each network must:

- Be diverse, accessible, and representative of the education sectors within their context.
- Ensure that the network serves its community, and all women can belong.

Following this introduction of our commitments and further definition of the roles of the network leaders, we have launched new European networks with increasingly diverse and representative teams in Spain, Belgium, Luxembourg, Italy, Switzerland and Germany as well as inspiring colleagues in Asia, the Middle East and North Africa as well as the Americas.

As the movement travels, there remains a bias toward internationally mobile teachers. However, we are cognisant of our mission and intention to create inclusive networks and now launch networks with a clear mandate for diversity and representation. With an awareness of the impact of westernised colonisation of education, we want to ensure that WomenEd celebrates its journey, travels when our members travel and remains firmly rooted in the needs of the network communities themselves.

As Liz describes, we were excited that our purpose and passion had taken us so quickly across the UK and Europe and the speed overtook our opportunity to think about the wider implications of representation and equity. Initially, if we were approached by a woman to set up a new network, we agreed immediately, and an orientation and a new twitter account followed rapidly. Now we have learned that it takes time to build a diverse network that reflects the country or regional needs of women educators, and this time is well spent as new network leaders understand the value each woman brings to the team building reciprocity and strong connections.

Canada
Our learning is reflected in Lisa Hannay's account of the development of networks in Canada. Lisa is a Senior Leader in a secondary school in Calgary and supports our networks in the United States and Canada as one of the current core team of seven Global Strategic Leaders:

WomenEd in Canada has recently grown and added three new regional networks making a total of four regional teams supported by the national @WomenEdCanada network team. Canada's geography being as large and spread out as it is means that much of the connection and networking must occur virtually. The various regional leaders connect women across Canada through slow chats over Twitter, with blog challenges and with the occasional in person event. Our regional leaders also participate in global events, enabling awareness of issues more specific to our country and bringing learning from other global networks back to their region. At in-person events, we seek out women leaders to share their truths and narratives, which creates their own agency and experience at being 10% braver. We have learned that participants relate to each other through the authentic sharing of individual experiences: 'Stories are huge to bring people together, to show no one is alone' (Khan, 2020: personal communication). There is always a palpable excitement at the conclusion of these events with various participants pledging to share at the next event, start their graduate program or enter a mentoring or coaching relationship to elevate their leadership development.

Since the inception of networks in Canada we knew that it was crucial to invite and include as many diverse voices as possible and look specifically at issues relevant to our region. In all our virtual and in-person sessions we looked carefully at including Indigenous teachings and voices. We have invited women Indigenous leaders to speak about their journeys and we look to incorporate Indigenous protocols as frequently as possible such as reading an Acknowledgment of the Land and sitting in circle. Whilst each WomenEd network works on our four campaigns set at the global level, it is also important to consider the local challenges and opportunities present in each region. In 2015, the Truth and Reconciliation Commission published 94 Calls to Action and these actions urge all Canadians to increase their awareness and knowledge of the legacy of Residential Schools in Canada and the contribution of First Nations, Metis and Inuit people.

At WomenEd's 2020 global unconference, @WomenEdCanada presented a session on Indigenous ways of teaching and learning and how each leader embedded these teachings in their leadership journey. Each region in Canada navigates the responsibility we have, to learn about, and incorporate Indigenous ways of knowing and being. As women leaders we believe we have a responsibility to increase representation of women leaders and underrepresented women in leadership positions. Each presenter shared their leadership experience with the Alberta representative talking about the Teacher Quality Standards and the British Columbia representatives talking about the British Columbia's First Peoples Principles of Learning. Our hope is that with increased awareness more First Nations, Metis and Inuit women leaders are represented in leadership and that all women will see that their voices must be at the table. During this exploration, participants were able to add their voices to the presentation and it was wonderful to see women connecting to each other and to the material. One participant voiced perfectly what encapsulates the heart of WomenEd: 'I stand on the shoulders of those who came before' (Everitt 2020: personal communication).

Agency creates impact. It is true to say that every time a woman stands up for herself, she does stand up for other women. The challenge comes when we commit to using our position and privilege to stand up for those whose voices have long gone unheard and unvalued. We must continue being 10% braver, true to our core beliefs and continue creating seats at the table.

Why we need positive disruption

WomenEd continued to grow through the stages of the pandemic with over 40,000 followers on social media, writing our second book *Being 10% Braver*, authored by 35 members of our global community and the development of new networks, totalling 36 at the time of writing. Ironically, the pandemic has simultaneously seen women 'in the front line' being celebrated (Fioramonti et al 2020) whilst also 'unwinding years of painstaking progress toward gender diversity' (Thomas et al 2020:6).

This paradox means the WomenEd global network has adopted a brave new world-view. We continue to share women's lived experiences, research papers and books; we organise unconferences, webinars, coaching and set up WomenEd networks in a new country or region and this networking is liberating women. The nature and purpose of networking, especially by women, is being changed. Dr Kay Fuller, a network leader for WomenEd, sees networking for women leaders as an 'under-researched field' (Fuller 2021a:116) and argues that 'women's professional networking comprises a cooperative that acts as a partial antidote to the fragmentation and competition' resulting from education reform (Fuller, personal communication 2021b).

We argue that global reforms have ignored the issues related to women educators and leaders. Women dominate in the global teaching workforce, yet men dominate as leaders. The moral question is how is this acceptable in a profession that should be both ethical and equitable? Pragmatically, we cannot afford the rate of attrition we see in women leaders leaving our profession, particularly because of a career break. In England, for example, 'one in four teachers who quit the classroom in recent years were women aged between 30 and 39' (Adams 2016). Research from National Foundation for Educational Research suggests that 'part-time teaching is most prevalent among women in their late 30s and early 40s' (2019:2). The lack of flexibility in teaching and support for women returning from a career break results in gender inequity at leadership levels. Our children see more men as leaders in schools and the inequity continues to the next generation. We must break this cycle to ensure our girls, who make up half of the world's population, are fully supported to realise their potential.

Through our engagement with women in education globally, women's personal stories exemplify the significant impact of gender on promotion and retention of female teachers, the large gender pay gap and the lack of flexible working opportunities, particularly in schools. Some stories demonstrate inequality from unconscious bias to overt discrimination. As recounted in *Being 10% Braver: Inspiring Women to Lead Education*, Claire Cuthbert was told she had been unsuccessful in achieving her first headship position because 'the local mining community would be more aligned to a male figure head' (Browne 2019:71). Claire is now a successful CEO of a growing trust. Sameena Choudry highlighted one woman of ethnic heritage was told by a senior male leader that 'there was little point in promoting her, and indeed other women [...] as they would just leave to go and have babies' (2019:59). In *Being 10% Braver*, Hannah Dalton and Kiran Mahil felt that 'after having children of our own, there was an assumption by management that we were no longer able to educate anybody's children' (2020:174). Jacinta Calzada-Mayronne was unsupported by female colleagues and was told that she 'had a bravado for being confident' (2020:155).

From the USA to Australia, it is well documented that there is a motherhood penalty (Gough and Noonan 2013; Monash University 2019): it is shocking this is reiterated in teaching, a supposedly family-friendly profession.

Through our global networks, WomenEd challenges such organisational and systemic issues which hold women back. Our campaigns highlight more equitable and ethical approaches and we call on the education profession to disrupt the status quo.

One example of a systemic issue is the recruitment process, the current outcome of which is an over preponderance of men at the top of education, too few Black, Brown and Asian women (and men) in senior leadership, a significant gender pay gap, and archaic working conditions as seen in the lack of flexible thinking. WomenEd offers more equitable ways forward for the way roles are advertised and how potential candidates are selected.

The advertisement

We will all agree that a post must go to the best candidate. However, 'if you lose people from the very beginning of the process, you may not see an application from the person you really need' (Porritt 2020). It is well documented that women and men use and respond to language differently due to gender stereotypes (Glick and Fiske 1996). Heilman (2001) reiterated that stereotypes posit men as agentic and women as communal. Gaucher et al demonstrated that words suggesting agentic appeal in job advertisements lead to 'less anticipated belongingness and job interest among women, which [...] likely perpetuates gender inequality in male-dominated fields' (2011:119). In leadership job advertisements, the 'types of words and phrases that lead to inequality' (Tickle 2018) need to be understood as such language can 'exert important effects on individual level judgments that facilitate the maintenance of inequality' (Gaucher et al 2011). WomenEd shares with our networks the research behind an online gender decoder (gender-decoder.katmatfield.com), which highlights stereotypically feminised and masculinised words. Using a balance of such words can attract more women to apply as does stating you support flexible working or want a diverse team. Women applicants can balance their more likely use of communal words with more agentic language and so diminish any unconscious bias on the part of the recruitment panel. Such a simple step widens the range of people who read and respond to an advertisement which must help education leaders to attract a wide field. Network teams then use such research in relevant discussions on Twitter or in events. Examples include our Thailand network which held an online Career Clinic with videos made available to our global networks: watch the full playlist on WomenEd's YouTube channel (2021). Blogs also share the learning within the Thailand network and across our global community (Brelsford 2021). Our networks in Spain and Germany have related videos with advice tailored to the needs of their community (WomenEd 2020). We then encourage our community to celebrate when new learning and positions are gained to amplify the messages across our networks:

'Someone in the #WomenEd CareerClinic shared this excellent tool to check the language in job advertisements for subtle gender bias. A really interesting point of reflection' (Elagha 2021).

'I have passed my MA and this woman cried tears of joy. Thank you @WomenEd. Thank you to everyone who encouraged and supported' (Stow 2021).

'@WomenEd Thank you for two very helpful sessions which have really focused my thinking and planning. I can't thank the WomenEd community enough; you gave me the courage to apply and then accept my new role as head of school' (Watts 2021).

The application form

Unconscious bias, which we all experience, affects the language used in advertisements and the application form. We encourage our networks to practise two disruptions that can reduce the inequity of the process.

Firstly, research is available on our website (WomenEd n.d.) as well as blogs which support education leaders to practise blind recruitment by redacting names, age, personal pronouns, universities, and qualifications before the shortlisting panel sees the personal statement. Blind recruitment has limitations, but it might stop what one study reported: 'White names receive 50 percent more callbacks for interviews' (Bertand and Mullainathan 2003).

And our networks then share their take: 'all employees should have bias training, employers should reject non-diverse shortlists, diversify job specs, use blind recruitment practices, have diverse recruitment panels (Plummer 2021).

Secondly, the majority of educational organisations require applicants to disclose their current salary in an application. This exacerbates the gender pay gap and is irrelevant to the person specification. WomenEd call for all organisations to remove this question and play their part in the reduction of gender pay gaps. If organisations have such a question, they are perpetuating the status quo and embedding inequity into their processes. Once you know this, it must be removed (Porritt 2021). We are beginning to see such change in many educational organisations:

'Delighted to confirm that we have taken away the "previous salary" box on our application forms as a positive step to reducing the #GenderPayGap in our organisation' (Prickett 2020). We are also delighted that the Teacher Vacancies Service in England and TES Jobs have removed this question from their application form to help reduce the pay gap for women. Our vision sees women's networks at the heart of bringing about systemic change for equity, diversity, and inclusion in the education sector: these simple disruptions are changing the systemic processes that hold women leaders back.

Moving forward

WomenEd will continue to challenge organisational and systemic bias but the pace of change in that respect is painfully slow. Therefore, we also challenge individual women to shake free of these stereotypes, to share their stories in our supportive and joyous community and to be 10% braver by:

- Challenging gender stereotyping
- Supporting women in underrepresented groups to become leaders
- Discussing the benefits of diverse teams in your organisation

- Challenging the gender pay gap in your organisation and working to reduce it
- Sharing the benefits of flexible working practices
- Doing leadership differently
- Using your voice to embolden women globally to lead

WomenEd also supports other grassroots communities and we are proud there are now many such focused on equitable support for our colleagues and our students. Examples include: BAMEEd, LGBTed, DisabilityEdUK, MaternityCPD, EdConnectNet. Our learning about growing such networks is to:

- have clear and simple values and purpose.
- be clear on the difference you want to achieve.
- exemplify your values in clear actions.
- celebrate your impact.

At a system level, we want all countries and organisations to know and share their gender pay gap and work to reduce it: we share ways forward for individuals, organisations, and the educational system (Porritt 2021). We also advocate that education systems need to have equity and diversity at their core and describe the ways they want to see such values enacted by their stakeholders. This would include gender equity for women leaders and more diverse representation of women and men of an ethnic heritage. Most importantly, 'The need to consider gender matters as part of the everyday discourse has become essential, not an add-on' (Featherstone 2019:145). We ask existing women and men who lead education in every sector and country to scrutinise the ways that they enable women's voices to be heard and how they develop future women leaders so they can lead education.

Finally, whilst support is paramount, a WomenEd network is not a cosy experience. We have 'warmth and humour but with a steely determination to challenge inequity relentlessly' (Peacock 2019:xiii). We challenge the passive acceptance of inequity, injustice, and discrimination. A radical change is needed to enable women to lead education and this change is being enacted by the collective voice and power of our network. Through positive disruptions to the status quo, we want to inspire and support women to rise, to influence, to lead and to reshape education so that it is an equitable profession in which every woman is enabled to achieve her aspirations and ambitions.

Be 10% braver for yourself and for others.

References

Adams, R. (2016) 'Teachers need flexible working to stop women leaving profession, says thinktank', *The Guardian*, [Online] 4 April. Available at: www.bit.ly/3uKFTKK.

Association of School and College Leaders, NAHT, National Governance Association, WomensEd (2012) 'Closing the Gender Pay Gap in Education: A leadership imperative', [Report] 1 December.

Bertrand, M. and Sendhil, M. (2003) 'Are Emily and Greg more employable than Lakisha and Jamal?', *National Bureau of Economic Research*, Working Paper 9873 [Online]. Available at: www.bit.ly/3qVw3V3.

Brands, B. and Fernando-Moti, I. (2017) 'Women Are Less Likely to Apply for Executive Roles If They've Been Rejected Before', *Harvard Business Review*, [Online] 7 February. Available at: www.bit.ly/3uNEa7q.

Brelsford, J. (2021) 'WomenEd Thailand Career Clinic', *WomenEd*, [Blog] 18 November. Available at: www.bit.ly/3LwHFG6.

Browne, A. (2019) 'Doing Leadership Differently' in V. Porritt and K. Featherstone (eds) *10% Braver: Inspiring Women to Lead Education*. London: Sage, pp. 67–81.

Calzada-Mayronne, J. (2020) 'Moving Mindsets and Failing Forward' in K. Featherstone and V. Porritt (eds) *Being 10% Braver*. London: Corwin, pp. 149–160.

Choudry, S. (2019) 'Concrete Ceilings and Kinked Hosepipes' in V. Porritt and K. Featherstone (eds) *10% Braver: Inspiring Women to Lead Education*. London: Sage, pp. 55–66.

Dalton, H. and Mahil, K. (2020) 'Pregnant and Screwed' in K. Featherstone and V. Porritt (eds) *Being 10% Braver*. London: Corwin, pp. 174–179.

Education Datalab (2015) 'Women dominate the teaching profession, but men are winning the pay game', Seven things you might not know about our schools, 22–25 [Online]. Available at: www.bit.ly/3uNumKp.

Elagha, M. [@Ms_Elagha] (2021) 23 October [Twitter] Available at: www.bit.ly/3qSfPfi.

Everitt, L. (2020) Zoom webinar chat comment (4 October). Personal Communication

Fuller, K. (2021a) Feminist Perspectives on Contemporary Educational Leadership. Oxfordshire: Routledge.

Fuller, K. (2021b) Email (5 May). Personal communication.

Featherstone, K. (2019) 'Still we Rise: Our Agenda for the Future' in V. Porritt and K. Featherstone (eds), *10% Braver: Inspiring Women to Lead Education*. London: Sage, pp. 141–151.

Fioramonti, L., Coscieme, L. and Trebeck, K. (2020) 'Women in power: it's a matter of life and death', *Social Europe*, Social Europe, [Online] 1 June. Available at: www.bit.ly/3u7daRj.

Gaucher, D., Freisen, J., Kay, A. C. (2011) 'Evidence That Gendered Wording in Job Advertisements Exists and Sustains Gender Inequality', *Journal of Personality and Social Psychology*, 101(1), 109–128.

Glick, P. and Fiske, S. T. (1996) 'The Ambivalent Sexism Inventory: Differentiating hostile and benevolent sexism', *Journal of Personality and Social Psychology*, 70(3), 491–512.

Gough, M. and Noonan, M. (2013) 'A review of the motherhood wage penalty in the United States', *Sociology Compass*, 7(4), 328–342.

Heilman, M. (2001) 'Description and Prescription: How Gender Stereotypes Prevent Women's Ascent Up The Organizational Ladder', *Journal of Social Issues*, 57(4), 657–674.

Khan, I. (2020) Zoom webinar chat comment (4 October). Personal Communication.

Peacock, A. (2019) 'Foreword' in V. Porritt and K. Featherstone (eds) *10% Braver: Inspiring Women to Lead Education*. London: Sage, pp. xiii–xiv.

Plummer, P. [@ParmPlummer] (2021) 1 September [Twitter] Available at: www.bit.ly/3wVrD4k.

Porritt, V. (2015) 'Connecting Women Leaders – the launch', *WomenEd*, [Blog] 13 October. Available at: www.bit.ly/3DxkfgJ.

Porritt, V. (2020) 'How to recruit a more diverse leadership team', TES, [Online] 21 February. Available at: www.bit.ly/3DumKjU.

Porritt, V. (2021) 'Women: Like men, only cheaper', WomenEd, [Blog] 18 November. Available at: www.bit.ly/3K1C623.

Prickett, S. [@ruralsbm] (2020) 19 October [Twitter]. Available at: www.bit.ly/3wW0xdt.

Sharp, C., Smith, R., Worth, J. and Van den Brande, J. (2019) Part-Time Teaching and Flexible Working in Secondary Schools. Slough: NFER. Available at: www.bit.ly/35v7gjb.

Stow, D. [@stowdawn] (2021) 13 October [Twitter] Available at: www.bit.ly/3DvQCfN.

The Future Leaders Trust (2015) 1700 female headteachers 'missing' from England's schools. London: Future Leaders.

Thomas, R., Behrer, A., Cardazone, G., Cooper, M., Coury, S., Huang, J., Krivkovish, A., Kumar, A., Lon, M., Prince, S., Urban, K. and Yee, L. (2020) 'Women in the Workplace', McKinsey & Company [Online]. Available at: www.bit.ly/3LwrzvT.

Tickle, L. (2019) 'Language in school job ads puts women off headteacher roles', *The Guardian*, [Online] 19 June. Available at: www.bit.ly/36H300P.

Van der Baan, A., De Haan, M., Leader, K. (2014) 'Learning Through Network Interaction: The Potential of Ego-Networks' in V. Hodgson, M. De Laat, D. Mcconnell, T. Ryberg (eds) The Design, Experience and Practice of Networked Learning. New York: Springer: pp. 225–240.

Watts, M. [@MoiraWatts10] (2021) 16 September [Twitter] Available at: www.bit.ly/3tXIVMj.

WomenEd (2020) 'Communicating Your Professional Identity & Landing Your Next Role', *YouTube*, [Online] 1 October. Available at: www.bit.ly/3JZh307.

WomenEd (2021) 'Thailand Career Clinic', YouTube, [Video] 23 October. Available at: www.bit.ly/3iTp2zF.

WomenEd (no date) Campaigns and Resources, WomensEd, [Online]. Available at: www.bit.ly/3wUafwU.

A digital asset
understanding your value and new possibilities in a pandemic/post–pandemic world

Kate Bancroft

Overview

In this chapter, the way each person wanting to network is, or will be, a digital asset in a pandemic/post-pandemic world is discussed. The context of this term in this chapter refers to how each person has value, whether that be to other education professionals, their wider school community or to their bigger multi-academy trusts. As a digital asset, they can provide a future benefit in terms of the professional growth they will experience through networking, and this professional growth will inevitably be needed to keep up with surges in the changes of pandemic/post-pandemic pedagogical practices. This chapter will focus on the new opportunities that Covid-19 has brought related to moving from being a physical asset to a digital asset. It will also discuss what this might mean for a person's future learning and progression when contained by and dependent on technology, as opposed to any form of physical presence.

Keywords
Networking
Post-pandemic
Mentoring
Online
Social networking
Job hunting

The rise of our virtual presence

The Covid-19 pandemic forced a new era of reinvention on all of us. During this unique period in time, national and long-term repeated lockdowns meant that societies changed. This was clear through global economies radically altering overnight, a dramatic culture shock when museums, heritage sites, art galleries all closed almost instantly, significant amounts of scientific research had to stop, and religious ways of life were dramatically altered with places of worship closing and 'digital church' becoming a new way of spiritually connecting for many.

Despite these significant changes to life as we knew it, we modified our way of living (as we knew it) quickly. Vaccines were promptly generated by the medical world, court proceedings switched online overnight, and we all quickly learned how to how to set up work stations in our homes, and our children quickly were forced to make the switch of being taught via Zoom, signalling a new era of digital education. Many of us went from being physical beings present at work, where generally our physical presence at something signalled our engagement and commitment to our work, to a different way of working overnight.

Although many education organisations were instigating remote working policies pre-pandemic, Covid-19 has fast-tracked this movement. For those of us working in education where sometimes our ability to use trends that the business sector has been employing well before us is lacking, our online presence suddenly meant everything. Whether that be through our digital attendance for lessons and lectures, meetings, CPD training and conferences, and whether this be via our digital avatars or cameras showing only our faces, logging in for live sessions signalled our interest in each online meet-up. When forced to 'go digital', our digital presence in our teaching delivery and attendance at online sessions, conferences and other events helped create and present ourselves as 'digital assets,' rather than 'in-person physical assets'. This meant the new service we offered were available in real-time and could be accessed from anywhere in the world instantaneously.

I would like to argue we became a new kind of asset to our organisations, but equally to ourselves. For example, we provided a benefit to our employers through upskilling ourselves via the surge in CPD offerings many of us engaged with during lockdown, for some individuals this was perhaps due to increased time with so many workers having no commute for the first time, and with networking and CPD activities being more accessible than ever before. Research has shown that there has been a surge in education CPD through virtual seminars, practice-sharing events, podcasts and the creation of open training resources and a 'general sense of coming together to help one another, and sharing best practice across the sector' (Headleand 2021).

The personal dividends of working virtually

I would also argue that despite increasing our worth to our organisations through the ways many individuals upskilled themselves during this time, we became more of a digital asset for ourselves. So, for instance, we perhaps developed into becoming more employable than ever before and, for some, finding the time to undertake activities that could help us achieve salary increases in the long-term through the increased free time the pandemic offered to some people. I witnessed a surge of colleagues who had been working on their PhD for years and years (and I include myself in this!), dramatically finishing their theses and securing more senior positions in academia as a result of this sudden change of living.

For me, this was down to the increased free time, the way that weekends suddenly became freer and time was saved from commuting at least an hour per day. I became more of a digital asset to my university through my online networking and presence, speaking at conferences, hosting online learning events with 350+ online attendees, and having open access to prestigious events that I would not have been able to attend before the pandemic due to them being less easy to access. I increased my value and using my skills as an online digital asset to benefit my life in a way I would not have been able to achieve before. In education now, it could be argued one does not need to physically be at an event to increase one's value as a digital asset; online engagement becomes the significant factor. This could mean we can increase our worth and value work-wise through far less effort than ever before in comparison to pre-pandemic work activities requiring more money and time.

The merits and demerits of online professional development

Naturally, this easier access to CPD via online methods also comes with some negative consequences. For example, previously, often travel time and possible overnight hotel stays for CPD, offered more freedom of time for reflection on current practice and new possibilities for change. For many employees with children at home, the pandemic offered no time for reflection when many individuals had to instantly return to childcare responsibilities the second the CPD ended due to the school, nursery and childminder services closing. Therefore, online CPD is not a solution without drawbacks for those wanting to increase their 'digital asset worth' in the current job market.

Technological devices and social media have provided a foundation of support for people feeling isolated during Covid-19. Despite its many faults, research has shown that messenger apps and video chat programmes were extensively used to support each other, but when considering how they can help increase a person's value work-wise as a digital asset, it is clear that they can be used as a fantastic tool for virtual social networking and connection (Shah et al 2020; Wiederhold 2020). Research has shown that tools like Teams and Zoom can be specifically used for providing cognitive support and vital information sharing. Virtual networking meetings have been extensively hosted across a range of sectors including education, medicine, music, which have all combined individual subject topics with online communication technologies, helping increase the availability of networking even more.

Networking

A way of increasing one's employability and value can be through high-quality networking and mentoring. Pre-Covid-19, networking in education would often take the form of physically meeting new people at education conferences, training events and other face-to-face events. However, online networking means that users can connect shared intelligence through utilising the millions of people who use social networking sites and attend online conferences to meet new colleagues working in their field to become collaborators together, increasing their worth as digital assets and benefiting each other's careers further.

This is often achieved since, whether it be in education or an education-related company (for example, those working for supply teaching agencies, private tutoring or creators of education-related products), networking is often undertaken to increase economic value, whether that be to the individual themselves searching for a salary increase in a new position, or to generate some form of cash flow income into the school/business through a new partnership. Generally, learning and growth come as a by-product of this networking process, and the positive effect online networking can have on the world of education is enormous (Garcia-Martinez et al 2020). New methods of online networking have emerged during the pandemic. A study from Harvard University over this time led by researcher Heather Staines (2020) argues for people who are seeking others to network with to spend thirty minutes with no set agenda phoning those they wish to form business/teaching contact with informally. She recommends this since many people dislike video calls and the novelty of video calls over face-to-face meetings swiftly wore off for many individuals very quickly due to the sudden and dramatic use of them in the early stages of the pandemic (Nesher Shoshan and Wehrt 2021). Other benefits of phoning those you want to network with include the flexibility of such an approach; for instance, connecting with someone whilst they are taking a walk, walking the dog or enjoying some different scenery and, therefore, away from their computer screens and less distracted by other tasks.

Online networking may become more authentic through an increase in transparency with people networking from the privacy of their own homes. So, for instance, online networking may enable people to be less concerned about networking with colleagues at rival schools/businesses, with less risk of being observed or colleagues overhearing what unfiltered, vulnerable truths might be being shared amongst the privacy of one-to-one digital conversations, and how these may result in a more meaningful experience for both networking parties. Online networking helps to avoid the distraction of crowded conferences and heavily-attended multiple school-based meetings and events. The white noise of other people's conversations and observations is eliminated, enabling two people to have their singular digital communication and this can help increase the value of each employee as a digital asset through their enhanced experience.

It is important to note also how networking has the power to improve communities by bringing together people who work in similar roles and who may use these opportunities to discuss innovative ideas that can enhance businesses and communities. For example, this may involve projects that enhance neighbourhoods, local districts and the wider public via the unique newly-made connections and ideas created at networking events. These can help add value to other people's lives since individuals who have networked together individually may wish to meet again through discussions about common goals and potential collaborations that can dramatically change their own and other people's lives.

A fascinating study from Harvard Business School explored this concept in depth. They specifically looked at the experiences of lawyers at networking events (Casciaro et al 2016). The study found that lawyers who, when networking, focused on the collective benefits of networking, such as 'helping clients' or 'helping the business they worked for', instead of personal ones such as 'helping my career', brought more authentic versions of themselves to networking events, and this led to an increase in the number of people they networked with and a higher level of work performance when not networking (such as more billable hours). The study also drew on how when helping women focus on how they were helping increase women's voices, who are traditionally underrepresented in business networking events and how attending might help generate more media coverage, they felt more likely and open to networking as a result of thinking about the bigger picture The study showed that by continually considering the wider benefit to the communities in which you work and serve you can become more effective at networking and that can help bring about positive change for many others simultaneously, whilst enhancing your own worth as an asset also.

Mentoring

A study published by the University of Massachusetts (Bryan and Vitello-Cicciu 2020) looked at how effective mentoring could be during the pandemic, and they looked specifically at nursing in the time of a worldwide health care crisis. The lead researcher specifically looked at how novice nurses joining the workforce at such a dramatic time could successfully be supported through mentoring. What she found out is relevant for all of us working in education in mentor-mentee relationships; she argued that mentoring culture can be enhanced by increased self-awareness from the mentee, conversations that foster resilience and preventing burn-out. These recommendations can be applied to other settings also like education. So, conversations based on burnout during the pandemic could help enhance a person's skill set by increasing the likelihood they can stay strong in the face of challenge and continue to grow as a digital asset and increase happiness and work satisfaction in life, even during the hardest of times.

A fascinating study led by organisational psychologist Dr Chantal van Esch at California State Polytechnic University (van Esch et al 2020) sought responses from a survey with 253 academics and discovered that females, and those more worried about the Covid-19 pandemic, were more likely to seek mentorship. The research team discovered that during the pandemic, role-modelling was one of the most commonly sought aspects of mentoring that the mentee was seeking, and this was more important than career or psychosocial support.

Readers may be aware of the seminal work by Bandura (1977) on role-modelling, which is an approach that argues that people are generally adopting the behaviour exhibited by strong models, and the repeated repetitions of a particular behaviour increase the likelihood of complete and accurate learning of particular behaviours being repeated. What is fascinating about van Esch et al's (2020) study is it looks at this traditional school of thought in the time of a worldwide pandemic. The research highlighted how important it is for aspects of mentoring to include role-modelling, especially for women who are seeking it, where perhaps traditionally it was thought that people sought mentoring predominantly for general career advice. According to this fascinating piece of work, by seeking this kind of mentoring, an individual can enhance their employability through the influence role-modelling from others can have on their sense of self-efficacy during uncertain times. Furthermore, when this is considered in the context of this book chapter, it could be suggested that this increase in skillset could enhance a person's worth as a digital asset and potential for career growth in the future through the use of this kind of highly influential mentoring.

Moving forward

Growing your worth and value in a post-pandemic world as a digital asset, both to yourself and your organisation in these are exciting times provides opportunities for growth with more flexible options for mentoring and networking than ever before. I believe these activities are going to be necessary for self-development and self-improvement and will be necessary to compete in a new kind of post-pandemic job market and help show eagerness and excitement, which can lead to enormous rewards.

The pandemic has brought new ways of improving one's skills and employability value to the surface and highlighted a new way of working life, helping individuals advance themselves as digital assets. This does not come without challenges or further questions. For example, what about those for whom the pandemic has left less alone time? What about those who do not have the money for IT and internet equipment for such activities? Does this advantage some people over others? For those of us with responsibility and leadership for employees, how can we help close that unfair gap? What about those who struggle with digital literacy but excel in face-to-face interactions? How can role-modelling best be done when so many of us are now working so much more via computers and having significantly less face-to-face contact with our colleagues? These are early days in research about employability during the pandemic. These are disruptive and dynamic days and as we progress towards a post-pandemic world; we need to consider how we can use these changes to support ourselves and our individual growth, as well as supporting those along the way who require support to overcome these modern day digital hurdles.

References

Bandura, A. (1977) *Social learning theory.* Englewood Cliffs, NJ: Prentice Hall.

Bryan, V. and Vitello-Cicciu, J. (2020) 'Effective Mentoring of Novice Nurses during a Healthcare Crisis'. Worcester, MA: University of Massachusetts Medical School Faculty Publications. Available at: www.bit.ly/3LuKDL6.

Casciaro, T., Gino, F. and Kouchaki, M. (2016) 'Learn to Love Networking', *Harvard Business Review*, 94(5), pp. 104–107.

García-Martínez, I., Tadeu, P., Montenegro-Rueda, M. and Fernández-Batanero, J. M. (2020) 'Networking for online teacher collaboration', *Interactive Learning Environments*, pp. 1–15.

Headleand, C. (2021) *Online CPD is one pandemic innovation worth fighting for,* *The Times Higher Education*, [Online] 24 September. Available at: www.bit. ly/3LBwpYL.

Nesher Shoshan, H. and Wehrt, W. (2021) 'Understanding "Zoom fatigue": A mixed-method approach', *Applied Psychology*, pp. 1–26.

Shah, S., Nogueras, D., van Woerden, H. and Kiparoglou, V. (2020) 'The COVID-19 Pandemic: A Pandemic of Lockdown Loneliness and the Role of Digital Technology', *Journal of Medical Internet Research*, 22(11).

Staines, H. (2020) Making connections in a disconnected world: Heather Staines discusses strategies for networking, mentoring and career advancement in the world of scholarly communications. *Research Information*, (111), pp. 20–22.

van Esch, C., Luse, W. and Bonner, R. L. (2021) 'The impact of COVID-19 pandemic concerns and gender on mentor seeking behavior and self-efficacy', *Equality, Diversity and Inclusion: An International Journal*, 41(1), pp. 80–97.

Wiederhold, B. K. (2020) 'Connecting through technology during the coronavirus disease 2019 pandemic: Avoiding "Zoom Fatigue"', *Cyberpsychology, Behavior, and Social Networking*, 23(7), pp. 437–438.

Dynamic, urban professional learning networks

David Woods

Overview

This chapter considers the effectiveness of professional development networking in challenging, urban environments, specifically the two largest cities in England, London and Birmingham, and by contrast a small, urban multi-academy trust. It is written from first-hand experience as well as evidence of successful practice and impact where networks have taken advantage of geographical proximity to develop a strong sense of place to promote collective endeavour in a determination to succeed in challenging contexts. Fundamental to their success is that they have had a collaborative vision and set of values firmly grounded in a compelling and inclusive moral purpose based on equity, social justice and unshakeable principles to be shared and acted upon by everyone. The chapter argues that developing an organisational culture with shared values and behaviours is vital in influencing the way professional development networks work in practice. Following on from this, there needs to be a coherent strategy for all networks based on an agreed theory of change and developing a model for collective improvement using professional experience and skills aligned to evidence and research. Only then can priorities and plans be successfully activated. Crucial to all plans and activities is an urgent and clear focus on improving teaching and learning. The chapter considers some key aspects of this including the mobilisation of intellectual capital, the use of joint practice development, reflective dialogue and the strengthening of professional judgment. It is further argued that without a strategy to share best practice effectively the impact of networks will be limited and that it is vital to develop strategies of identifying, validating and disseminating this practice for the benefit of teachers and pupils. The chapter finally argues that post-Covid there is now an enhanced opportunity to build back stronger and put into place more rigorous and resilient systems establishing dynamic communities of practice.

Keywords
Urban
Collaborative values
Theory of change
Joint practice development
Systemic leadership
Best practice

The challenges and potential of urban learning networks

This chapter seeks to examine professional learning networks, present and future, in challenging urban communities and draws upon practice in London and Birmingham as well as a small MAT in Telford offering macro and micro perspectives. It is based on the work and legacy of the London Challenge and London Leadership Strategy as well as the Birmingham Education Partnership where the author has been in leadership positions, and also the experience as a Trustee of developing a professional learning network in a deprived part of north Telford since 2018.

Despite the challenges urban learning networks do have more advantages in that they can develop a strong sense of place and identity to promote collective endeavour whether across an entire city or in distinct communities (Riley et al 2018). Creating a sense of place with purpose and partnerships is an ideal stimulus to develop dynamic, professional learning networks focused on improving learning for every school community. Another advantage is the geographical proximity of schools to facilitate joint practice development and peer review as well as school to school support. Of course, Covid-19 has partly changed this dynamic but there is every reason to believe that 'communities of practice' can be restarted physically as well as virtually and indeed build back stronger taking advantage of enhanced digital learning accelerated through the pandemic.

Part of the sense of place in specifically urban communities are the common concerns and challenges urgently facing teachers and schools; for example, working with a range of disadvantaged and vulnerable groups of children and young people who are disproportionally represented and also working intensively with parents and families ensuring stability and continuity. These challenges can be a powerful motivator for change bringing networks together in a determination to succeed against the odds.

Collaborative values and vision

If professional learning networks are to be really effective, they have to be firmly grounded in a compelling and inclusive moral purpose based on equity, social justice and unshakeable principles to be shared and acted upon by everyone. This especially applies to those who work in a challenging, urban context where children and young people deserve the best possible education whatever the realities of race, poverty and other social barriers. In the best networks, there is a recognition by school leaders and staff that although their first responsibility is to their own schools they should also support other schools and children and seek support from others as required. There is a strong emphasis on the importance of articulating the mutual gain from working in professional networks which we might term 'system altruism', rather than simply focusing on the success of individual schools. Generally, moral purpose is expressed in terms of making a real difference to the lives of children and young people. As Christine Gilbert says in her paper on 'Optimism of the Will' (2017), 'for area networks to have any permanence it is crucial that they accept collective responsibility for local outcomes' (Gilbert 2017).

The evidence from London in particular is that successful professional development networks are not only based on strong values but that they are inclusive and fully engage practitioners offering a range of opportunities from those beginning their career in education to those in senior leadership positions. Although structures are important, as we will see later, developing a culture with a shared vision and shared behaviours is vital. Ensuring an organisational culture influencing the way individual practitioners work, underpins structural change focusing on high aspirations for the learning community (Woods and Brighouse 2014).

A coherent strategy based on an agreed theory of change

What draws staff to participate in professional development learning networks is to be part of a community of practice beyond their own school and setting. Most commonly this is around subject development particularly in secondary schools but also in curriculum development in primary and special schools. There are many other communities based on 'phase' specialism such as early years or post-16 education. Some are drawn to particular aspects of a school's provision such as special needs, safeguarding and pastoral care where they seek to examine comparative practice. Others want to join 'research' communities giving them the opportunity to explore in-depth particular education challenges. However, although there is a bond of common interest and experience, these communities often lack a coherent strategy focusing on what they are trying to achieve. The very best networks have worked out the answers to these questions or at least are continually reviewing them:

- What is the overarching purpose of the network?
- What are the agreed values and principles?
- What is the organisational structure?
- What are the agreed success criteria and how is progress to be reviewed?
- Have we identified the bodies of knowledge, research and emerging, effective innovation?
- Have we identified and disseminated effectively the best practice in our network? (Brighouse and Woods 2013)

Many networks have spent time on working out their purpose and priorities although less on values. Very few have spent time devising and articulating a model for collective improvement, particularly how knowledge and skills are to be developed and shared and what this means for the way they work. They have not really thought through their theory of change but concentrated instead on what 'offer' they could make to participants. Too many professional development networks have become 'communities of the willing' and have failed to engage and include many practitioners because it is unclear what they could contribute to, and gain from, the network.

As well as the expansion and enhancement of digital learning it may be that the experience of Covid-19 has given us time to reflect and re-evaluate the purpose and value of professional learning networks and the chance to reset for the future. Certainly, in London and Birmingham, the most successful networks have a clear model of change, using professional experience and skills aligned to research and evidence to develop an inclusive culture of openness, trust and mutual accountability. They want to be seen to make a difference and to be able to review their work against agreed criteria.

An example from Birmingham is the work of the Birmingham Education Partnership in fostering and developing specific curriculum groups in primary education. The strategy and rationale are clearly set out describing principles and purpose. They make clear that the purpose is to secure teacher subject knowledge but also rigorous planning of the taught curriculum to ensure effective teaching and learning. Teachers clearly enjoy collaboration when it is purposeful and of immediate benefit to their practice and they relish communicating with fellow practitioners engaged in the same work. Similarly, curriculum and school leaders have enjoyed the benefits of expert guidance and evidence-based practice building trust between schools and professional obligation (Birmingham Curriculum Strategy 2019). Another example includes the various leadership development programmes with a strategic emphasis on system leadership originating from the London Challenge and Leadership Strategy experience with a model of change that:

- empowers real leaders to make things happen.
- creates time and space for innovation.
- keeps the work where it needs to be – close to the front line.
- sustains a sense of shared endeavour and a climate for improvement.
- influences the educational system at both vertical and lateral levels.

Put at its simplest, system leadership refers to the form of leadership that goes beyond individual schools to influence the education, achievement and wellbeing of children and young people more widely. School leaders extend their reach so that all schools improve. There is a system that focuses on collaborative partnerships between schools sharing knowledge and expertise. System leaders realise that classroom, school and system impact one another and seek to engage with this in a meaningful way, as can be seen in recent research on the concept of ecosystems in schools (Godfrey and Handscomb 2019). At its most mature system leadership goes beyond headteachers and senior leaders and included a range of others in leadership roles – going deeper and wider. We sometimes refer to this as 'systemic leadership' where other school leaders at different levels share a strong professional motivation to collaborate. In providing support and challenge to other schools they seek reciprocal benefits leading to self-improvement through observation, evaluation, reflection and joint practice development as well as the dissemination of the most effective practice (Woods 2020a).

A dynamic and urgent focus on improving teaching and learning

This is at the heart of any professional development learning network but sometimes it is poorly articulated and lacks a clear focus and plan. Once context and shared values have been established it is critical to have a tight strategy and strong rationale including models of knowledge and learning. Key questions include:

- What do we want children and young people to know and master?
- How can we verify that they are attaining their learning objectives?
- How can we respond if they do not learn and develop the way we want them to?
- How do we ensure continuous progress?
- How can we strengthen our professional judgment?

All networks depend on the knowledge that participants themselves bring – their accumulated understanding, experience and insights gained in particular contexts. Networks must also be grounded in external, validated knowledge, the best that is known generally about practice which can be used to challenge the knowledge and thinking that participants bring. A good example is the Education Endowment toolkit, another is the various universities and Ofsted research papers. Teaching and learning networks may seek to have partnerships with higher education which are greatly beneficial to various networks in Birmingham and London and are more easily accessible in urban centres. Such networks also need to aim to acquire new knowledge that is collaboratively constructed and developed through dialogue and interactions.

David Hargreaves has written about the importance of intellectual capital and that 'the capacity of a school and network to mobilise its intellectual capital is crucial for this is what fosters new ideas and creates new knowledge, which leads to sustained innovation'. Hargreaves defines intellectual capacity as an 'endless supply of focused intellectual curiosity with effective knowledge sharing which builds capacity' (Hargreaves 2003; Hargreaves 2010; Fullan 2005). Professional development networks should use the techniques of modelling, peer learning, team talking, coaching, peer review and action research to build up their knowledge of what works in improving teaching and learning in particular contexts. Joint practice development in a network cannot be effectively replaced by digital learning although it can be supplemented by this. Similarly, the strength of professional judgment is mainly dependent on teachers meeting together, both inside and outside their schools.

In a strong learning network participants can help to diversify ways of analysis and solve practical dilemmas. It is always difficult for individuals to reflect on their own way of doing things because mindsets and practice get confused but good networks should be able to free themselves from inhibiting assumptions and fixed ways of working. Reflective dialogues are a core element of professional development within and between schools and we need to retain where possible opportunities to apply critical and investigative methods on a wider scale. A good example would be Birmingham's peer review model based on first-hand observations, evidence gathering, peer dialogue and the strengthening of professional judgment.

Identifying and disseminating best practice

Professional development networks can do many things but unless they can share best practice effectively to the benefit of teachers and pupils their impact will be limited. This was one of the London Challenge's major successes that is still sustained today followed to a lesser extent by the Birmingham Education Partnership. However, large cities do have some advantages in knowledge dissemination. As far as possible, we need to avoid a situation where what is said about best practice is based on opinion, assertion and reputation rather than robust evidence of what works best in particular circumstances. To develop a coherent strategy for professional development networks we need to examine the identification, validation and effective dissemination of best practice.

To help the process of identification education networks should offer some defined criteria and reference to particular evidence, reports from education consultants, peer review and a range of data properly contextualised and benchmarked. However, we know that not everything can be measured in this way. If we wish, for example, to record best practice in working with vulnerable children, or working with parents and the community, we have to be confident about the use of self-evaluation and evidence from a range of stakeholders. In my view, every school and network have some best practice it can securely identify through self-evaluation which can be validated externally. We need to get to the situation where most schools are prepared to identify at least one area that it believes to be best practice and confident to share this with others. Furthermore, we should encourage professional development networks to write up their very best practice in the form of a case study with a common structure of elements – context, aims and objectives, the story, audiences, impact and results, evaluation, next steps, and then publish online or hard copy as can be seen best in the contributions from London's schools (Woods 2020b).

The greatest challenge for professional development networks is the effective dissemination of identified and validated best practice. A good knowledge mobilisation strategy includes a range of approaches making full use of digital learning but also considering the means of social interaction. Of course, sharing knowledge is only the first step. The real test is whether this new knowledge about best practice actually changes practice for the benefit of children and young people. The best way to spread best practice is through peer champions. Champions are of two kinds – practitioner champions who have devised and successfully applied the practice with beneficial outcomes and advocate champions who have some authority in the field, e.g. education consultants and researchers. Effective champions are well connected to other practitioners and networks and have the skills both to demonstrate and explain best practice in different contexts. A checklist of dissemination processes in networks would include the following:

- Develop a 'spread the word' toolkit

- Workshops, conferences, webinars and websites
- Focused excellence visits to schools
- Peer reviews which always include an example of validated best practice in reports
- TeachMeets through Zoom or Teams
- Video libraries
- Twitter, blogs, Google and virtual learning platforms
- Publications
- Case studies and think pieces online

At the end of all this, a question needs to be asked of all networks, does the network know what the network knows? To answer the question there should be a clear strategy identifying and disseminating both innovative and best practices an essential element of professional development and a summary of the outcomes achieved.

Multi-academy trusts and professional development networks

The majority of schools are now in MATs of various sizes and geographical reach and as such, they would seem to be in an ideal position to develop excellent professional development networks given their rationale and structures which should provide efficient use of resources, economies of scale, and effective strategic management. As regards strategic planning all MATs have central boards of trustees making sure that the trust operates as a collaborative project rather than a collection of individual schools. However, the evidence so far from regional commissioner reports would indicate that, apart from some larger trusts, few local and smaller trusts have developed their potential to create dynamic professional learning networks. This should be a cause for significant concern. The direction of travel from the government would seem to be that eventually all schools will be in MATs so we need to consider how they can be better at networking for the benefit of everybody and the pandemic has offered the chance for a reset.

This is an example of how one small MAT of nine schools, the Learning Community Trust, operating in a deprived part of North Telford, has put professional development networking at the heart of its school improvement strategy. Its mission is to be an outstanding trust for the whole community with a strong set of values relating to equity, inclusion and moral purpose. The trustees and chief education officer have thought through an overarching strategy with four major objectives – engaging learners, quality teaching, committed leadership and governance and continuous improvement with a culture of collaboration across the trust. This Learning Community Trust operates a very successful cross-trust 'hub' model that brings leaders and staff together to develop further and ensure consistent practice whilst allowing for institutional differences.

It has a number of principles and working practices:

- High levels of trust.
- Full participation in trust programmes.
- Quality opportunities for professional growth.
- Collaborative practice and sharing across schools for the benefit of all including the identification and dissemination of best practice.
- Striving to make a difference to the life chances of children and young people and the community as a whole (Learning Community Trust School Improvement Strategy 2020; Greany et al 2018).

The structure of professional development networks is kept simple but designed to be inclusive. There are phase, subject leaders and leadership forums meeting half termly and all staff participate in working groups designed to share practice and ideas.

Although the trust has had to fall back on digital meetings and learning during Covid-19 from the summer term of 2021, it has sought to build back stronger and taken the opportunity to review and strengthen structures and procedures regarding face-to-face networking building greater relational trust whilst securing better communications through digital links.

Moving forward

This chapter has attempted to describe and analyse highly effective professional development networks in challenging urban contexts. It suggests that more consideration needs to be given to the development and establishment of collaborative values within a culture of shared behaviours. Networks do need to be very clear about their organisational culture that should be open and inclusive. Further, it is fundamental to devise and articulate a model for collective improvement in the network – an agreed theory of change within a particular context and set of objectives. Otherwise, there is a danger that the network might simply represent a somewhat random set of activities and 'offers' that will not motivate many potential participants.

Although Covid-19 has disrupted the work of many networks in terms of opportunities to meet and work together across schools, it has also enhanced opportunities for digital learning. Critically, it has provided some time and space to re-evaluate and reset network strategies. This chapter argues that professional development networks should build back stronger by not only paying more attention to values and culture but re-thinking models of change to put into place more aspirational, inclusive, rigorous and resilient systems. We should aim to deepen and deliver the best of what works strengthened by the experience of designing new digital networking systems. There needs to be a dynamic and urgent focus on improving teaching and learning, particularly through the strengthening of joint practice development, reflective dialogue, sharing innovative and best practice and professional judgment. Networks should also be clear about success criteria and assuming collective responsibility for outcomes. Moving forward multi-academy trusts in particular should strive to become dynamic communities of practice rather than simply aggregates of schools, which are focused upon cooperation, relational trust, maximum participation and professional obligation.

References

Birmingham Curriculum Development Strategy (2019) as part of the Birmingham Education Partnership which is a city network for professional learning.

Brighouse, T. M. and Woods, D. C. (2013) *The A-Z of School Improvement: Principles and Practice*. London: Bloomsbury.

Fullan, M. (2005) *Leadership & sustainability: System thinkers in action*. Thousand Oaks, CA: Corwin Press.

Gilbert, C. (2017) Optimism of the will: the growth of area-based improvement partnerships. Paper presented to the London Centre for Leadership. London: UCL Institute of Education.

Godfrey, D. and Handscomb, G. (2019) 'Evidence use, research-engaged schools and the concept of an ecosystem' in D. Godfrey and C. Brown (eds) An ecosystem for research-engaged schools: Reforming education through research (pp. 1-18). London: Routledge.

Greany, T. and Higham, R. (2018) Hierarchy, Markets and Networks. London: UCL Institute of Education.

Hargreaves, D. H. (2003) Working Laterally: How Innovation Networks Make an Education Epidemic. London: National College for Teaching and Leadership.

Hargreaves, D. H. (2010) Creating a Self-Improving System. London: National College for Teaching and Leadership.

Learning Community Trust School Improvement Strategy (2020)

Riley, K., Coates, M. and Martinez, S. (2018) Place and Belonging in Schools – unlocking possibilities. London: UCL Institute of Education.

Woods, D. C. and Brighouse, T. M. (eds) (2014) *The Story of London Challenge*. London: London Leadership Strategy.

Woods, D. C. (2020a) Lessons from the London Challenge, a whole system approach to Leadership development', in E. Jackson and A. Berkeley (eds) *Sustaining Depth and Meaning in School Leadership*. Abingdon, Oxford: Routledge.

Woods, D. C. (2020b) Best Practice in Birmingham. Birmingham: Birmingham Education Partnership Discussion paper.

Part two:

Flourishing practice

Creative collaboration
professional learning in and through the arts

Steven Berryman

Overview

This chapter will explore recent approaches to building local and national networks of arts, culture and creative educators in a range of settings. These approaches include the use of dedicated websites that align with arts and cultural policy in England, the use of collaboration platforms to facilitate the exchange of ideas, content and sustainable dialogue and the use of thematic professional learning to engage with academic literature for music educators. The author will place these more recent approaches in the context of previous collaborative networks for educators, and how the most effective collaboration and professional learning for arts educators is through art, for example, educators working with practitioners to develop their skills. The Durham Commission for Creativity revealed the value of teaching for creativity, and the chapter will discuss attempts to build a national network that reaches beyond the confines of individual subjects that seeks to champion, at scale, creativity as a whole-school and sector-wide endeavour.

There is an interesting tension for arts educators in how they perceive their identity; this chapter will explore how working with educators as artists, and creating an effective balance between arts practice, pedagogy and the more literature-based learning is the most effective approach to build networks in and through the arts.

Keywords
Arts
Culture

Music
Practitioner
Creativity
Collaboration

The solitary plight of the arts specialist

Arts educators, depending on the nature of their educational setting, can experience a level of professional isolation not experienced by those educators of subjects that are taught more often throughout a week and for a longer period of time (for example, English). Educators may work in small departments, potentially working as a department of one, and without the counterpoint of arts colleagues much of the work can be solitary; the design and delivery of the curriculum becomes a solo effort. Whilst this may involve the seeming benefit of the chore of securing the consensus of others when preparing teaching materials, it does prove to be demanding to devise and resource a curriculum free of collaboration. 'There is a clear recognition that fostering peer collaboration among arts and music teachers is particularly challenging, much more so than for teachers specializing in other content areas' (Bautista et al 2021) due to the lack of time to connect with colleagues beyond their own settings, and typically the lack of fellow specialists within their own setting. Additionally, the practices known to be beneficially for professional learning are often not available to specialist arts educators (Ibid). 'Teacher growth… requires improving the quality of teachers' socio-emotional experiences, reducing their stress, and establishing communities of practice and social networks.' This chapter will share recent work at connecting arts educators and building the professional networks to minimise the effects of professional isolation.

'Art education students who become art teachers are, for the most part, educated first as artists and second as art educators. Given this dual education, there is some evidence to suggest that they may experience contradictions in their career development that seriously impact the construction of their professional role and identity as art teachers' (Zwirn 2002). This is an important point as it sets the tone for the networks that arts educators seek to join and interact with; and how the educator considers their identity will drive the professional learning choices they make throughout their career. I suggest education does not always recognise or value artistic practice as a form of professional learning deserving of central funding and support; pedagogically driven professional learning and networks may be considered more valuable to those who fund professional learning activities.

Models of professional learning for arts educators

Krutka et al (2016) identified five common activities in professional learning networks: engaging, discovering, experimenting, reflecting, and sharing. These activities very much underpin the typical way artistic practitioners of many creative domains experience their art and craft; for example, experimentation can play a significant role in creating new work, most readily in improvisation in music but doodling and sketching are also a manifestation of artistic experiments. Much of this experimentation will form part of an artist's practice; whilst many arts are built on a process of training and study, creative risk-taking and improvisation will play a role in the development of craft. Collaborative forms of improvisation and experimentation exist in all artistic domains and it is through these activities that professional learning can be fostered; practitioners working in an ensemble can respond to others, and through this work, networks are formed (or more commonly known as ensembles).

During the challenges of the Covid pandemic, it was evident all elements of Krutka's model were components of virtual professional networks. For example, the Music Teachers Association offered a series of webinars that provided discovery of new resources, provoking reflection on current practices. The webinars offered the opportunity to consider change in practice in addition to the space for music teachers to share their current approaches and offer insight into their own classrooms and thinking. This is seemingly a typical model of a professional network in the arts, where subject associations provide a mixture of engagement and discovery opportunities, increasingly online due to the challenges of the pandemic, coupled with discussion and reflection space. There remains the challenge of activating colleagues' creativity when meeting online and a range of tools have been deployed to provoke the very creativity teachers in arts subjects extol in their students.

For arts educators, keeping connected to practice by working with other practitioners is an under-recognised approach to professional learning; some amateurs may consider artistic endeavour as therapeutic, for example, whilst professionals will see their craft as work. Considering practice as learning means that: 'If teachers are to continually develop their practice then [they will] benefit from broad, holistic, and flexible networks as they navigate shifting professional landscapes' (Trust et al 2016).

Domain specific professional learning

An educator's approach to developing their own artistic practice will determine the kind of professional learning they will invest time and effort in cultivating. Puppe et al (2020) et al showed that expert artists valued social interaction with peers less than intermediate artists value such interaction. These authors showed 'that networks change over the course of artists' lifetimes. Experts usually have several different networks, while novices have fewer and smaller networks' (ibid). Educators will value a range of networks depending on how they conceive their artistic and educational identities; they could seek professional learning through networks that allow them to interact with their artistic peers, as well as networks that champion their educational interests.

Music, specifically, involves solitary practice in developing instrumental skill. Networks for collective learning can exist in the form of group courses, such as residential programmes, than bring together groups of musicians to pursue a particular style of music, for example. It is disputed whether such practice can be considered as research; 'the university model of knowledge exchange that separates the researcher from the industry does not apply to the [music] conservatoire, since the notion of the 'networked' artistic community which defines the conservatoire culture, makes it difficult to neatly divide the academic and professional realms' (Dogantan-Dack 2016). By permitting artistic practice to be deemed research it opens up a variety of knowledge exchange networks for enhancing professional learning. 'The pursuit of practice-based doctoral training in the creative and performing arts has opened up a space for artistic practitioners to contribute to the development of knowledge … and growth of these programmes indicates that artistic practitioners are attracted to the possibilities offered by practice-based doctorates' (Bendrups 2021).

Research activities for practitioners in and beyond educational settings will include a variety of ways of engaging with the craft as well as the literature that can develop the understanding of the craft. Visits to see live performances, exhibitions and meeting authors, for example, provide an immediate professional learning and can be activated through networks that champion certain practices (for example, a journal or book group). A range of professional associations, that may or may not permit membership to those deemed professionals (by virtue of qualifications or particular accreditations), often cultivate these networked opportunities through their membership. Some arts, particularly music, have an array of qualifications that provide a structured approach to gaining recognition for continued development of one's craft, but these typically exist as activities to be pursued on an individual basis.

The following approaches outlined are an example of attempts to connect teachers by providing the space to share and reflect on their practice, particularly during the challenges of the Covid pandemic. It is evident that provocation and discovery play a key role in the professional networking for arts educators; organisations are typically offering interaction with an expert to encourage teachers to reflect. Increasingly the promise of online platforms to share and capture thinking in a range of settings is being enabled, with a large number of online spaces for sharing and amplifying the work of teachers.

Teacher–led networks

ResearchED has become an international venture, with conferences taking place around the globe that unite classroom-based educators with academic research and researchers. As a movement, it appears to have been remarkably successful at building a network that promotes engagement with ideas that could inform the practices of classroom-based educators and in equal measure provides the space for academics to connect with the reality of the classroom.

There are networks in arts and culture that are member-led and often driven by a shared cause or mission. The network called *What Next?* is built on chapters, over thirty across the UK, to facilitate conversation and knowledge sharing around the value and practice of arts and culture. Chapter chairs meet regularly to bring together the bigger picture, and 'Chatham House rules' enable free and open debate in the chapter meetings, many of which involve a visiting speaker to provoke debate. In a sector that has the potential to be fractured and fragmentary due to the small size of some arts organisations and the individual nature of many artists' work, What Next? is an ideal vehicle and approach to building sector-wide strength.

Such an approach adapts well to an educational theme, and *Open Drama UK* was established with a similar chapter structure to connect theatre practitioners who are working in school settings or learning and participation in theatre settings. Events bring colleagues together to discuss specific issues, and a podcast helps promote debate and discussion. Like *What Next?*, *Open Drama* is a volunteer-led venture, as is the Music Teachers Association. The *Music Teachers Association* championed various forms of networking for their members throughout the challenges of the Covid pandemic; their usual annual conference moved to an online event, and to promote more sustained engagement from their membership a series of webinars were devised around specific themes to enable discussion and practice sharing.

Bridging the academic and classroom divide

Bautista et al (2021) noted the one-way nature of classroom practice and educational research; the latter feeding into practice more than practice was feeding into research. To address this disconnect the Music Teachers Association (a UK based association of music educators mostly based in classroom settings) devised a peer-learning project to promote engagement with academic literature to help cultivate reflection on practice. The confidence of educators to interact with academic literature is seemingly thriving (on social media) with a growing number of educator blogs, articles and books that champion 'what the research says' and how the research plays out in classrooms. For music education, the work of academics in the field appeared to be dislocated from the reality of the classroom; the British Journal of Music Education is ranked 238 out of 263 in educational/education research (in 2019) with typically low citations and views of the articles; access appears minimal when we consider the size of the music education workforce in the United Kingdom alone. Building a network of teachers to engage with this literature and respond to it took the form of a blogging exercise; a series of articles were selected by the journal editors and a member of the Music Teachers Association committee with one designated article a week over an 11-week period. Teachers were encouraged to read the article and share their reflections. Reflections were collated and shared as one blog post published each week over the course of the project.

It was apparent how the pandemic provided some increased capacity for teachers to engage in academic literature; increased homeworking for some colleagues allowed them to engage with the blogging project, though conversely for some this added to the challenge of taking part. Pandemic challenges aside, it takes considerable will to engage with a blogging project of this nature and teachers needed regular encouragement to take part and submit responses. Feedback from those involved revealed they found the experience valuable but additionally that was challenging to sustain engagement.

It was demonstrated that during the collaborative blogging project a community of practice developed; the metrics on the journal website revealed a spike in views of the articles featured in the project (Berryman 2021) and anecdotally a community was developing where educators with an interest in the blogging project were able to coalesce on social media to discuss the issues in the articles. Further research would be welcome to ascertain the effectiveness of promoting reflective writing as an engagement mechanism for classroom music educators to build a community of practice that focused on academic literature. With the isolation mentioned previously, there appears to be considerable merit in building such networks to combat the disconnection and under confidence classroom educators in the arts can feel.

Creativity exchange

The Durham Commission on Creativity and Education (2019) sought to champion the importance of creativity beyond the realm of arts subjects alone. One of the recommendations of this research involved the creation of 'a national network of Creativity Collaboratives should be established, in which schools collaborate in establishing and sustaining the conditions required for nurturing creativity in the classroom, across the curriculum'. At the time of writing, the competitive process to recruit the pilot networks has completed and the networks awarded funding will work over three years to pilot ways of working as a group of schools with a range of partners to investigate teaching for and with creativity at a whole-school and system-wide level.

A web-based network, 'The Creativity Exchange', was established as 'a space for school leaders, teachers, those working in cultural organisations, scientists, researchers and parents to share ideas about how to teach for creativity and develop young people's creativity at and beyond school' (see www.creativityexchange.org.uk). The platform signposts a range of articles that provide examples of practice that exemplifies the whole-school ambitions of the Durham Commission research; creatives and school-based leaders and educators share blog posts on their work, with recommendations on how to apply these approaches. The future of evaluation of these network building endeavours will be important reading for creatives and arts educators; is this website (and will the Creativity Collaboratives) likely to remain up to date with new content or will it age quickly once a new endeavour is championed? The challenge of online networks is the need to refresh the content regularly and to generate sufficient interest to cultivate new authors.

Moving foward

The isolation of arts educators is unlikely to change in the near future and the need for peer-learning, thematic and professional-led networks will remain. The arts sector can be increasingly fragmentary as those involved in the creation of work may not always connect with those who teach, and those that work in non-educational settings may not always connect with school-based educators. System-wide organisations that bring a range of perspectives, particularly in championing arts and cultural education and the professional learning of the broader workforce will remain vital.

There is further research needed to understand the distinct learning needs of cultural learning professionals in contrast to arts educators based in school settings; the range of professional learning activities will remain broad and include the necessity (and desire) to attend live work, if appropriate, as well as keeping connected to broader debates and literature in the field. Educators in school settings can find it increasingly difficult with the demands of classroom teaching to have the capacity to engage with professional learning networks and social media and other online platforms will remain vital for maintaining connections and asynchronous content viewing.

Arts teachers conceive their identity as a teacher in a variety of ways; as an artist teaching, as a teacher of the arts, or as an artist-educator and there may be other permutations of these identities. These identities will evolve and change over the career of the teacher. This identity, of those working in arts education, will drive the nature of professional learning activities and the nature of networks such educators will join or create. For those artist educators, they may continue to undertake a range of practice developing activities that necessitate working alone, and may draw on activities aimed at amateurs (such as evening classes) to sustain their desire to develop their creative practices. Professional activity as an artist (for example, putting on an exhibition or performing in a concert) could be reimagined as a form of professional learning and networking. There is further work to do with regards to what is valued as professional learning for those in school settings so such activities can be appropriately rewarded with the time to undertake them or the necessary funding for them to be afforded by educators. It will always remain likely that arts educators will join a range of networks to enable them to develop their knowledge and understanding to cope with the complex and varied demands of their work.

References

Bautista, A., Stanley, A. and Candusso, F. (2021) Policy strategies to remedy isolation of specialist arts and music teachers, Arts Education Policy Review, 122(1) 42–53.

Bendrups, D. (2021) 'What attracts arts industry professionals to undertake practice-based doctorates? Three Australian vignettes', *Research in Post-Compulsory Education*, 26(3) 353–367.

Cordingley, P. (2015) The contribution of research to teachers' professional learning and development, *Oxford Review of Education*, 41(2) 234–252.

Dogantan-Dack, M. (ed) (2016) *Artistic practice as research in music: Theory, criticism, practice.* Abingdon, Oxford: Routledge.

Dwyer, R. (2020) '"Music is special": Music teachers navigating professional identity within a process of arts curriculum reform', *International Journal of Education & the Arts*, 21(20).

Hickman, R. (2010) 'Self portrait – An account of the artist as educator', *International Journal of Education & the Arts*, 11(Portrayal 2).

James, S. J., Houston, A., Newton, L., Daniels, S., Morgan, N., Coho, W., Ruck, A. and Lucas, B. (2019) 'Durham commission on creativity and education', Project Report. Arts Council UK.

Krutka, D., Carpenter, J., and Trust, T. (2016) 'Elements of Engagement: A Model of Teacher Interactions via Professional Learning Networks', *Journal of Digital Learning in Teacher Education*, 32(4), 150–158.

Puppe, L., Jossberger, H., Stein, I. and Gruber, H. (2020) 'Professional Development in Visual Arts', *Vocations and Learning*, 13, 389–417.

Trust, T., Krutka, D. G. and Carpenter, J. P. (2016) '"Together we are better": Professional learning networks for teachers', *Computers & Education*, 102 15–34.

Zwirn, S. G. (2002) To be or not to be: The teacher-artist conundrum. New York: Teachers College, Columbia University.

Discovering professional identities

a networked Theatre in Education approach to support early career teachers

Chris Bolton

Overview

This chapter will demonstrate and explore how a collaborative network, made up of university academics, teachers and Theatre in Education practitioners, supports early career teachers (ECTs) entering the teaching profession with the formation of their teacher identity through a hybrid Theatre in Education approach and research. Extending the professional education of ECTs beyond their university training and into their professional contexts creates challenges around professional identity formation. The recent and on-going 'pandemic context' has meant that a hybrid approach to collaborative networking has been particularly prescient, and has generated significant creative opportunities. Developing meaningful and durable cross-sector 'communities of discovery' (Coffield and Williamson 2011) that exist betwixt and between the formalities of university education and the day-to-day realities of school life are complex. However, considering that these meaningful opportunities and complex problems, are held in the tension between various 'economies of performance' and 'ecologies of practice' (Stronach et al 2002), this chapter will demonstrate the impact of an artful relationship between theory and practice. Becoming aware of changes in teacher identity through artful pedagogical approaches, the community of discovery questions how professional identities can affect new ECTs in creating their own. Whilst it is acknowledged that teaching is measured using various performative outcomes that lead to a 'performance culture' (Ball et al 2012: 514), our community of discovery attempts to subvert this by re-valuing artistic approaches to learning about identity and pedagogy. This not only meet the requirements of a performative culture but also has a lasting and affective impact for both ECTs and their pupils. In the chapter's conclusion, I argue that a greater awareness of the complexity of identity formation has clear implications for academics, senior leaders, and teachers looking to develop as confident and innovative educators.

Keywords
Professional identity
Early career teachers
Theatre in Education
Professional learning
Teacher research

Community of discovery in pandemic times

The teaching profession has been characterised as one that 'eats its young' (Halford 1998:33). Early career teachers (ECTs) in England not only face the demands of surviving in the profession but existing in one that has been sharpened, shaped and altered by the current pandemic context. Among other issues created by the Covid-19 global pandemic, it is useful to consider how initial teacher education (ITE) and the collaborative networks that exist within it have creatively responded to constraints in pedagogical interaction. How have they morphed into adaptive and hybrid ways of learning and teaching whilst, at the same time, preparing and continuing to support new teachers for an uncertain educational world?

Azorín (2020:2) suggests that despite the restrictions that have arisen from the pandemic, it has offered a 'golden opportunity' to 'rethink what matters most in education'. However, considering what it is that matters most, particularly in ITE, is not clearly understood as new teachers entering the profession face an ever-changing and unstable context. This context is not only affected by the Covid-19 global pandemic but also on a national level through policy initiatives such as the implementation of the Department for Education's (2019a) Early Career Framework (ECF) and the promotion of narratives such as 'the recovery curriculum'.

In this chapter, I consider that the continued development of our meaningful 'community of discovery' (Coffield and Williamson 2011) is potentially one golden opportunity that matters most in terms of networked professional development. Alongside the pandemic, our community of discovery has been shaped by the tensions that exist between 'economies of performance' in school contexts and various 'ecologies of practice' (Stronach et al 2002). What we mean by 'Economies of performance in a school context' is a concern with the potential negative effects of an audit culture. For example, the impact of lesson observations or the demands of performance management targets. Ecologies of practice relate to the professional dispositions and commitments individually and collectively engendered, such as school ethos or teacher values. Both of these concepts have been significantly affected by the pandemic. However, we have explored what these tensions mean for ECTs and trainee drama teachers within our community.

We have done this through the artful application of a Theatre in Education (TiE) programme provided by Big Brum Theatre in Education Company.[1] I define the term 'artful application' as the use of artistic or arts-based experiences and environments, such as Theatre in Education, that affect individual teachers cognitively or emotionally (Chemi 2014). I will explain, using the case study example that follows, how university academics, drama teachers and Theatre in Education practitioners have collaboratively and creatively worked to develop a meaningful and durable cross-sector community of discovery. This community is one that exists betwixt and between the formalities of university education and the day-to-day realities of school life. The space created through our collaborative work is one that has adapted to the pandemic context in an attempt to understand what 'being a teacher' means. It has seen our work move between live experiences and the virtual world to form a hybrid. One potential future development, in terms of networked professional learning, is that increasing the awareness of the tacit complexity of professional identity formation has clear implications for academics, senior leaders

---

1   Big Brum (bigbrum.org.uk), formed in 1982, facilitates Theatre in Education programmes and community projects for young people primarily across the West Midlands but also nationally and internationally.

in schools and teachers who wish to develop as more confident and innovative educators. In this way, a collaborative networked approach within ITE, either in-person or virtually, becomes future-forming.

Context

Demonstrating and exploring collaboratively how new teachers in the teaching profession can develop and sustain their emerging identities and practice is an ongoing, troubling and complex problem that faces many ECTs and academics working in ITE alike (Darling-Hammond and Hyler 2020). The ongoing global pandemic has strengthened issues around 'authenticity in training', which has led to further complexities about 'what it means to be in the classroom' (La Velle et al 2020:603–604). ECTs are not only planning what learning would look like but what it might also look like 'virtually' and 'online'. These issues inevitably affect the development of teachers' identities. This is particularly so in the early stages of their career, as new teachers grapple with the tension between 'the real' and 'the imagined' and the possible and the potential. This uncertainty also creates a sense of teacher fragility in which new teachers are constantly questioning if they have done enough, if what they have planned is good enough, and even if they are 'being' a teacher in the traditional sense. Perhaps foretelling this, Stonach et al suggested that 'professionals do not conduct their practices in the 'real' so much as they traffic between the twin abstractions of the ideal [...] and the unrealised' (2002:25). The pandemic has made this idea tangible as ECTs have shifted between notions of idealism and the unrealised in their practice, particularly as the traditional reference points of what it means to be a teacher have been shifted and changed.

The early career drama teachers with whom we work, like all teachers, are facing a more uncertain and restricted educational world with the '…implications and effects of the pandemic' becoming '…more challenging for educators and learners… in more fragile and unstable contexts' (Flores and Swennen 2020:453). Understanding how professional learning networks that consist of ITE providers, in partnership with arts organisations, such as Big Brum Theatre in Education Company, might support and strengthen the academic and social provision of teacher education through a creative professional network is potentially one way to stabilise this situation. Supporting ECTs beyond their formal ITE university training, and their subsequent, ongoing identity formation in the profession, offers opportunities to develop meaningful and lasting cross-sector communities of discovery. However, these opportunities can also create complex problems, when considering the tension between 'economies of performance' and various 'ecologies of practice' as defined by Stronach et al (2002).

The creative and collaborative network between Birmingham City University and Big Brum Theatre in Education Company is one successful way to facilitate teacher identity development and practices. The professional learning network continues to support drama ECTs and drama teachers more generally, which demonstrates the power of a hybrid community of discovery. Since 2014, our community of discovery has been evolving and includes ECTs, drama teachers studying part time for a master's in teaching and learning (MTL) alongside their professional responsibilities, drama teachers with an interest in our work generally, and school leaders and theatre professionals more widely. This cross-sector melting point of ideas and thinking has proven a useful crucible for stirring knowledge around collaboratively – as each member seeks to understand their personal perceptions of teaching and learning, cultural experiences of education and understanding of their professional contexts within their practice. What unifies this community is their goal of genuinely supporting each other's development. We aim to do this by taking ownership of our own and each other's professional learning and putting to work artful and creative research approaches. Alongside the development of professional knowledge, this unity influences the development of ECTs' professional identity, as they become competent and confident teacher-researchers. This can only be a good thing in that as ECTs become more assured of their professional identity they take more ownership of their own development. Realising this demonstrates that a professional learning network can support ECTs beyond their formal ITE experience. This has been done despite the recent pandemic context forcing our practice to adapt to a hybrid approach, which has led to a more flexible, agile and adaptive style of collaboration.

Economies of performance versus ecologies of practice

Facilitating the development of new drama teachers as artful, risk-taking and sophisticated practitioners faces specific challenges in the current context. These challenges are further troubled when considering notions of professional teacher identities and how they are traditionally constructed and monitored within a 'performance culture' (Ball et al 2012:514). Research into the nature of teacher professionalism provides a useful space for some of these considerations with the idea of the professional as a teacher being defined as, 'an indefensibly unitary construct' (Stronach et al 2002:2).

Teachers have different types of knowledge, different understandings of their role, and disparate reasons for teaching. These differences all combine to construct different teacher identities. Conceptually, however, this unitary construct of what a teacher '... is already too much of a generalisation' and creates views of teacher identity as 'typified, staged and judged' (ibid). This linear conceptual thinking about professional identity development is important to consider when seeking to support ECTs beyond their formal ITE provision. Early career drama teachers may be thinking about their own professional identity construction in these ways: through the collation of evidence, practice in the classroom and integration into the life of a school. Indeed, university tutors, like myself, who assess that progress may also reflect on their own professional identities in a similar fashion. Likewise, school-based mentors who support professional practice and the policies of the ITE provider itself might also need to reconsider this conceptual linearity.

The pandemic itself has disrupted this conceptual thinking and revealed the fragility of this linear approach to identity construction. Understandably, the various agents involved in the construction and monitoring of new professional teacher identities, require a method of tracking development. They may do this through various professional practices and be guided by education policies, or they may not. For example, trainee teachers' development during a Postgraduate Certificate in Education may be tracked through observations or the gathering of evidence in meeting their ITE curriculum. For Stronach et al (2002:3) this monitoring approach to developing views of teacher professionalism and the role of the teacher trainer demonstrates a simplistic and crude view of that development.

Here they argue that a result of focusing too much on an 'economy of performance (manifestations broadly of the audit culture) rather than various 'ecologies of practice' (professional dispositions and commitments individually and collectively engendered)' can result in a one-dimensional view of how teacher identity is formed. In other words, the instruments that are used to audit and monitor the progression of professional teacher identities and practices are often imprecise and fail to notice the subtleties and nuances of identity formation. Using economies of performance without thinking about the ecology of professional identity formation can be reductive. This can also be said about the development of relationships within traditional teaching and learning spaces in the formation of identity. The outcome of this fails to register or acknowledge that the formation of identity takes time and can be imprecise. This imprecision in the nuance of identity formation has been exacerbated by the move to hybrid forms of pedagogy brought about by the pandemic. For example, how can an ECT's impact be measured in the new virtual learning space? However, this raises new and exciting questions about what it means to be a teacher. Similarly, the pandemic has allowed our community to address and reconsider our ecology of practice in a meaningful way beyond 'school life' and the formalities of an ITE curriculum or master's qualification, themselves examples of performance economies.

Simultaneously exploring both how identity and practice have reformed through hybrid pedagogies, whilst learning about how these pedagogies have impacted on ECTs, has formed the foundation of the recent research discussions within our professional learning network. What our community of discovery has found is that notions of professionalism, in this sense, are much more subtle and organic, particularly if new drama teachers are developing aspects of their teacher role, as discussed. This is something recognised by Stronach et al (2002:3) in that 'the question of "professionalism" is bound up in the discursive dynamics of professionals attempting to address or redress the dilemmas of the job'. New drama teachers' professional identity formation involves the stitching together of a number of elements. These are almost inevitably non-linear, sequential or tangible nor are they typified, staged or easily judged. Professional development in this sense is much more subtle and organic, particularly if ECTs, drama teachers and theatre professionals are developing aspects of their 'teacher-ness' in various educational contexts.

Resisting emblematic figures

Although beyond the boundaries of this chapter, the recent pandemic also saw examples of toppled monuments, such as the statue of Edward Colston in Bristol, as a result of the increasing awareness of the Black Live Matters movement. Using monuments as a metaphor has also proved useful for our network as we have considered the role of 'emblematic figures' (Stronach et al 2002: 3) in the teaching profession, whereby the notion of being a teacher means much more than the day-to-day realities of actually doing the job. The pandemic has revealed this in a very real sense as traditional notions of being a teacher have now collapsed.

This work around metaphor within our network has steered us toward considerations around 'affect' in our work, which has led '…to a focus on embodiment' and 'to attempts to understand how people are moved, and what attracts them' (Wetherell 2012:2). For example, when considering my own role as a professional lecturer in ITE, I am mindful that the idea, or ideal of, being a 'drama teacher' is not constructed, promoted or celebrated. Being mindful of this enables me to resist the promotion of a professional drama teacher as an emblematic figure and creates spaces for ECTs to develop their own sense of teacher self and approach to practice in schools.

This is a useful element of self-spectatorship where I am seeking to explore how my own identity and practice can affect the formation of new drama teachers' identities. At the same time, individual ECTs and drama teachers are seeking to explore how their identity affects their practice. The same could be true of subject mentors working in schools as they seek to support, develop and challenge the emerging identity(ies) and practices of new drama teachers. Resisting an emblematic figured approach to the formation of drama teacher identity and practice also challenges and disrupts the idea of the professional as '… an expression of the zeitgeist' (ibid), which is both something we believe should be opposed and something that the pandemic has affected – what is the zeitgeist now?

Through our community of discovery we have learned to be mindful that the construction of ECT or drama teacher identities are not formulated based upon an idealistic view of that identity, nor based upon an idealised view of what a drama teacher 'should' or 'need' be. The risk of doing so, and enforcing one's own views of drama teacher identity might prevent the personal and professional growth of those entering the profession. Historically, research exploring new teacher identity formation can be seen in the work of Cooper and Olson (1996), Olsen (2008) and Oruç (2013) who suggest that professional identity is informed, formed and reformed through experiences and interactions with others. In addition, Olsen (2008) also suggests that any identity, including a recognisable professional identity, may need to be negotiated; therefore a new drama teacher's identity will be in a constant state of flux as internal and external factors influence its formation, either positively or negatively. However, through the meaningful and creative work of our community members, we have pushed the boundaries of identity formation further by putting to work creative approaches to research and learning and realising that our identities as teachers are shifting, hybrid and changeable.

Case study: socially distant/socially connected

Developing notions of self-spectatorship and reflexivity has become a clear focus for our community as a result of our context, which has been promoted by Big Brum's latest work entitled 'Socially Distant' written by Chris Cooper. The filmed monodrama explores the impact of the pandemic on a man whose son has died, as he attempts to understand the meaning of his identity as both a father and a teacher. This filmed content, explored and framed through virtual meetings, live seminars and creative experiences, facilitated a strong and powerful space for trainee drama teachers and ECTs to consider their own rationale for becoming/continuing to be a teacher during a global pandemic. Using theatre and imagination as ways to know the world, therefore, has become a central aspect of the creative approach to research within our collaborative network.

The work of our community has usefully combined face-to-face experiences where possible with online virtual events. We have used pre-recorded digital theatre to frame live experiences when considering research and vice versa. Primarily, this has been conducted through the use of digital platforms, such as Zoom, and break-out room functions. This approach is complemented by live group seminars during which we share responses to pre-recorded digital work. Sitting within this, the community has also been able to meet and discuss at 'non-traditional' times beyond the formalities of a university or school timetable. Similarly, we have collaborated beyond geographical boundaries with colleagues across Europe! This has enabled our community to re-consider our creative approach to networked learning.

One specific example of how our professional learning community work can be seen in a whole day hybrid event called 'Socially Connected-Drama, Theatre and Education'. The aim of this day was to bring together the various members of our community to discuss and explore the monodrama 'Socially Distant'. This hybrid event mixed together live explorational work with virtual inputs in order to challenge teachers' thinking about their identity. However, for trainee drama teachers and ECTs specifically, the preparation started a week beforehand.

As part of their live, face-to-face training in university, the community was asked to create and build a shared imaginary space – the bedroom of a teenage boy. Unbeknown, the space they were physically creating was the bedroom in which the virtual monodrama was set. This process was guided by myself as their university tutor using the dramatic tool of 'givens' and 'negotiables'. In this sense, a 'given' is something that we know to be true. For example, in the bedroom were particular objects, such as a suitcase and a red hoodie, which also featured in the monodrama. A 'negotiable' is something that can be discussed that 'might' be true. So, for instance, the layout of the bedroom, the objects on a desk or the books on a shelf. In creating the space through these 'givens' and 'negotiables', the community collaborated to imagine the set of the monodrama. This 'imagineering approach' (Nijs 2015:17) built toward and framed our online work. It was not necessarily focused on an objective truth but rather the use of collective imagining to create a fascinating narrative to explore.

Following this live experience, the community then watched episodes of the filmed monodrama online over the next four days. To frame the thinking of the community, a particular question was asked beforehand. For example, in this episode 'what is being revealed and/or concealed by the action of the character'. The community then recorded their responses, either through writing or pre-recording short filmed responses on their phones. During the final event, these responses were shared as part of the day. To explore the responses, we again combined live dramatic exploration with virtual inputs. We also asked members of the community to look for creative spaces in their own homes from which they might respond artfully to the questions posed by the monodrama, for example: show us where you felt most connected or disconnected to yourself during the lockdown period. This hybrid experience was then taken as part of ongoing auto-ethnographic research within the network and is building toward similar events and experiences in the future.

Using a hybrid approach to professional learning networks in the way I have described is built upon the active and collective use of the imagination. Bond (2014) posits that drama is the imagination in action and that it is the imagination – the ability to recognise the 'other' – that makes us human; it creates human value and reflects the idea that drama involves an act of 'self'-creation and becoming. This is further supported by Katafiasz's (2005) belief that reasoning imaginatively, animates the 'other' and makes people more socially engaged. For both, using the imagination to reason and examine fictional situations, participants in a drama process can test their social, moral, political and cultural values in a safe social context. This is particularly useful when applied to the professional learning that has taken place within our network.

Using the hybrid Theatre in Education programme has enabled ECTs to engage with a range of autoethnographic research to explore their emerging and changing selves. Autoethonograpy is an approach to research that examines the self in a particular context. For example, a teacher might explore their own experience (auto) of teaching in a school context (*ethno*) and typically express this through writing (*graphy*) (Ellis and Bochner 2000). Often using artful approaches, such as theatre experiences, metaphor, journaling and composite characters (Gutkind 2008), the ECTs have engaged in conversations with themselves through the application of fictional others and imagined situations. This self-reflective and imaginative approach to research has re-affirmed and challenged the rationales for those entering the profession at this time and for those continuing to practise as a teacher. Usefully, this approach to research has transcended the 'typified and staged' approach to teacher performativity, as discussed, and has truly deepened thinking imaginatively around what it means to be a teacher. More than this, the TiE used within our collaborative network has created spaces to attempt to answer what it means to be human in the world right now, which is a central question at the foundation of all theatre.

The community has conducted research into their own practice using various applications of research methodologies and methods. The results of these approaches can be seen in diverse pieces of research. These include: 'Fearriculum: An analysis of pedagogical choice and change made by secondary level educators', 'The Pied Piper of Hamelin and the Flipped Curriculum: a case study', and 'The play's the thing: An Auto-Ethnographic Reflection of my Teaching Persona, Using Metaphor'. The research conducted by our teacher-researchers demonstrates how through our community, ECTs have engaged with critical reflection, by engaging in high-quality professional development in order to improve. Furthermore, not only have the ECTs strengthened their 'pedagogical and subject knowledge by participating in wider networks' as suggested in the Early Career Framework (Department for Education 2019a:24), but they have also engaged critically with research and discussed the evidence, of their own research and that of others, with their school-based colleagues. In this way, they have securely linked theoretical perspectives to their teaching practices in a meaningful way that is future-forming. This positive contribution to the wider school culture has also developed ownership and responsibility for improving the lives of pupils within schools and thus serves as a way to meet the requirements of an economy of performance, such as the Early Career Framework, in a meaningful way. More than this, by re-identifying as teacher-researchers, the community members have demonstrated how the requirements of an economy of performance can be achieved through considerations and research about their ecologies of practice.

Moving forward

Through the community of discovery, we have explored how identity and practice have and continue to be shaped, challenged and affirmed by ECTs' entry to, and continuance in, the teaching profession in England. This process has led me personally, as a university lecturer, to question my complicit role within the system of ITE and collaborative networked learning. The exploration of new teacher identity and pedagogy, revealed in part by the pandemic, is intentionally in marked contrast to the quick-fix-disco-finger techniques promoted by educationalists such as Lemov (2015). The professional development in our community of discovery is a slow, developmental and organic process. The pandemic has afforded us time and space in which to deepen our critical understanding of what being a teacher means. It is acknowledged that there are particular challenges to this process from economies of performance and the auditing culture that frames education more generally.

By becoming aware of shifting and emerging identities and by focusing on the meaning of teaching and learning in a pedagogical sense, the community of discovery values less the measurement and comparison of practice with others and questions instead how professional identities can affect ECTs and drama teachers to re-create their own. Can new drama teachers learn that the value of their practice and the formation of their teacher identity is a learning process for all involved rather than it being an outcome-driven product that is measured? The answer is simply, yes. The combination of competition between schools, exam results, assessment and Ofsted requirements create for schools and teachers, what Ball et al (2012:514) call a 'performance culture'. In contrast, we know, through our community of discovery, that a stronger valuing of the artistic and artful approaches and processes of learning about identity and pedagogy is fundamental. By doing this, particularly for new drama teachers, it not only meets the requirements of a performative culture but also, more importantly, has a longer-lasting, deeper and more affective impact for both new drama teachers and, in turn, their pupils.

To continue the future-forming aspects of our collaborative network we are now collectively developing a project called 'Socially Distant Stories from Beyond the Screen'. This aims to explore not only the impact of the pandemic on ITE generally, but also how collaborative approaches between ITE and arts organisations can be developed to strengthen the academic and social support for ECTs. Additionally, our network has grown to include colleagues from other ITE providers. We aim, through the development of this project, to capture and explore the stories of drama ECTs working in secondary schools during a global pandemic and hear the impact on their experiences of hybrid learning and teaching in relation to the development of their teacher identity and practice. Furthermore, we also aim to develop an understanding and produce recommendations about a new approach to ITE that puts to work a hybrid Theatre in Education methodology by asking:

- What can ITE learn from applied hybrid Theatre in Education methodologies in regard to the ITE curriculum?

- How does an art-based pedagogical approach to ITE enhance academic and social support in the ITE curriculum?

This creative future-forming project, therefore, offers potential for impact, as there is currently an apparent research vacuum on the effect an applied hybrid Theatre in Education approach can have in ITE. It will also help to trace the impact that TiE methodologies can have on the formation of teacher identity(ies) and practices in the classroom. The vacuum deepens by considering the impact of hybrid approaches to ITE that combine virtual and live experiences within a TiE methodology. It is intended that this will help to trace the impact that hybrid TiE methodologies can have on the formation of teacher identity and practice in the classroom using Big Brum Theatre in Education Company's work.

Emerging evidence, which does exist, about the impact of hybrid-pedagogies in drama and theatre education, focuses on different pedagogical approaches within the field, such as 'online process drama' (Cziboly and Bethlenfalvy 2020; Po-Chi 2020) and 'verbatim digital story-telling' (Gallagher et al 2020), but this is not focused on ITE specifically nor on the development of professional identity(ies). The project is also important given the forthcoming statutory guidance about induction for early career teachers (Department for Education 2021), which is underpinned and shaped by the Early Career Framework in schools (Department for Education 2019a) and the core content framework in ITE (Department for Education 2019b). This context, in combination with the pandemic, is challenging for ITE providers and this project is one future-forming way to reconsider potential new approaches to teacher education.

References

Azorín, C. (2020) 'Beyond COVID-19 supernova. Is another education coming?' *Journal of Professional Capital and Community*, 5(3). Available at: www.bit.ly/3EGKz92.

Ball, S. J., Maguire, M., Braun, A., Perryman, J. and Hoskins, K. (2012) 'Assessment Technologies in Schools: 'Deliverology' and the 'play of dominations'', *Research Papers in Education*, 27(5) 513–53.

Bond, E. (2014) in D. Davis, *Imagining the Real*. London: Institute of Education Press.

Chemi, T. (2014) 'The Artful Teacher: A Conceptual Model for Arts Integration in Schools', *Studies in Art Education*, 56(1) 370–383.

Coffield, F. and Williamson, B. (2011) *From Exam Factories to Communities of Discovery: The Democratic Route*. London: Institute of Education Press.

Cooper, K. and Olson, M. R. (1996) 'The multiple 'I's of teacher identity'. In M. Kompf, W. R. Bond, D. Dworet and R. T. Boak, *Changing research and practice: Teachers+ professionalism, identities and knowledge*. London: Falmer Press.

Cziboly, A. and Bethlenfalvy, A. (2020) 'Response to COVID-19 Zooming in on online process drama', *Research in Drama Education: The Journal of Applied Theatre and Performance*, 25(4) 645–651.

Darling-Hammond, L. and Hyler, M. E. (2020) 'Preparing Educators for the time of COVID… and beyond', *European Journal of Teacher Education*, 43(4) 456–465.

Department for Education (2021) *Induction for early career teachers (England)*. Available at: www.bit.ly/3xJ0H8k.

Department for Education (2019a) *Early Career Framework (ECF)*. Available at: www.bit.ly/3L7v9gc.

Department for Education (2019b) *Initial teacher training (ITT): core content framework*. Available at: www.bit.ly/3K3f4Hf.

Ellis, C. and Bochner, A. (2000) 'Auto-Ethnography, Personal Narrative, Reflexivity' in K. Denzin and Y. Lincoln (eds) *The Handbook of Qualitative Research* (2nd ed., pp. 733-767). Thousand Oaks, CA: Sage Publications.

Flores, M. A. and Swennen, A. (2020) 'The Covid-19 pandemic and its effects on teacher education', *European Journal of Teacher Education*, 43(4) 453–456.

Gallagher, K., Balt, C., Cardwell, N. and Charlebois, B. (2020) 'Response to COVID-19 – losing and finding one another in drama: personal geographies, digital spaces and new intimacies', *Research in Drama Education: The Journal of Applied Theatre and Performance*, 25(4) 638–644.

Gutkind, L. (2008) *Keep It Real: Everything you need to know about researching and writing creative nonfiction*. New York: Norton.

Halford, J. M. (1998) 'Easing the way for new teachers', *Educational Leadership*, 55(5) 33–36.

Katafiasz. K. (2005) 'Addendum to Glossary of Terms' in D. Davis (ed) *Edward Bond and the Dramatic Child*. London: Trentham Books/Institute of Education Press.

La Velle, L., Newman, S., Montgomery, C. and Hyatt, D. (2020) 'Initial teacher education in England and the Covid-19 pandemic: Challenges and Opportunities', *Journal of Education for Teaching*, 46(4) 596–608.

Lemov, D. (2015) *Teach like a Champion 2.0: 62 Techniques that Put Students on the Path to College*. San Francisco: Jossey-Bass Publishers.

Nijs, D. E. (2015) 'The Complexity-inspired design approach of Imagineering', *World Futures*, 71(1-2) 8–25.

Olsen, B. (2008) 'How reasons for entry into the profession illuminate teacher identity development', *Teacher Education Quarterly*, 35(3) 23–40.

Oruç, N. (2013) 'Early Teacher Identity Development', *Procedia – Social and Behavioural Sciences*, 70 207–212.

Po-Chi, T. (2020) 'Response to Covid-19 "Now I send you the rays of the sun": A drama project to rebuild post-Covid-19 resilience for teachers and children in Hong Kong', *Research in Drama Education*, 25(4) 631–637.

Stronach, I., Corbin, B., Mcnamara, O., Stark, S. and Warne, T. (2002) 'Towards an Uncertain Politics of Professionalism: Teacher and Nurse Identities in flux', Journal of Education Policy, 17(1). Available at: www.bit.ly/3K5X9j0.

Wetherell, M. (2012) *Affect and Emotion: A New Social Science Understanding*. London: Sage Publications.

Covid–19 driven emergence of an informal network to support vulnerable students

Dana Braunberger and Sarah Hamilton

Overview

The educational response to the Covid-19 pandemic included intense disruptions in the delivery of learning for students from kindergarten to post-secondary. Moves to online learning and hybrid model were undertaken by many schools and districts, resulting in significant diversity in the responses to the pandemic and unpredictable environments for students, educators, and families. Students with learning difficulties experienced disproportionately adverse effects as these disruptions and unpredictability resulted in the loss of structure and stability many relied on for both their learning and mental health. Teachers who worked with these students became increasingly concerned that these students and their learning were being negatively impacted by a lack of face-to-face teaching and a reduction in the availability of student support services. To build knowledge and share real-time learnings in a complex and fluid environment, school faculty and staff with a variety of roles reached beyond their schools to self-organise into a dynamic, informal professional learning network. This network not only met a need driven by crisis but also established relationships that extended members' collective influence and led to the support of new, non-pandemic related initiatives. The authors describe how the organic and emergent development of a professional learning network was used to help support vulnerable learners during this time of global crisis. Through a shared desire to provide meaningful, impactful, and quality learning for all students, the authors co-constructed a network of experts who work with students with learning difficulties in a desire to ensure these students were not left in their moments of need.

Keywords
Professional learning networks
Learning differences
Complexity

The move for students from kindergarten to post-secondary. Shifts to hybrid models, online course delivery and variations in approaches to managing the pandemic within the same geographic area resulted in unpredictable learning environments for students, educators, and families.

These changes exacerbated what had previously been noted with vulnerable student populations. These students experienced disproportionately adverse effects as learning moved from in-person classes to emergency online learning and back again. The unpredictability of shifting school environments resulted in the loss of stability that many students with learning and attention difficulties relied on as a key element of their success. Teachers working with these students were increasingly concerned that their learning was negatively impacted by the lack of physical proximity, the reduction in student support, and lack of teacher experience in addressing the complex demands of this changing context. As is often seen in moments of crisis, the initial phase of government and district response focused on the general school population and the needs of vulnerable students were not always prioritised, nor fully anticipated. As a result, in an effort to access knowledge and real-time learning in a fluid environment, school staff and faculty with a variety of roles reached beyond their school to self-organise into dynamic, informal professional learning networks.

The learning ecosystem

This new approach to responding to student needs during a time of heightened change made explicit the interconnected ways the subsystems of our schools are organised, supported, and enacted. Godfrey and

Handscomb (2019) described the application and design of these subsystems within school 'ecosystems', and the considerations necessary to understand their organisation and impact (see figure 1). The rapid onset and prolonged uncertainty of the Covid-19 pandemic resulted in abrupt changes as the microsystem, i.e. the classroom environment, was changing with as little as a few days' notice and teachers were forced to pivot and adjust. Some of these changes included new protocols, new classroom configurations, changing cohort groups, as well as adjustments to teaching practice to minimise contact between students. Further, restrictions were placed on the support services within classrooms to limit the exposure of people to different cohort groups. Accompanying these changes to the microsystem included mesosystem changes in school policies, enacted to prevent and minimise outbreaks, and changes to operational schedules. Further, faculty meetings and professional learning moved online, and some staff members shifted to full-time remote work.

As our micro and mesosystems rapidly underwent adjustments, the exo and macrosystems were unable to keep up with the pace of change. For instance, the exosystem, as manifested in the form of government policy, provided broad guidelines, allocated additional school level responsibilities, such as providing support for contact tracing, but left many other decisions to school boards and individual schools. Guidance for school boards varied in direction as did consistent communication between cities and regions. This lack of consistency and coherence contributed to much confusion and uncertainty for educators. Individual schools prioritised their immediate needs, while the wider community remained largely divided on the measures that were necessary for student learning to continue in a safe and effective manner. Many in-school supports were not translatable to online learning, while others, including educational assistants who worked with students with specific learning difficulties, had their funding redirected when student learning shifted online (Joannou 2020).

When students were at home due to government directives, parents of students with learning needs often felt ill-equipped to provide a learning environment that was commensurate with productive learning. Professionals in all areas of education sought to increase their capacity to deliver effective and impactful learning to students. However, most available resources were focused on supporting the 'typical' learner. An urgent need for a more fulsome understanding of the complex learning, social, emotional, technological and environmental needs of changing learning environments emphasised the need to move away from a siloed approach to more relevant and integrated professional learning. Additionally, there was limited research available to inform teachers specifically working with students with learning difficulties in this shifting environment. Further, research for practitioners who sought to better understand how to support these learners in blended and online environments was even more limited.

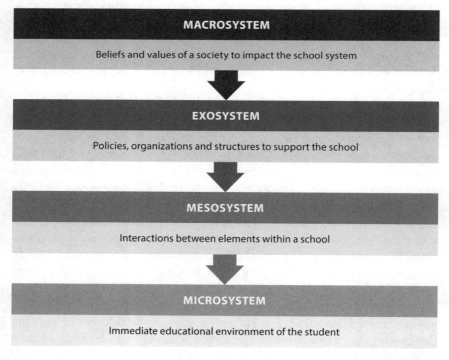

Figure 1 Ecosystem levels in the school system (Godfrey and Handscomb 2019)

Since the rate of change experienced within each subsystem of the school ecosystem was significant and unevenly distributed, it was often beyond the existing capacity of each subsystem to manage effectively. The misalignment of the chronosystem, the pace of change at each sub-level of the ecosystem (Godfrey and Handscomb 2019), created a noticeable gap where teachers, leaders and policymakers struggled to provide for the immediate and pressing needs of the students, particularly the needs of a vulnerable learning population. As a result, there was a lack of a coherent approach or service delivery within the education ecosystem.

This urgent need for teachers, administrators, and specialists to work cohesively to support students with learning difficulties resulted in the development of an informal network to generate and mobilise knowledge beyond any single school-based community. Although professional learning networks (PLNs) are increasingly used by leaders to promote bottom-up educational improvement at scale (Brown and Poortman 2018), PLNs were not formally present among designated special education schools. While traditionally competitors, these schools recognised that the learning of vulnerable students in unpredictable contexts was too complex and entangled for individual schools to solve within their own communities. Prior to the pandemic, there were limited, formal instances of professional learning networks. These included a now-defunct traditional professional learning conference and an advocacy network that currently meets bi-annually.

Both formal learning networks were not well-known and were not generally viewed as opportunities for impactful learning. With the inability of more traditional, top-down professional development to be agile in the face of large-scale and rapid change, the pandemic offered the opportunity to develop an approach that was 'self-improving and school led' (Brown and Poortman 2019). This provided a context for dynamic knowledge mobilisation structures to support learning during times of uncertainty. Further, within this evolving professional learning network, an increasing focus was to engage with and develop research-based approaches and innovative practices. The move to take ownership for not only being consumers of research but also partners in creating new knowledge highlighted the need for collaborative structures across jurisdictions to support the collective generation of possibilities.

The professional learning network and the emergence model

The origins of this network were unique in this community. For the first time, a number of different members with different roles, experience and expertise within a single school community found it challenging to overcome the obstacles to learning during the Covid-19 pandemic. Students with learning differences were struggling, and professionals were struggling to learn and employ approaches to support them. Without an existing structure or network, members began to reach out to others in similar positions in different schools who they knew had some expertise. Following some gingerly initiated conversations, those contacted then reached out to their colleagues. In this way, an informal network organically grew out of the nature of the needed learning and a shared urgency in seeking solutions. These self-organising origins and the subsequent evolution of this network can be understood in the context of complexity and emergence, how something comes into being.

Complexity has been employed to explain a variety of phenomena, including network structuring (Andriani and Passiante 2001; Newman et al 2006), innovation (Lichtenstein 2011) and strategic adaptation (Baumann and Siggelkow 2011; Eisenhardt and Piezunka 2011). In this way, the organic shift of professional learning from a hierarchical or top-driven enterprise to a more grassroots, generative and ecosystem-based approach has underscored the need to create space for self-organisation and emergence in complex educational systems.

An emergence model provides a valuable lens with which to view this change as it includes four essential steps: disequilibrium, amplification, recombination and stabilisation (McKelvey and Lichtenstein 2007). This model reflects the complex nature of networks and supports the insight that there is an opportunity for catalytic change out of disequilibrium. Within this, new circumstances and learnings emerge. Leadership in this model takes a significantly different role than traditionally considered, one of cultivating the conditions to support innovation rather than 'driving' or 'leading' it from the top down. As a result, out of the disequilibrium, seeds of innovative ideas can be developed, tested, and if proved valuable, amplified for broader application. Additional space created for reflection and problem modelling for capacity building can also promote new thinking. Creating space for emergence within informal professional learning networks can therefore position leaders and organisations to thrive in environments where they face complexity and are inundated by the need for adaptive, responsive decision-making in real time. Rather than seeking to impose a prescribed order, leaders and organisations can be more responsive and open to moments of insight and possibility.

Network activities

In addition to providing a space for real-time problem solving to spark learning in urgent areas of need, the network supported activities such as a comprehensive exploration of approaches to literacy instruction, knowledge mobilisation of research-based mathematics instruction, and co-development of a graduate certificate program focused on supporting learning difficulties in the classroom. These are outlined in the following section.

As literacy was a perennial topic regarding learning for students who struggle, accelerating literacy development became even more challenging with the shifts in learning modes and time away from in-person instruction. As a result, one PLN-coordinated initiative included a series of consultations that offered access to leading university researchers, resources, assessments and publications from a variety of providers. Interestingly, after this engaged exploration took place, each participating school selected a different approach. The value of this work was described as collaborative and autonomous. The membership of this network effort was diverse, including university faculty, school-based leadership, professional learning coordinators, service providers and teachers. In this way, the PLN served as a holding space for varied perspectives and the exploration of both novel and familiar issues as they emerged.

A shared understanding by both university faculty and members of designated special education schools was that there was room for growth in educator understanding of how learning difficulties present and how these students might best be supported. As a result, teachers, researchers, learning leads, psychologists, and administrators were invited to collaborate on the development of a four course specialisation within the Interdisciplinary Masters of Education programme at the University of Calgary. This was a new and unique experience for all non-university faculty. Upon its launch this past summer, it was one of the most popular graduate program offerings.

As we further developed our informal network and reached out to educators and researchers in post-secondary contexts, a new opportunity for collaboration and learning emerged. School-based network members noted their students were struggling specifically with self-regulation online, and teachers encountered difficulties finding solutions. As they sought recommendations and strategies to support their students in building skills, they noticed a lack of professional literature or easily accessible information to guide them. Discussions with colleagues, specialists and academics in post-secondary showed similar observations and a desire to learn more about this phenomenon.

Out of these discussions emerged an opportunity to pursue a research partnership as a provincial grant became available. Despite the value of school-based research partnerships to build the capacity of educators to engage in research, scepticism has often resulted in ineffectual impact or a lack of lasting change in practice (Abodeeb-Gentile et al 2016; Godfrey and Brown 2018; Henrick et al 2017). Mindful of these considerations, five members designed a research study based on the challenges our teachers were facing each day as they sought to meet the learning needs of LD students in online or shifting environments.

The grant application was successful and, being aware of some of the pitfalls of research-practice partnerships (RPPs), the design of this RPP was intended to generate knowledge and actionable results for our vulnerable learners regarding mathematics and self-regulation. Partnership conversations focused on shared leadership, shared goals, the democratisation of participation and opportunities to engage in open discussion to learn from and with each other. The development of this partnership and intervention was also a process new to the school and the university partners. The research project is currently entering phase one of what we hope will be a multi-year partnership by leveraging the expertise of the group to expand this project beyond the current site.

Learning from network activities

These occasions to share experiences, ideas, successes, and challenges in informal spaces have emphasised how networks can be leveraged to provide additional support for students with the greatest need of assistance and care. Our experiences also highlight the need for research to support a better understanding of how teachers in special education might establish, develop and use networks to design learning in changing environments. This is particularly important as predictable structures and processes have often been the cornerstone of most educational approaches. To support vulnerable learners, the need to move towards a collective, common goal approach requires consideration for both individual knowing and learning, and collective knowledge. This recognises these 'dynamic phenomena to be inextricably intertwined and continuously co-emergent' (Davis and Francis 2021). There is a simultaneous consideration for both the individual and the collective that honours individuals, valuing their role not only as a group member but also as an entangled part of the collective whole.

Whereas informal connections between these schools were limited or typically focused on policy environments at a leadership level, these new emergent networks focused on real-time problem solving of complex problems at a variety of levels. These self-organising networks focused on pedagogy for vulnerable students, access points and new opportunities for professional learning, and the vehicles to share this learning through post-secondary and professional communities. This collective learning and knowing was a key feature noted upon reflection of our developing network. We continued to each seek new knowledge and means to support students and teachers during times of unanticipated change, rapidly evolving contexts and unpredictable learning environments. However, we were also arriving at new knowledge we would not have anticipated as conversations and direction from collaborators and peers continued to expand our possibilities and potential next steps.

According to Davis and Sumara (2008:38), 'a successful collective is not just more intelligent than the smartest of its members, but that it presents occasions for all participants to be smarter'. Within the networked relationships amongst systems, a shift from considering the learning and knowledge of the individual within a group to the collective knowledge of the group recognises the critical importance of the collective knowledge production and individual sense making within systems cannot be untangled and attributed back to the individual members of the system.

Reflection on theoretical framework

The emergence of our informal PLN reflects the theoretical construct of complexity theory. At the heart of complexity theory lies unpredictability, emergence and decentralised control that recognises the diversity and co-existence of multiple facets within the system, including physical, biological, social and psychological perspectives in multiple dimensions of time and space (Kaput et al 1999). Complexity theory emerges from an active, social perspective to recognise the dynamic entities that develop in a non-linear manner and are unpredictable. This is of particular importance in education as the sheer number of variables that exist within each interaction between individuals cannot be separated and independently deconstructed. This results in the co-entanglements of learning and knowing cannot be attributed to the individual members within the community, but the community as a whole (Kimmerle et al 2015). Thus, the complexity which exists in each interaction requires educators to embrace the fluidity and ambiguity that accompanies such work.

Complexity theory provides an underlying explanation for the challenges that come with generalising professional development. The learning experienced is often deepened through application to individual classrooms, honouring the internal diversity, organised randomness and decentralised control within a school ecosystem. Complexity helps to provide perspectives for the disparities and intricacies present within classrooms, learning organisations, and society (Davis and Simmt 2003; Davis and Sumara 2008). Following the decentralised model at the heart of complex systems, professional learning networks offer occasions from which learning emerges, with the network members self-organising to foster the rise of new knowledge and understanding in an unpredictable and emergent manner.

As we begin to look to continuously improve learning opportunities for our students with LD, the need for space – both figuratively and literally – for conversations to evolve remains a key feature of our developing network. This offers opportunities to consider how educational communities can better work amongst each other, inclusive of both specialists and researchers, to develop richer conversations, foster organic and emergent knowledge production, and offer opportunity to reconsider what support looks like for vulnerable students. If given the time and space to redesign what this support would entail, how might we integrate knowledge that emerges from a collective, holistic vision to result in emergent and unanticipated learning and knowing. How can learning and knowledge in a PLN reflect a Gestalten phenomenon, where the whole is greater than the sum of the parts?

Dynamic networking arising out of pandemic chaos

Out of a pandemic that was experienced as 'chaotic' by many, the creation of the informal PLN for vulnerable students was prolific. The members created a strong relational base which resulted in sufficient joint working to identify problems of practice and to collaborate in real-time to discover solutions. Some of these solutions included advocacy work for the needs of vulnerable students, the development of new pedagogical approaches, and partnerships to engage in research to fill existing voids. The network was sufficiently dynamic to shift its scope to be responsive to diverse issues, such as student social emotional needs, mental health and contacts for innovative forms of assessment. Rather than driven by policy, this network was driven by the ever-changing needs of vulnerable students and the professionals who serve them. In this way, membership in the network was sufficiently diverse (e.g. psychologists, university faculty, researchers, teachers, administrators and professional learning leads) to promote interdisciplinary thinking, but sufficiently homogenous to build a shared purpose and foundational understandings.

Moving forward

As this PLN was established organically due to an emergent need during a global pandemic, we anticipate maintaining this same urgency and energy for continued collaboration will be challenging. We expect participation to wane while we shift from a pandemic to an endemic period. The imperative to provide a place to collaborate might not be the same as when there were more significant, novel changes in learning for students and teachers. Further, to habituate the practice of continued collaboration, there may need to be more formalised processes for the rhythm of meetings, the topics of focus, and the nature of shared ownership. We will explore how we might better understand why members may continue or discontinue their membership and the reasons for this decision. For instance, might the network itself fade away as the expediency of meeting student needs is enveloped into daily in-person school routines or might it be retained for other reasons, such as seeking to maintain relationships or recognising untapped opportunities that membership in a PLN might provide?

In summary, we found that when it was initially formed, the work of this PLN focused on specific tools, just-in-time learnings to support vulnerable students through changing educational environments, and projects, including the development of a graduate course certificate. Moving forward, a question for further exploration might be whether a project-driven or a continuous learning focus would provide a more meaningful draw for continued participation in the PLN. Given the diversity of this PLN's membership, clearly identifying the benefits of continued collaboration may need to be made more explicit.

A deeper understanding of how PLNs that are initiated during times of crisis evolved, once immediate needs subsided, could offer a richer understanding of how these organic networks can be both responsive to emerging needs while also providing a construct to fuel and advance innovative practices.

References

Abodeeb-Gentile, T., Pedro, J. and Tapper, J. (2016) 'Translational research in education: The benefits of a partnership that examines the impact of professional development on early-literacy outcomes', *Delta Kappa Gamma Bulletin*, 82(3) 1–15.

Andriani, P. and Passiante, G. (2001) *Complexity Theory and the Management of Networks*. London: Imperial College Press.

Baumann, O. and Siggelkow, N. (2011) 'Complexity and competitive advantage', in P. Allen, S. Maguire and B. McKelvey (eds) *The SAGE Handbook of Complexity and Management* (pp. 494–505). New York: Sage Publications.

Brown C. and Poortman C. (2019) 'Professional Learning Networks: Harnessing Collaboration to Achieve the Scale-Up of Effective Education Practices', in M. Peters and R. Heraud (eds) *Encyclopedia of Educational Innovation*. New York: Springer.

Brown, C. and Poortman, C. L. (eds) (2018) *Networks for learning; Effective Collaboration for Teacher, School and System Improvement*. Abingdon, Oxford: Routledge.

Davis, B. and Francis, K. (2021) 'Discourses on Learning Collectives', in *Discourses on Learning in Education*. www.learningdiscourses.com.

Davis, B. and Simmt, E. (2003) 'Understanding learning systems: Mathematics education and complexity science', *Journal for Research in Mathematics Education*, 34(2) 137–167.

Davis, B. and Sumara, D. (2008) 'Complexity as a theory of education', *Transnational Curriculum Inquiry*, 5(2) 33–44.

Eisenhardt, K. M. and Piezunka, H. (2011) 'Complexity theory and corporate strategy', in P. Allen, S. Maguire & B. McKelvey (eds) *The SAGE Handbook of Complexity and Management* (pp. 506–523). New York: Sage Publishing.

Godfrey, D. and Brown, C. (2018) 'How effective is the research and development ecosystem for England's schools?', *London Review of Education*, 16(1) 136–151.

Godfrey, D. and Handscomb, G. (2019) 'Evidence use, research-engaged schools and the concept of an ecosystem', in D. Godfrey and C. Brown (eds) *An ecosystem for research-engaged schools: Reforming education through research* (pp. 1–18). Abingdon, Oxford: Routledge.

Henrick, E. C., Cobb, P., Penuel, W. R., Jackson, K. and Clark, T. (2017). *Assessing research-practice partnerships*. William T. Grant Foundation.

Joannou, A. (2020) 'COVID-19: Alberta temporarily cuts funding for educational assistants, transportation while classes cancelled', 29 March [Online] *Edmonton Journal*. Retrieved from: www.bit.ly/3L9dDbs.

Kaput, J., Bar-Yam, Y., Jacobson, M., Jakobsson, E., Lemke, J., Wilensky, U. and collaborators (1999) 'Two roles for complex systems in education: Mainstream content and means for understanding the education system itself', in *Planning Documents for a National Initiative on Complex Systems in K-16 Education*. New England Complex Science Institute. Retrieved from: www.bit.ly/3Osam9j.

Lichtenstein, B. (2011) 'Degrees and levels of emergence: toward a matrix of complexity in entrepreneurship', *International Journal of Complexity in Leadership and Management*, 1(3) 252–274.

McKelvey, B. and Lichtenstein, B. (2007) 'Leadership in the four stages of emergence', in J. Hazy, J. Goldstein and B. B. Lichtenstein (eds) *Complex Systems Leadership Theory* (pp. 93–108). Institute for the Study of Coherence and Emergence Press.

Mitleton-Kelly, E. (ed) (2003) *Complex Systems and Evolutionary Perspectives on Organizations*. Elsevier Science/Pergamon.

Newman, M., Barabási, A-L. and Watts, D. J. (2006) *The Structure and Dynamics of Networks*. Princeton, NJ: Princeton University Press.

Scottish Island Schools Network

bringing the remote rural voice to networked professional development

Suzie Dick and Stephanie Peat

Overview

The Scottish Islands School Network is a community of practice for leadership teams working in schools that include primary and secondary students in Scotland. This chapter reflects on the emergence of the network as a digital community of practice within a rural island community context. Using Wenger's 'Community of Practice' concept, the chapter discusses how the emergence of an island network for school leaders fits in with characteristics of domain, community and practice. It explores the practical and professional learning needs met by the network and the subsequent opportunities and benefits to the members and their school communities, particularly focusing on how digital has been a crucial enabler for the network. Drawing on the OECD (Dahlman 2016) report on rural education, this chapter seeks to highlight specific issues of rurality, benefits and challenges. It considers why a network such as this has a place within the island schools in Scotland and where the potential risks associated with the network's impact and development are also discussed. For example, the chapter explores the limitations for those in less digitally connected rural areas. Lastly, the chapter discusses the next steps for the network and how the unique experiences of rural educators may offer insights which are useful for the wider education population going forward post-Covid-19.

Keywords
Rural education
Community of practice
Teacher social capital
Networked professional learning
Identity
Place based education

The emergence

The Scottish Island School's Network is a community of practice that emerged spontaneously as a result of conversations between senior school leadership colleagues in different island schools who felt they needed a home for their identity as island school leaders. A community of practice is defined by Wenger (1998:1) as a group of people who share a concern and a passion for something they do and learn how to do this better through regular interaction.

As Stern (1994) states, opportunities to share ideas and collaborate with colleagues can be limited by the size and geographical isolation of certain rural schools. This can result in some rural teachers feeling professionally isolated, and it was the aim of the network to begin to reduce the isolation and join together teachers to provide mutual support and a collective voice. The OECD report (Dahlman 2016:43) on learning in rural schools recognised that rural life and community relations may be one of the factors that attract some teachers and school leaders to work in a rural school, but it may also act as a barrier for others. One of those barriers, related to the small size of rural schools, is the risk of professional isolation and limited access to professional learning (Echazarra and Radinger 2019). The design of the network was that it would be set up online, informally, and be used as and when needed by the relevant leadership teams in the Scottish island secondary/all through schools.

Though communities of practice are about developing knowledge, networks are about relationships and it was key to the group moving forward that relationships could be formed between members for mutual support, but also that knowledge and experience could be shared. The group is not affiliated to any organisation and, as such, practices are able to reflect members' own understanding of what is important, they are not bound by organisational affiliations and they can span institutional structures and hierarchies (Wenger 2011:2–3). This reflects the position taken by Borko (2004) that teacher learning should be interactive and social, with teachers developing their own communities of practice within and across schools, with the group being one that emphasises the learning that people have done together rather than the school or local (government) authority they report to (Wenger 2011).

Previous research has highlighted that a lack of opportunity for professional dialogue could be a frustration for rural education professionals (Coker 2021). Being cognisant of the social nature of professional learning (Philpott 2014) and the value of social capital (Hargreaves and Fullan 2012) the network seeks to extend this opportunity for interaction to colleagues through the power of technology and digital means. As previously mentioned the feeling of isolation can mean that educators feel that they are working on the periphery of the education community. Through the use of technology, those on the periphery can more easily be pulled into the fold of the communities' narrative and be afforded the crucial social interaction and ongoing dialogue that is arguably more easily achieved by urban colleagues (Coker 2021).

Community of practice characteristics

Wenger (2011) talks about the three characteristics of a community of practice: the domain, where identity is defined by a shared interest and an identity that they identify or live with. The community, where members support each other and engage in joint activities and discussions. Lastly, practice, where practitioners come together to create shared resources, experiences and problems, i.e. shared practice (Wenger 1998:2). Community practice is a combination of these three characteristics and this is what the Scottish Islands Schools Network aims to support among its members.

Domain

One aim of the network was to build the social capital within those leading schools in an island context using a place conscious approach (as defined by White 2015). The identity was that all members live and work in an island environment with the shared interest of leading island schools and providing mutual support to each other. Coleman

(1988) talks about this in terms of social capital, which is inherent in the 'structure of relations between and among actors' and as a productive entity, which make possible achievements 'that in its absence would not be possible' (Coleman 1988:98). As such ,social capital is built through meaningful interactions with peers about instruction based on feelings of closeness and trust (Fullan and Hargreaves 2021) by providing a space for those teaching in like-for-like schools there was a new opportunity for a unique domain to emerge, and teacher social capital can be enhanced (Bourdieu 2011). Coleman (1988) explains this in terms of increasing the density of social obligations, where 'the overall usefulness of the tangible resources of that social structure is amplified by their availability to others when needed (Coleman 1998:103). The benefit of networks as a response to the professional learning need of rural schools is that it is embedded in the 'situatedness' of the context; the social and cultural nuances of rural places and spaces (Kostogriz 2007; Roberts and Green 2013). Coker (2020) explains that those leading and contributing to a network already possess the human capital necessary to boost the perceived value of the network because they live and breathe the rural experience; their positionality mirrors that of the members they wish to attract and retain.

Subsequently, the network is one of the professional learning avenues that is best placed to understand the local differences in knowledge, need and opportunity for teachers and schools (Quinn et al 2020). Conversely externally provided professional learning can be perceived to exhibit 'placelessness' – a disconnection from rural reality (Quinn et al 2020). Stack et al (2011:13) explain this as, 'the whole of the context is initially unknowable to the facilitator as "incomer." This unknowability is increased by the social and spatial distance confronting the usually urban-based expert facilitator in the rural situation.' Riley (2013) talks about this in terms of leadership of place and that this begins with the 'outside-in' construction of community and the need to be connected to the 'external realities and possibilities'. Often the external expert may have little or no knowledge of the community and, as suggested by Riley, being a 'leader of place' is a 'proactive approach to leadership which recognizes the ways in which leaders can work with others – to cross boundaries, to influence and shape communities and to unleash potential'.

Community

In the OECD report on rural education by Dahlman (2016) it was highlighted that teachers in rural schools tend to be more supportive than teachers in city schools (Dahlman 2016:27) and the benefits of a rural community are that each one is unique and deeply influenced by the cultures and traditions of its place. The report goes on to state that it is also possible to see similarities across the rural communities (Hunt-Barron et al 2015:5). It is these similarities for this network that help bridge the island communities' schools together to recognise the similarities between the schools and the benefits of this. It also enabled support with similar difficulties when geographically dispersed schools and the varying specific needs of teachers based on their unique context make providing professional development particularly perplexing (Peterson 2012). Some of the issues include things unique to the island context e.g. weather and ferry/flight timetables, but also more generic rural issues such as those highlighted by Stewart and Matthew's (2015) research; problems of funding, travel access to professional development, infrastructure, financial ability to create budgets, and facing accountability measures on their own were pervasive struggles for rural principals. Social capital helps teachers accomplish things they cannot do alone (Demir 2021) and can be built further when individuals reach beyond their immediate groups and networks (Putnam 2000). Members of the community are informally bound by what they do together in the context of this network, sharing ideas, resources, and advice (Wenger 2011).

The relationships between members of a professional learning community form the 'connective tissue' of networked professional learning (Katz and Earl 2010). The Scottish Island Schools Network is a social space that evolves when its members participate and negotiate the meaning of what it is to 'be' in the community (Wenger 1999, cited in Coker 2021). Through this dialogic process, the network members negotiate their shared values and beliefs as a way to establish group cohesion. The enactment of these values and beliefs in practice forms part of their collective professional identity as rural teachers (Wenger 1999). Through being part of the Scottish Island Schools Network the members are learning with, from and on behalf of one another which highlights the argument made by Stoll and Seashore Louis (2007) that professional learning communities are not just about professional learning but are about fostering a sense of belonging and a mutual investment in the people and growth of the respective schools.

Practice

This sharing of ideas, resources and advice, helps tackle a particular need (Bouck 2004). Rural schools often have the advantage of smaller classes and a strong sense of community, but they also face issues of underfunding and a lack of resources. There is also the feeling of being more isolated from resources that are specific to, or work in, a small island context. The network recognises the social and symbolic capital that exist there, rather than elsewhere. It means using the resources of the people who know (White 2015:272). The very practical side of this community of practice was that by joining together, rather than each small school re-inventing the wheel when it came to creating a new resource or policy following a shift in government perspective or to keep up to date with the latest educational thinking, the work could be shared out between schools.

It is worth highlighting however that a community of practice is different from a team in that it is defined by knowledge rather than by task and exists because participation has value to its members (Wenger 2011). Resources and know-how were contributed because people wanted to, rather than because they were obliged to.

Historically, we have focused on learning as the individual formation of knowledge but more recent learning theory has expanded this to include learning as being a process and product of participation with others (Katz and Earl 2010). This is exemplified in the following figure.

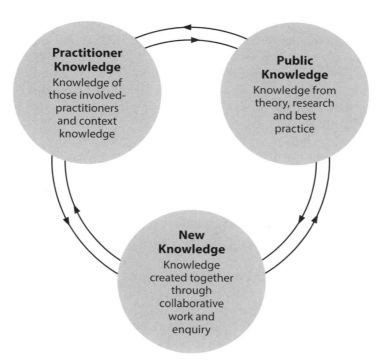

Figure 1 National College London's Three Fields of Knowledge diagram (Temperley and Jackson 2006)

Regarding *practitioner knowledge*, Katz and Earl (2010:29) explain that 'when the strength of attachment between schools and networks is strong, school-level learning communities can upload their ideas and practices into the network'. Individual network members take their learning and experience from their local context and share it with the wider group. This leads to a growth in *public knowledge* where the network member's individual knowledge is then combined and added to by research, policy and theory that is also shared. In turn, this results in the growth of *new knowledge* where the network members' interactions and dialogue make for a collaborative process of enquiry, whereby members question, reflect, advise and support each other. This allows for the explicit and tacit knowledge each member holds to be made visible and available for exploration by the network (Katz and Earl 2010). By bringing together colleagues from across the islands, the network allows for members to engage with a broader range of ideas and perspectives that normally wouldn't be available to them. Hakkarainen et al (2004) go on to explain the impact of that: 'It is in these conversations that new ideas, tools, and practices are created, and the initial knowledge is either substantially enriched or transformed during the process (cited in Katz and Earl 2010:28).

Ultimately the individual school learning communities can then 'download' and use ideas and practices from the network to be used and adapted at local level (ibid:29). Emphasising the point made by Skott (2019) that teachers are part of multiple, intertwined 'social constellations' of practice that not only benefit the individual but are mutually beneficial to each other and are part of a wider feedback loop.

Opportunities

The benefits of the practice outlined are twofold. Firstly, in terms of time. In rural primary schools, composite classes are commonplace. This small number of students and teachers means that the timetable and set-up can change from year to year depending on the demographics and needs of those attending (Mulcahy 2009). In addition, secondary school teachers may have to teach a variety of subjects, including some outside the area of expertise for which they have not received training (Echazarra and Radinger 2019:39). This can mean that rural areas find it more difficult to take advantage of scale economies and network effects, and the long distances increase the travel, communication and training costs (ibid:8).

By sharing knowledge, experience and resources between those in a similar context, it has the opportunity to create a critical mass of knowledge, resources and students to expand the education programs, specialised support, extracurricular activities and professional development offered to students and teachers that the OECD report (2019:51) suggests. Hopkins et al (2019) similarly found that social capital, measured as teacher interactions and access to resources through relationships, contributed to teacher self-efficacy over time (Demir 2021).

Secondly, in terms of creating that critical mass of bringing school leaders together, to collectively shout louder for the rural standpoint to be heard. Being island based brings with it positionality, based on that rural people and communities matter, and that that is what defines our learning and our actions first and foremost. White (2015:56) explains this as instead of concentrating just on classroom ready focus to encompass a broader 'school and community readiness'. So that the best approach to the decision and preparation to teach in a rural community is by looking at the benefits of the community rather than from a deficit viewpoint (Thomson 2002). This would help smooth the way for the vast majority who work in education in Scotland who are not island based to begin to hear different rhetoric from the mainstream. This bringing together of the collective voice has the benefits of unlocking expertise and building an atmosphere of trust and respect, but it does come with some risks, including the possibility of network closure where government policies sometimes may hinder social capital cultivation (Demir 2021).

The online dimension of our community of practice

The Covid-19 pandemic has highlighted for us all how connecting colleagues using digital platforms can effectively enable the continued flow of knowledge and support that is jeopardised when face-to-face interaction is not possible. Embracing digital is not a new concept for many rural educators. Adequate technology can mitigate the challenges of distance, cost and time that impact rural professionals' access to professional learning. Having the Scottish Islands Schools Network facilitated online means that the need for lengthy travel (sometimes involving overnight stays) and the associated drain on time and money are eliminated (Coker 2021). The impact of this is that more time and headspace is freed up to allow rural teachers to reflect on and actually practice what they have learned from their engagement.

The risks

'Autonomy, practitioner-orientation, informality, crossing boundaries – are also characteristics that make them a challenge for traditional hierarchical organisations' (Wenger 1998:4). This network is grassroots and operates on an online closed platform. Members know of the existence of the network primarily through word of mouth and a phone call/email from other members of the network explaining its existence and purpose. As the network slowly grows, there is the potential for suspicion at local and national level that there is a network that is not controlled and is operating outside of official collaborative networks, or particularly given the partly raising the rural voice agenda to a national level, may be as slightly 'agin the government', which is not the intent.

Demir (2021) highlights this when she states that too much bridging, on the other hand, can lead to distrust for members of the immediate group. This is also backed up by a study by Hunt-Barron et al (2015) where 'a few noted that they were in a small close-knit department and felt they were getting all the advice and ideas they needed from one another (Hunt-Barron et al 2015:10). It is important to highlight that the network is not only about professional development, but that means that those involved need to be able to see that online activity is something from which they will directly benefit. Too often, professional development is seen as one more activity added to teachers' ever-growing to-do list (Knight 2000). If it is not about professional development then what is it about?

There are several potential risks associated with a purely online network. The most significant is that it is widely acknowledged that rural areas have poorer internet connectivity than urban areas (Coker 2021). Coker goes on to explain that in Scotland, the current roll-out of broadband has seen an increase in connectivity from 4% of the Highlands and Islands in 2013 to 86% coverage in 2017 (2021:256). The data highlights that there is still a large percentage of rural educators working without access to stable connectivity. Consequently, this means that there are teachers who cannot reliably access and benefit from the Scottish Island School's Network. This generates a domino effect; if the network membership is limited by members' connectivity it is at risk of becoming stale and insular without the fresh, re-energising input of new members and their perspectives.

Furthermore, online learning is different to traditional face-to-face approach in the way that it is facilitated and experienced (Coker 2016 cited in Coker 2021). However there is an unfortunate narrative ascribed to and circulated by some educators that difference in this instance equals 'less than, especially if the learning was perceived to be poorly designed and facilitated (Quinn et al 2020). This tacit resistance combined with a lack of skill or confidence with technology can be a barrier to the network's sustainability and growth (Coker 2021:664), 'Rural educators who then default to face-to-face dialogues have less opportunity to access social capital compared with those in more populated areas'.

Moving forward

As we move into a post-Covid-19 pandemic phase, the unique experiences of rural educators during this time may offer insights that are useful for the wider education population going forward. The first is the strong sense of place-based identity that they retain whilst connecting with each other. The rural place in which the Scottish Island Schools Network teachers are from will continuously influence their 'cognition, personality, creativity, and maturity' (Shepard 1977:32), because of this there is a deep 'sense of rootedness, responsibility and belonging' to the places and people within those communities (Orr 2013:184). So, supporting teachers to connect their professional identities to the place in which they teach can 'merge geographical ways of living and learning' (Lavina 2020:242). The consequence of this, in the context of the Scottish Island Schools Network, is explained by Orr (2013:186) as the individual 'microsystems' in various rural places becoming better connected to a wider educational 'ecosystem'. Godfrey and Handscomb (2019:7) exemplify this when they explain that professional networks can impact a school's ability to be innovative, the professional development of a teacher and improve teacher practice and student outcomes.

Among many other things, the Covid-19 pandemic has significantly influenced the professional learning taking place in the Scottish education system. The rural approach to professional learning is another insight which would benefit the wider system. The International Council of Education Advisors Second Formal Report 2018–2020 recommends that: 'Scotland should move still further beyond what has become known as a self-improving system – a term that is perhaps overly rooted in the idea of creating coherence and improvement in more fragmented and market-competitive educational systems – to become a Networked Learning System (NLS).' They describe an NLS as:

- connected through networks across physical, professional and virtual boundaries; and
- driven by design-based research and collaborative inquiry to innovate, test and refine practice and build leadership capacity through practice-based professional learning. (2020:22)

A next step for the Scottish Island Schools Network and other networks like it would be to consider how they can adapt to ensure that they capture and value the expertise and learning of everyone in the education system, not just teachers. So that collectively we can drive improvement for children and young people. The International Council of Education Advisor's report suggests that the Regional Improvement Collaboratives could achieve the necessary dynamism but their potential is still not fully realised (2020). The value of the community of practice model is that by using domain, community and practice as the building blocks for the wider system, there is a prompt for a balanced approach and equality of focus on what makes a community sustainable within the context of support and practice. Having a networked learning system in Scotland would mean that we would achieve a truly inclusive, responsive, agile and collaborative system (2020:23); one that focuses on, 'building collective agency and efficacy, horizontal challenge and continued shift in the ownership of change and responsibility for making judgments about change towards people who are closest to the practice' (2020:23).

References

Borko, H. (2004) 'Professional development and teacher learning: Mapping the terrain', *Educational Researcher*, 33(8) 3–15.

Bouck, E. (2004) 'How size and setting impact education in rural schools', *Rural Educator*, 25(3) 38–42.

Bourdieu, P. (1986) 'The forms of capital', in J. Richardson, *Handbook of Theory and Research for the Sociology of Education*. Westport, CT: Greenwood, pp. 241–258.

Coker, H. (2021) 'Harnessing technology to enable the flow of professional capital: exploring experiences of professional learning in rural Scotland', *Professional Development in Education*, 47(4) 651–666.

Coleman, J. (1988) 'Social capital in the creation of human capital', *American Journal of Sociology, 94, Supplement: Organizations and Institutions: Sociological and Economic Approaches to the Analysis of Social Structure*, pp. 95–120.

Dahlman, C. (2016) *A new paradigm for rural development*. Paris: OECD Publishing.

Demir, E. (2021) 'The Role of Social Capital for Teacher Professional Learning and Student Achievement: A Systematic Literature Review', *Educational Research Review*, 33(1).

Echazarra, A. and Radinger, T. (2019) *Learning in Rural Schools: Insights from PISA, TALIS and the Literature*. Paris: OECD Publishing.

Fullan, M. and Hargreaves, A. (2021) 'Reviving teaching with professional capital', *Education Week*, 31(33) 30–36.

Godfrey, D. and Handscomb, G. (2019) 'Evidence use, research-engaged schools and the concept of an ecosystem' in D. Godfrey and C. Brown (eds) *An ecosystem for research-engaged schools: Reforming education through research* (pp. 1–18). Abingdon, Oxford: Routledge.

Hakkarainen, K., Palonen, T., Paavola, S. and Lehtinen, E. (2004) Communities of networked expertise: Professional and educational perspectives. Amsterdam: Elsevier.

Hargreaves, A. and Fullan, M. (2012) *Professional capital: transforming teaching in every school*. London: Teachers College Press.

Hopkins, M., Spillane, J. and Neugebauer, S. (2019) 'Social sources of teacher self-efficacy: The potency of teacher interactions and proximity to instruction', *Teachers College Record*, 121(4) 1–32.

Hunt-Barron, S., Tracy, K., Howell, E. and Kaminski, R. (2015) 'Obstacles to enhancing professional development with digital tools in rural landscapes', *Journal of Research in Rural Education*, 30(2) 1–14.

Katz, S. and Earl, L. (2010) 'Learning about networked learning communities', *School Effectiveness and School Improvement*, 21(1) 27–51.

Knight, J. (2000) *Another Damn Thing We've Got To Do: Teacher Perceptions of Professional Development*. Paper presented at the Annual Meeting of the American Educational Research Association (New Orleans, LA, April 24–28, 2000).

Kostogriz, A. (2007) 'Spaces of professional learning: Remapping teacher professionalism', in A. Berry, A. Clemans and A. Kostogriz (eds) *Dimensions of professional learning: Professionalism, identities and practice*. Rotterdam: Sense Publishers, pp. 23–36.

Lavina, L. (2020) 'Identity and place-based teacher identities: what connects across diverse personal and professional landscapes?', *Journal of Early Childhood Teacher Education*, 41(3) 241–261.

Mulcahy, D. (2009) 'Developing government policies for successful rural education in Canada', in C. Khupe, M. Keane and A. Cameron (2009) *Improving Equity in Rural Education*. Armidale, New South Wales: University of New England, pp. 23–32.

Orr, D. (2013) 'Place and pedagogy', *The NAMTA Journal*, 38(1), 183–188

Peterson, S. (2012) 'Action Research Supporting Students' Oral Language in Northern Canadian Schools: A Professional Development Initiative', *Journal of Research in Rural Education*, 27(10) 1–16.

Philpott, C. (2014) *Theories of professional learning: A critical guide for teacher educators*. St Albans: Critical Publishing.

Putnam, R. (2000) *Bowling alone: The collapse and revival of American community*. New York: Simon and Schuster.

Quinn, F., Charteris, J., Adlington, R., Rizk, N., Fletcher, P. and Parkes, M. (2020) 'The potential of online technologies in meeting PLD needs of rural teachers', *Asia-Pacific Journal of Teacher Education*, 50(1) 69–83.

Riley, K. (2013) *Leadership of Place: Stories from schools in the US, UK and South Africa*. London: Bloomsbury.

Roberts, P. and Green, B. (2013) 'Researching rural places: On social justice and rural education', *Qualitative Inquiry*, 19(10) 765–774.

Scottish Government (2020) *International Council of Education Advisers: Report 2018–2020*. Available at: www.bit.ly/3v4oJJc.

Shepard, P. (1977) 'Place in American culture', *The North American Review*, 262(3) 22–32.

Skott, J. (2019) 'Changing Experiences of Being, Becoming, and Belonging: Teachers' Professional Identity Revisited', *ZDM: The International Journal on Mathematics Education*, 51(3) 469–480.

Stack, S., Beswick, K., Brown, N., Bound, H., Kenny, J. and Abbott-Chapman, J. (2011) 'Putting partnership at the centre of teachers' professional learning in rural and regional contexts: Evidence from case study projects in Tasmania', *Australian Journal of Teacher Education*, 36(12) 1–20.

Stern, J. (1994) *The condition of education in rural schools*. Washington, DC: U.S. Government Printing Office.

Stewart, C. and Matthews, J. (2015) 'The lone ranger in rural education: The small rural school principal and professional development', *The Rural Educator*, 36(3).

Stoll, L. and Seashore Louis, K. (2007) *Professional Learning Communities*. New York: McGraw-Hill Education.

Temperley, J. and Jackson, D. (2006) 'From Professional Learning Community to Networked Learning Community', International Congress for School Effectiveness and Improvement (ICSEI) Conference 6. Fort Lauderdale, FL, 3–6 January.

Thomson, P. (2002) *Schooling the rustbelt kids: Making the difference in changing times.* Sydney: Allen & Unwin.

Wenger, E. (1998) 'Communities of practice: Learning as a social system', *Systems Thinker,* 9(5) 2–3.

Wenger, E. (1999) *Communities of practice: learning, meaning, and identity.* Cambridge: Cambridge University Press.

Wenger, E. (2011) *Communities of practice: A brief introduction.* Available at: www.bit.ly/3K7UEwO.

White, S. (2015) 'Extending the knowledge base for (rural) teacher educators', *Australian and International Journal of Rural Education,* 25(3) 50–61.

Global networking for sustainable futures

collegiality and intellectualism as network norms

Alexander Gardner-McTaggart and Paul Armstrong

Overview

This chapter reports on the start-up and roll-out of a blended MA programme in educational leadership at the exact time that Covid-19 hit the world stage. The MA rolls out internationally but aims to be sustainable and ecologically responsible as a blended programme that groups cohorts in worldwide centres served by flying faculty. It has a focus on practice and networking, considering the individual participants as valuable co-constructors of knowledge in the online and digital space with this being balanced by an iterative personal-professional reflective process throughout the programme. The students are practitioners, most work internationally, and so this course fulfils an increasing demand for global networking among educational professionals who often work in countries with emergent systems and little or no professional representation beyond fee-paying consultancies.

We describe the thinking behind this networked course to then analyse data from student feedback and interviews to show how in an increasingly privatised and disconnected educational landscape, the value and appeal of professional networks through education are in strong demand. This chapter aims to show how connecting with others through intellectual, non-remunerated work builds different types of professional networks that are based on mutual understanding, respect and recognition, providing a powerful space that facilitates professional growth through collegiality rather than competition. Despite the impact of Covid-19, our model remained robust, maintaining a network through dark times, and providing fresh scope for educational practices in the future that aim to increase networking and practice focus, whilst at the same time reducing carbon footprint, and working towards a more socially just world.

Keywords
Networking
Educational leadership
Higher education
Covid-19
Intersubjectivity
Teaching and learning

The vital need to connect with others

This chapter reports on the master's degree programme at the University of Manchester's Institute of Education in Educational Leadership, belonging to the largest humanities faculty in Great Britain. MA Educational Leadership in Practice (ELiP) is notable for being a winner of 'Best Programme in the Faculty of Humanities 2021' while at the same time a new programme and one in development and roll-out through the disruption of the Covid-19 pandemic. Much of the success of this programme is due to its conception in the intellectual tradition of equitable and emancipatory thinking, but also in its flexible blended delivery and a strong emphasis on networks and networking. This chapter explores how grouping and interaction have come to play such an important role in a learning space, and what implications this may have for the future of learning in a post-Covid landscape.

Networks and networking are a professional way of articulating a deeply human requirement to engage and act socially and to connect with others and explore the richness of intersubjectivity and all the potential it holds for growth, comfort and inspiration. It is obvious that humans are innately social creatures, yet sociability is more than simply a way to pass the time, it is in fact central to how our species functions, understands reality and adapts. Interacting in networks is constitutive of creating meaning and understanding existence in a continual dialectic between individuals (agents). In so doing, human agents establish systems and processes which are intended to be helpful and productive for all, in other words, emancipatory action (Habermas 1981). So central is this component of human existence that such practice is linked to reward within the brain, as it is reported to account for happiness, and good cognitive health in adults. It appears that humans involved in meaningful interactions build 'cognitive reserve', compensating for pathology, with a buffering effect on stress where such social ties promote positive health behaviours. Benefits are understood to be generous and include a reduction in stress, which positively influences memory, and executive functioning or social network interactions, which assist with reasoning attention and processing speed (Kelly et al 2017). These important effects of networks and networking emanate from a biological-cognitive interface ability that exists in most mammals, particularly apes, and is most strongly developed in humans. Much of this may derive from the ability to mentalise '[...] the ability to understand and manipulate others' behaviour in terms of mental states (Frith and Frith 1999:1692). It follows that many of the positive effects of self-actualisation, fulfilment and connectivity are achieved in a process that is driven by agents themselves, rooted in their own sense of agency, and driven by the individual urge to find connection and identity with the group (Bandura 1977; Vygotsky 1986).

Despite the complexity afforded by millions of years of evolution, many networks and networking experiences are now experienced in the non-corporeal. Networks are often delineated as either social or professional and the relatively new phenomenon of computer interaction has brought forth emergent social-professional online networks such as LinkedIn or ResearchGate as pertinent examples of how the two may be conjoined (Brandão and Moro 2017).

A question of power and agency

In a world where online interactions are becoming the new norm, it is easy to lose sight of power relations; who controls the process of selection and grouping, but also who is included, or excluded, and how are people directed to think. The issue can be viewed as one of agency versus structure. What is meant for the purposes of this chapter is that increasingly, the agency of humans in digital spaces is replaced at the system level with algorithms. As this chapter will argue, MA ELiP reverses this process in the online space. It provides scaffolding of learning rather than preselecting students' choices and therefore places agency with the learner (Wood, Bruner and Ross 1976). While Brandão and Moro point out that 'social network' is a 'very prolific research area' (ibid:21) they illuminate six 'clustering' techniques by which groups and grouping are corralled in online social professional networks. These are: exclusive and non-exclusive, intrinsic or extrinsic, and partitional or hierarchical (ibid:25). The authors highlight that key in these interactions is finding information, yet in an increasingly over-saturated data landscape, finding like-minded groups (i.e. clustering) within specialisms is vital, and finding experts is hard. This online process is managed in an artificial and linear action of clustering, recommendation and ranking (ibid:24) – it is automated and achieved through algorithms. The computerised algorithmic process which accelerates interaction and networks in online spaces is unlikely to afford the human user similar levels of agency as the physical interactions resultant from evolutionary processes and experienced in the corporeal, as presented. Online and computer interactions 'steer' people towards goals and groups that are predefined by third parties, often those with significant market-driven interests, exploitative in nature, not emancipatory. That is not to say that the online medium is bereft of benefits for networks, and this chapter aims to reflectively demonstrate how such networking processes can and do function positively in blended and online spaces with agentic and self-selected actors, when emancipatory and intellectualised thinking is prioritised, as is student agency, from start to finish.

The interplay between the individual and the social is key in understanding how people prosper, learn, and generate positive futures. As Vygotsky (1986) makes clear, social interaction defines the ways in which humans learn and as this chapter will argue, it confirms research on the benefits of socialised learning (Frith and Frith 1999; Kelly et al 2017) and on the positivity of networks if they are able to:

1. Place agency in the individual.
2. Facilitate emancipatory and collaborative spaces for growth.

The emancipatory domain of thinking and action is linked with improvement and positive change (Habermas 1981). Through work in the networked spaces of a master's degree we are witness that emancipatory endeavour is experienced as beneficial and productive, both for the social, but more pertinently, for the professional outlook and identity of those involved. Whilst this may appear as an obvious fact, we highlight that such networking is often overlooked in more competitive settings typical of social and professional networks. This lack of recognition can be particularly prevalent in online spaces where individual agency is assumed, *yet actually algorithmic* (Brandão and Moro 2017) and resultantly directed and ordered at the system level. In short, this chapter shows how increased planning for self-directed network activity couched in an emancipatory process promotes positive personal/professional growth and learning.

A sustainable programme

Education and its leaders face a century of unprecedented firsts in human history, most poignant among them the climate crisis (Gardner-McTaggart 2020). The warming of the earth through the release of carbon that was previously bound up in the earth's crust in the form of hydrocarbons has set in motion a chain of predictable changes (IPCC 2021). These changes are experienced by human beings as critical to their own survival, and education still struggles to keep up with the magnitude and scale of this man-made crisis, particularly as our own thinking remains embedded in an evolution now out of synch with the Anthropocene age. This is an epoch where human activity is in itself a significant geological force, which began around 200 years ago coinciding with James Watt's invention of the steam engine (Crutzen 2006). This 'slow burn crisis' acts as provocation for educational leadership to respond in ways that can think of nurture as an inclusive good that transcends the classroom, and becomes indelibly linked with the wider world. It is a challenge that demands social practice and intersubjective truth (Gardner-McTaggart 2020).

The master's degree in question was conceived from the outset to take the best of what education and technology have on offer, and work towards a sustainable programme, in line with the University of Manchester's sustainable goals (University of Manchester 2021).

Globally ranked number one on sustainability by the Times Educational Supplement, the thinking behind the MA accepts the affordances of man's technology, but aims to pursue a pathway that is more respectful of people and planet. Where the UK sees tens of thousands of students flying in and out multiple times a year contributing to the enormous carbon footprint of air travel, this programme rolls out in smaller global centres and decarbonises the process. It does this by providing a total of four learning conferences over two years in those centres where resident Manchester University scholars are flown to, thereby decreasing the carbon footprint of the program by an order of hundreds. For the rest of the teaching, the programme is blended and utilises Blackboard, Pebblepad and Padlet to create social spaces of learning and interaction, but also encourages student agency in setting up other groups in various mediums, such as WhatsApp or Instagram. The experience for students is one that is founded upon regular face-to-face interaction, with each other and teaching staff, but also allows professionals to work asynchronously for the rest. Rather than blocking face-to-face time in summer schools, the four conferences provide more continued connection for students and the online medium continues and intensifies the processes of intersubjectivity that began in the embodied and corporeal.

The evaluation of the course programme

Students enrolled on the course were vocal in their support of this approach and collectively voted the course to the apex of 'Winner of best Humanities programme', a clear sign of the Master's effect on the teaching and learning process. As part of a review of this programme, students were solicited with four questions as follows:

Briefly describe your experience of collaboration and networking in MA ELiP.

1. Have you been able to find any comfort and reassurance and support by discussing your professional role in and through ELiP – if so, please give a little detail.
2. How do you think the programme has facilitated this, if at all?
3. Do you think this kind of networking has a future in professional education?

4. What particular benefits do you think you may have experienced through the programme in the Covid-19 pandemic as opposed to more traditional courses?

13 students responded from the then enrolled number of 59, and are addressed by statements and questions on the following pages. This section is not presented as findings as the authors recognise their own hermeneutic (Habermas 1981) in understanding them.

The masters consisted at the time of five cohorts, three based in the Manchester location, one in Dubai and one in Shanghai. The first intake was in February 2020, just as the Covid-19 pandemic began to take effect, and so six of the students from this first cohort were able to attend the face-to-face conference (one of four over two years) and as the section that follows will show, these students retell a marked different experience of networking and interaction, even just from one three-day conference. All other cohorts have only experienced an online course.

Student voices

1. Briefly describe your experience of collaboration and networking in MA ELiP.

On this question, most students noted the debilitating effects of the pandemic in preventing the face-to-face component in the conferences. This is a core component of the MA, and without it the programme is an online not a blended programme. It is clear that the lessened physical interaction has a detrimental effect upon students' perceptions of networking as expressed by student as follows:

'In my experience there has been limited opportunity to network as the online nature of our interactions have removed the incidental and side conversations you would have before and after tutorials etc.'

'Due to the Covid-19 situation, I have not met up with my classmates at all. As such, I think my collaboration and networking with them have been limited.'

By contrast, a student who was in the first cohort and came to the face-to-face conference relayed an entirely different view of networking and their response speaks for itself.

'The networking opportunity at the initial conference, March 2020, was excellent as I felt that this contributed to my enjoyment and engagement of the course. The opportunity to meet face-to-face, discuss professional challenges and have more social interaction meant that the relationships formed created a sense of collegiality. Moving onto the online conferences, they have not had quite the same collegial effect, as it has resulted in superficial interactions with other colleagues and limited interaction with tutors.'

Students also reported using their own social media to make up for a less formalised space 'We used mobile app to chat because we couldn't meet face-to-face due to Covid-19 restrictions', and one student commented on the importance of visual interactions as follows 'I enjoy the tutorials when you can speak to people, although I do wish people would put their camera on to build connection'. Making clear the limitations of a purely online medium as enforced by Covid-19: 'I wouldn't say that I have *networked* in the sense that the other students are now a *contact to call upon* as we have not had the platform to really get to know people and that is where networking start'. Yet one more student made plain the importance of the face-to-face conference aspect for networking: 'I am looking forward to the possibility of face-to-face networking at the future conferences, which will enable me to draw from experiences of fellow colleagues'.

All in all, responses to question one made clear how valued the face-to-face component of this MA is for networking and positive student experience. It is clear that the exigencies of the pandemic have pressed students to 'make do'. However, their responses are unanimous in voicing support for the corporeal experience at the bi-annual conferences. It is clear that those 'incidental side conversations' and 'being able to discuss professional challenges' develops 'a sense of collegiality', consistent with the wellbeing and sense of fulfilment associated with networks and social interaction (Brandão and Moro 2017; Frith and Frith 1999).

2. Have you been able to find any comfort and reassurance and support by discussing your professional role in and through ELiP?

Responses to this question sought to uncover the particular nuance and challenge involved in the pandemic itself, and whether the programme had provided any form of social and professional reassurance.

It emerges that those who experienced initial face-to-face interactions (at the first and only conference) were much more positive about the effects of the subsequent online learning and networking. 'The relationships which I developed at the initial conference allowed me to discuss with others the challenges facing educational leaders in day-to-day settings and future developments'. This demonstrates how embodied face-to-face interactions accelerate and intensify subsequent online interactions. A second student who had been present at face-to-face conferences commented: 'Throughout the pandemic it was useful to know that my experiences as a school leader were not unique – the stress, indecision from government and constant changes were universal'; finally noting, '... that my colleagues have been useful sounding boards for how best to approach each of these changes with colleagues and encouraged me to create networks in my area'. This last shows a potential for learned behaviour in the programme to cascade in interactions outside of the programme, underscoring the value of networking practice in this course as a professional conduit.

Another participant commented how 'I have had a few opportunities to discuss my role but this has not resulted in comfort and reassurance through verbal discussion with fellow students' yet countered this with the assertion that, 'the discussion groups, tutorials, learning materials, conference, and assignments have really helped develop my leadership and given me a greater understanding of my "big picture" role'.

So, while the online interactions do not appear to have provided social comfort, they have promoted professional development. People are different and react in different ways, and so one student expresses this by saying: 'I feel that when I discuss my professional role with other students they are very supportive and we support each other where we can through this journey.' In reviewing the data, it becomes clear how very different these individuals are, despite their interest in educational leadership. For example, a further student commented that they felt 'out of their depth' in the programme. She was surrounded by ambitious leaders, but not a leader herself. However, the discussion groups in the online medium led to positive 'lateral thinking' and a firmer understanding of professional identity, noting that, 'It has also been useful to discuss issues within the school with colleagues who are not emotionally attached to the school, or have preconceived ideas, and issues can be discussed rationally and impartially'. This last highlights the value of allowing a group of like-minded 'specialists' to find each other through education, from an emancipatory ontological starting point. Resultantly, they come from a wide array of hierarchy, experience and ability, known in clustering as intrinsic and non-exclusive (Brandão and Moro 2017). However, in this case, these groupings are helpfully mixed and inclusive because they have not been pre-selected, rather they have selected themselves. In other words, the exclusivity afforded through clustering algorithms is replaced by human agency.

Finally, the sharing and collaborative nature of the programme, appears to encourage students and reinvigorate practice as was asserted in several answers but best captured here: 'Yes – I think its energizing to see so many others who have a desire to shape education and outcomes for students'.

3. How do you think the programme has facilitated point two, if at all?

The spectre of Covid-19 is writ large on all responses, as here: 'The online nature of the course and the restrictions on travel due to Covid-19 have clearly made this a challenge, as spending extended periods of time on video calls would not be ideal'. Participants at the first face-to-face conference are able to provide helpful contrast and one states: 'I would say that the initial face-to-face conference had a deeper impact on the ability to communicate and develop a collegial network than the online work has'. He continues to say how the online medium is well-intentioned, but functionally unable to make up for actual physical contact:

> 'The online conference has tried to develop the networking atmosphere which the face-to-face conference had, but it fails to do so as the networking small chitchat of going for coffee, or breakfast, or lunch breaks etc. are missed which means when you turn off the conference from your laptop the conference is over with no real interaction with others.'

A further aspect of the programme that enables more networking are the tutorials, which are online but allow smaller breakout sessions and the ability to have a more intimate smaller space, which the unit leader/tutor as expressed: 'Discussion forums are a great source to facilitate collaboration. During tutorials, we engage in tasks that generate discussions and help to connect with each other.'

One further student made quite clear how helpful the programme design was in facilitating change: 'I now have access to professionals outside my regular context which has provided me with an objective critical voice which enables me to look at issues within the context of my school from an outsider's perspective and challenge situations in my own context.' Another makes clear how the emancipatory ontology of the programme underscores the students' outlook and appreciation of leadership: 'The programme has enriched my understanding of leadership as a positive influential role of change and fairness rather than power'. There also exists firm empirical evidence of instrumental progression through the programme as expressed here: 'The course made me re-evaluate my views and made me see myself as a school leader. I am without doubt that I would not have received my promotion were it not for the course', and another says, 'Encouraging collaborative work, the collaboration module itself and opportunity for individuals to speak on the tutorial sessions'. Finally, another student stresses how online interactions can become stilted, whereas the face-to-face equivalent is more lively, engaging and ad hoc. This is firm confirmation of the power of blended approaches and vindication for this type of hybrid learning for flexible learning in uncertain futures.

4. Do you think this kind of networking has a future in professional education?
Participants make it abundantly clear that such networking has a strong future, yet their comments highlight the need for embodied face-to-face interactions in order to make this a reality. One of the few who experienced the online conference states, 'From my personal experience opportunity to network face-to-face is easier. Once a relationship is established then online connections can work' [sic], echoed by another in this way, 'Face-to-face conferences at the start of every semester would definitely have an added value to this kind of networking'. By contrast, one student who experienced the one and only face-to-face conference made clear that: 'It opens professionals to research which creates a more critical approach in their work and promotes the practice of reflection, which is still underestimated and underused by professionals.' One who did not experience face-to-face contact pointed out the helpful nature of this kind of medium-melange for international educational professionals, but stressed the need for more openness, supporting the view that

even short bouts of corporeal contact bring great interactive positivity and potential for networking. A further participant commented on the benefits resulting from the pandemic: '… there has been more professional collaboration during the Covid pandemic than at any other point in my career.' Yet pointed out how market-driven algorithms were already seeking to dominate this trend, '… teachers are now much more willing to share, although I am tending to notice an increase in paid resources popping up again on social media.'

One of the most powerful vindications of this type of course for educational leaders was expressed in this way: 'I believe that a lot of leaders in education feel isolated and struggle to discuss their roles with like-minded people so to have contacts within different schools across the globe would be very beneficial even just to gain ideas and learn from one another.' It seems that leadership professionals gain great insight and reassurance from listening to the stories of others in different educational contexts where a programme like MA ELiP and its cascading network: '… opens doors to gain experience in other schools if solid connections are formed outside of the course.' The same participant also highlights the intellectual approach taken as an emancipatory mechanism for positive change '… I do think this critical approach to leadership is the way forward in encouraging leaders that feel educationally and academically able to challenge the norm' stressing the value of reflective practice for '… professionals to use the experience of others as well as their own to do so.' And one goes as far as to recommend this form of networking to all educational leadership professionals, 'This kind of networking with professionals in contexts so far outside your own should form part of professional education for all school leaders as it makes you better able to review your own context with a critical eye'. In thinking about futures, it emerges that educational leadership can indeed be motivated by reflection and emancipatory, intellectual efforts to create change. The experience is best summed up by this student's observation:

'I do believe that this style of networking is valuable and will continue in the future. Due to the time constraints that professionals have, an online forum is an excellent way to allow for discussions to take place. I do strongly feel that there still needs to be an element of face-to-face interaction as this allows for deeper conversations to take place as online networking and discussions are only surface level and do not allow for the "filler" conversations that happen during a break, lunch, toilet trip! This is where connections are formed, which allows for deeper networking opportunities. It is easy to forget someone you have met online compared to meeting someone in the flesh.'

5. What particular benefits do you think you may have experienced through the programme during the pandemic as opposed to more traditional courses?

Most students point out how the MA programme and its affordability for networks and networking was an unexpected advantage in the Covid-19 crisis. Reasons given range from reduced pressure to travel to work, to increased focus on intellectual pursuits due to isolation in lockdowns, even to bringing to life the real-life policy struggles that became quite apparent through the pandemic.

One of the participants who experienced the face-to-face interaction found that the course was 'not dramatically changed' their conception being that due to its predominantly online rollout that it had been 'designed for online learners'. This perception underscores how easy it is to take for granted the face-to-face component once it has been experienced. This sentiment rests in stark contrast to others who did not experience the face-to-face component as expressed in the previous section.

Reassurance is important in such blended spaces and particularly through the pandemic. The teaching team had been briefed to provide feedback in a timely manner and students' felt this was crucial as expressed here: 'Feedbacks were prompt and made available in a range of ways such as written and even recorded that helped to overcome challenges in the Covid-19 pandemic. Academic tutors were readily available to provide support if needed.' Indeed, flexibility was crucial too as this same student continues: 'The meeting timings are flexible and cater to everyone's needs, such as the tutorials that are offered twice a day instead of once a day, which makes these sessions even more inclusive for everyone from around the world.' Finally, this flexibility went beyond teaching and learning even into the reduction in course fees as a response to the Covid-19 pandemic as the student comments here: 'Our annual fee structure was also reduced as many had faced financial loss during Covid-19.'

The shift to purely online during the pandemic was seen by at least one student to make things more difficult: 'Although there are fewer face-to-face lectures/instructions, the requirements for autonomous learning are even higher.'

Moving forward

The future of learning will by necessity be ever more conceived to be sustainable, both in conception and delivery. This MA programme demonstrates how the blending of face-to-face and online provide the affordances for networks and networking that are founded upon non-antagonism and non-competitive principles in line with education and sustainable educational leadership (Gardner-McTaggart 2020). They are emancipatory (Habermas 1981) and, as a result, they work upon students in positive ways, enhancing careers and benefitting all, however, this formula is not magical. It is contingent upon human nature, human agency and collaboration. It requires precise adherence to a mix of ingredients that should not be substituted.

Firstly, these networks are likely to work effectively because they are, from the outset, inclusive, open and non-algorithmic. This encourages a variety of professionals to congregate and collaborate, based on values of education, and not of profit. Creators of similar higher education programmes will be well advised to privilege the thinking of education and allow emancipatory aims to drive unit development, marketing, recruitment and rollout.

Secondly, *real physical interaction cannot be substituted*. This point cannot be stressed enough, as the embodied face-to-face component of such interaction acts as a springboard which appears central to activating the positivity associated with social-professional interaction (Kelly et al 2017). It is a measure that truly goes a long way towards influencing subsequent online interactions and represents the tip of the spear in networked learning. Without it, the process emerges from the data presented as impoverished and blunted. The danger facing course programmers and busy departments is that it is all too easy to 'make do' and revert to (or conceptualise) the online medium. Once the online variant has been set up, it requires less organisation and is ultimately cheaper. The appeal of a market-driven and utilitarian way of thinking is clear. The face-to-face component can and is easily overlooked or taken for granted, because it appears that people privilege more functional ways (Habermas 1981) of thinking about the processes and goals associated with education (Gardner-McTaggart 2020) than with the nuance and connection that is so central to it (Vygotsky 1986). The lesson for programme success is to not 'make do' with the inevitable creep of economic thinking that will question the efficacy of face-to-face contact. Deploy economic language where it counts by stressing that face-to-face is the brand, the selling point and what the 'customer' wants.

Thirdly, the data shows how students appreciate programmes that prioritise emancipatory and intellectualised learning for leadership. It reveals how the networked space becomes, in itself, an alternate test bed for ideas and shared experiences that provides as much comfort and reassurance as it does inspiration. It can do this because it is predicated upon a collection of individuals who have self-selected into this course without clustering techniques or algorithms (Brandão and Moro 2017), but based on their own scholarship and education. Their trajectories are extremely diverse, as are their hierarchical positions, yet in this safe space these differences become valuable and instrumental learning capital. The takeaway for programme developers is that education is itself the internalised human algorithm and that diversity and collegiality require no external, digitised guiding hand, but a very human one in the form of colleagues and mentors who are real, embodied and collegial.

Finally, the experience of the pandemic has shown how resilient a programme of this nature is, with an ability to change and remain flexible in the face of crises. It demonstrates how learning is sure to evolve in the coming century, as individuality and agency merge with online networks and embodied interaction. It shows that travel should be a luxury, not an arbitrary necessity. It highlights that online alone is far less effective in producing networks. It demonstrates that antagonism and competition do not belong in learning spaces, and the power of a university education department to foster leadership in increasingly powerful and connective ways.

References

Bandura, A. (1977) *Social Learning Theory*. New York: General Learning Press.

Brandão, M. and Moro, M. (2017) 'Social professional networks: A survey and taxonomy', *Computer Communications*, 100, 20–31.

Crutzen, J. (2006) 'The "Anthropocene"', in E. Ehlers and T. Kraft (eds) *Earth System Science in the Anthropocene*. Berlin: Springer, pp. 13–18.

Frith, C. and Frith, U. (1999) 'Interacting minds a biological basis', *Science*, 286(5445), 1692–1695.

Gardner-McTaggart, A. (2020) 'Educational leadership and global crises; reimagining planetary futures through social practice', *International Journal of Leadership in Education*.

Habermas, J. (1981) Theorie des kommunikativen Handelns. Band 1: Handlungsrationalität und gesellschaftliche Rationalisierung. Band 2: Zur Kritik der funktionalistischen Vernunft. Frankfurt am Main: Suhrkamp.

Kelly, M. E., Kelly, S., Duff, H., McHugh-Power, J. E., Brennan, S., Lawlor, B. A. and Loughrey, D. G. (2017) 'The impact of social activities, social networks, social support and social relationships on the cognitive functioning of healthy older adults: a systematic review', *Systematic Review*, 6(1), 259.

University of Manchester (2021) Leading the world on sustainable development. Retrieved September 13, 2021, from Ehlers E., Krafft T. (eds).

Vygotsky, L. (1986) *Thought and language*. Cambridge, MA: MIT Press.

Wood, D., Bruner, J. and Ross, G. (1976) 'The role of tutoring in problem solving', *Journal of Child Psychiatry and Psychology*, 17(2), 89–100.

Creating a virtual staffroom
dynamic and organic CPD conversations with colleagues, at a distance

Haili Hughes

Overview

Although for many teachers, schools continued to provide CPD opportunities online for their staff during the first lockdown, what many teachers missed were the informal professional conversations they had with colleagues in their department. Continuous professional development takes many forms and subject knowledge is often not given the time it deserves in school's training calendars. That is why the informal discussions with colleagues in the same department are so valuable, as they are an opportunity to discuss a fresh interpretation of a text or suggest some reading on a contextual matter that would illuminate the analysis. Distance teaching and the isolation from colleagues in departments over lockdown left a huge void and created pedagogical loneliness, which made planning and conceptualised thinking more challenging.

With this in mind, 'CPD Conversations with the Inked Scholar' was created – a YouTube channel where English teachers from across the country can come together and have informal professional conversations about texts or something to do with English teaching via a video. There are no PowerPoints or resources, the conversations are dynamic and organic. They are then shared on Twitter and the conversations are continued with other practitioners from across the country. It is a virtual staffroom where teachers can grab a cup of tea and develop their subject knowledge – even in the isolation of lockdown.

Keywords
Professional development
Subject knowledge
Virtual communities
Collaboration
Networked learning
Teacher identity

Towards becoming an extended professional

Teaching has sometimes been labelled 'the learning profession' (Darling-Hammond and Sykes 1999; Kennedy 2003) and there is certainly an expectation that teachers will undertake and seek out professional development opportunities which will help to enhance their practice. Recently, policy change from the Department for Education has focused on teacher education for early career teachers, with the roll-out of the Core Content Framework for student teachers and the Early Career Framework for new practitioners.

While development opportunities for novice practitioners are absolutely vital, ensuring that continuous professional development (CPD) opportunities are available for experienced teachers has also grown in significance. These opportunities may too often take the form of sessions delivered by others in the school setting, which are linked to whole school priorities. Due to this tight control on the types of development offered to teachers, Hoyle (1980) has labelled teaching as a 'restricted' profession, where teachers sometimes do not perceive their classroom activities in a broader concept, or consider how theory might guide their teaching. If teachers really want to improve in any kind of meaningful way, they could move towards more of an 'extended' professional model, where they become involved in a variety of professional activities to develop their pedagogy, rather than just existing on a diet of more traditional forms of training (Davies and Preston 2006).

The power of social learning

Increasingly, teachers are beginning to realise that schools are relatively small worlds which do not in themselves provide opportunities for teachers to share in the broader educational community's growing and constantly changing body of knowledge and experience of teaching (UNESCO 2008). This has led to many teachers seeking their own opportunities for CPD, outside of their school contexts, in their own time and sometimes at their own expense. Yet, choosing the right type of CPD can sometimes be a challenge, due to a plethora of different options now available.

Research has revealed that if CPD is to impact on pupils it needs to be accessible and sustained (Fletcher-Wood and Zuccollo 2020), while also being attuned to a teacher's individual needs (Murphy and de Paor 2017). Yet, professional growth is not only fostered through listening to the ideas of others, Dadds (1997) highlights the value in the exchange of ideas, the critique and exploration that occurs when teachers collaborate with others. Through this collaboration, learning becomes more of a social experience, which can help teachers explore new perspectives and ideas.

This opportunity to collaborate is something that teachers value but feel that they do not get enough time to do (Harris et al 2006). Teachers in this study also indicated that they valued the informal professional learning opportunities which present opportunities for collaboration in schools, such as staffroom discussions, or the organic formation of teacher groups to discuss particular issues. This engagement with colleagues can be critical for a teacher's professional development, so when schools were closed in March 2020, due to the Covid-19 pandemic, many teachers now found themselves cut off from the collegiate environment of the school. It is no wonder then, that some felt isolated and adrift.

A pandemic problem

On Wednesday 18 March 2020, Boris Johnson announced in a televised press conference that all schools in the UK were to close until further notice in an attempt to respond to the pandemic. At the time, confirmed cases were steadily rising, so teachers were asked to deliver content remotely, this applied to all children except for vulnerable students and the children of keyworkers. To some teachers, this announcement may have come as a relief as for weeks the situation in schools was becoming untenable; students were exhibiting symptoms of the virus and being sent home and departments were decimated, as staff absence soared. Yet despite the relief, many teachers felt when schools were closed, the new conditions forced teachers into a new way of working that they had never experienced before – one which was much more isolated than ever. For some, this meant teaching solely online, talking to a screen with little feedback or interaction with students or their colleagues. For others, it meant balancing their teaching commitments with caring responsibilities and home schooling their children. For all teachers though, there was a sense of professional isolation, after working in such a collaborative and immersive environment as a school. The situation starkly challenged teachers' abilities to learn and develop.

If teachers are not given the opportunity to interact with other educators, it reduces teaching into what Hargreaves (1995:26) terms 'a narrow, utilitarian exercise', where the socio-cultural aspects of learning, such as becoming part of a community, are missing. Research has found that it is much more challenging to learn in a vacuum and that an expert in isolation has limited capacities (Hadar and Brody 2010). It is the communal conception of learning that can be so important for educators and this has certainly been the case in my own practice, where I have enjoyed being a part of English departments where there is a culture of further learning, which is stimulated and supported by peers. Belonging to a community of learning can help to bridge the gap between theory and practice and help innovate and enhance pedagogy (Stevens, Kahne and Cooper 2006).

Of course, working in isolation is not a new challenge for teachers. For much of the time that teachers are at school, they work alone with groups of students in separate classrooms, but there are opportunities for professional dialogue and support throughout the day and some of these opportunities can even be informal chats in the corridor or staff room about particular aspects of subject knowledge or student needs. To combat the isolation of the classroom, a supportive community of practice is vital and during the pandemic, teachers found themselves cut off from this, no longer having the opportunity for those vital informal discussions on pedagogy or subject knowledge. Many schools still held department and whole staff meetings using online platforms, but agendas were tight and staff could not always attend due to caring responsibilities. There seemed to be little room for spontaneous and organic conversations, where practitioners shared their innovative knowledge and ideas with one another. Many teachers, including myself, felt this loss and this is where the idea for 'CPD Conversations with the Inked Scholar' was conceptualised.

A virtual staffroom

For me, teaching had always been a collaborative craft, where we all worked together for the common good, drawing on the wisdom of one another's expertise. White (2013) called for a kind of associated teaching, where teachers can celebrate one another as scholars so that nobody 'swims alone' (2013:46) and his views align with my own. For teachers who were missing the interactions with their peers, I created a YouTube channel called 'CPD Conversations with the Inked Scholar',[1] where I recorded and uploaded videos of me having informal discussions with other English teachers, on aspects of subject-specific pedagogy or GCSE English Literature texts. The conversations centred around one topic but were fluid and organic in their nature, as myself and the participant engaged with and learned from one another. The informal structure was important to me, as I wanted the space to feel like a staffroom and even encouraged people to 'grab a brew' while they watched.

From its conception, I wanted the online community of practice to subscribe to Wenger's (1998) three dimensions to promote collaboration: engagement, imagination, and alignment. I was keen for as many English teachers to engage as possible, which is why videos were shared on social media platforms, such as Twitter, after they were uploaded, with viewers being encouraged to contribute to the discussion.

When teachers engaged, it created a collegiate environment, where we were all bound together by our shared identity of being English teachers. For those of us who were struggling with our identities as teachers, as we spent long periods of time away from our students and colleagues, the channel became a lifeline and mode of belonging that people invested in, a place where they were able to reaffirm their professional identity and re-ignite their passion for subject knowledge. Despite not teaching in the traditional classroom environment, teachers engaging with the channel reported that they still felt like they were being professionally developed, despite not receiving any formal CPD during the school closures. It was the opportunities for dialogue, conversations about relevant theories and ideas for their practical application that participants found so valuable,

---

1   "Inked" is a nickname we used because the author is a scholar with over 200 tattoos!

as well as the feeling that they were never alone – that there was this ongoing, continuous support available when needed.

Although much CPD in schools still involves formally provided courses, the importance of teachers sharing their knowledge and experience is being increasingly acknowledged as a powerful vehicle for change. Unlike traditional educational research completed by academics, who do not work in schools, teachers possess 'knowledge [that] is situated in the day-to-day lived experiences of teachers and best understood through critical reflection with others who share the same experience' (Vescio, Ross and Adams 2008:81). However, due to teachers' busy timetables and lack of free time, attending face to face teacher network events can be difficult and this problem was only exacerbated by the Covid-19 pandemic, when people were asked to isolate in their homes and avoid socialising with others outside of their bubble. This is why I felt it was important that 'CPD Conversations with the Inked Scholar' remained an online community, as it can be engaged with on an individual, self-directed basis, in teachers' own time, when most convenient.

One particular group of teachers who seemed to benefit from engaging with 'CPD Conversations with the Inked Scholar' was the newly qualified and recently qualified teacher, who found themselves isolated from the support and wisdom of more experienced colleagues. There has been a great deal of research which has highlighted how challenging it can be for trainee English teachers to acquire the vast amount of subject knowledge required to teach English well (Gordon 2012; Daw 2000; Daly 2004). For new entrants to the profession, who suddenly found themselves deprived of their subject knowledge CPD and the wisdom of more experienced colleagues, the closure of schools could have been quite disarming. I wanted the YouTube channel to be not only a source of support but also an opportunity for new teachers to collaborate with teachers from different settings and stages in their careers and in turn, develop their pedagogy.

It was also important that all teachers felt empowered by engaging with the videos and subsequent discussions, by knowing they had contributed and updated their subject knowledge at the same time. To enable this, I ensured that teachers who engaged with the videos on Twitter and contributed the most to discussions were offered the opportunity to take part in a video chat and join the community through a sense of 'shared expertise and passion for a joint enterprise or goal' (Tseng and Kuo 2014). Many teachers have been motivated to join the community and collaborate and even when schools returned, the channel has continued to be popular. Perhaps this can be explained by the opportunity that the channel offers to collaborate and network with teachers outside of the school setting.

Collaboration is key

Peter Goodyear (2004) argues that Networked Professional Learning operates at two levels:

- collaboration with others to learn how to tackle a current task, and
- collaboration with others to improve one's capabilities for tackling future tasks.

This process – where individuals work together for mutually beneficial interests – works well in English secondary school teaching as, sometimes, little time is designated in CPD schedules for the development of subject knowledge. The social space that the channel provides for collaborative inquiry, creates a new kind of learning experience, where teachers can all collaborate towards the same goals.

This kind of collaborative networked learning assumes that our understanding of the world and our subject knowledge is enriched by interactions and relational dialogue with peers. Hodgson, McConnell and Dirckinck-Holmfeld (2011:295) wrote about the values that underpin successful networked learning:

- Cooperation and collaboration in the learning process
- Working in groups and in communities
- Discussion and dialogue
- Self-determination in the learning process

I will now explore how each of these values are present and exemplified in the 'CPD Conversations with the Inked Scholar' YouTube channel.

Cooperation, collaboration and working in communities

There is already a strong sense of community for English teachers in the UK on social media sites such as Twitter, with the hashtags #TeamEnglish often being used when discussions are taking place or resources are being shared. The channel built on this sense of collaboration by also utilising the familiar hashtag. This enabled users to see the content shared and get involved in the discussions after viewing the videos, while also adding a layer of credibility by association with an already established network. Many teachers who engaged tagged other members of their departments and also used it as subject CPD enhancements during their department meetings. Teachers who disagreed with the ideas or wanted to build on these ideas with a different perspective were subsequently invited to make a video, to feel more part of the community.

Discussion and dialogue

After the videos were uploaded and shared, discussions often appeared on the Twitter post and this learning dialogue often resulted in the teacher who had presented then developing their perspective or recommending further reading for the teacher initiating the dialogue. Sometimes, a teacher was so interested in the conversation that they re-tweeted parts of it to engage in an even wider debate so that the dialogue included teachers from many different points in their careers and with varied expertise and subject knowledge.

Self-determination

As engagement in the channel would be entirely voluntary and need to be undertaken in a teacher's limited free time, the tone was informal and those who engaged in it often spoke about sitting and watching the video with a hot drink, as they would in a real staff room. For teachers to voluntarily seek out the channel in their own free time, outside of working hours, there needed to be a direct link to material they could use in their lessons, so after discussions, lesson ideas and activities were always explored. Some teachers who actively engaged also regularly spoke about further reading they would now seek out after watching the videos or how they might use the ideas in school.

Recently, the teacher-centred approach to pedagogy has been gaining popularity, where lessons are more didactic and led by teacher talk. The teacher is centred as the expert at the front of the room and possessing the relevant subject knowledge is the bedrock of the expert (TES 2018). Ofsted has also stated how important subject knowledge is in their research on the EIF framework, 'If curriculum lies at the heart of education, and subject lies at the heart of curriculum, then it follows that teachers need solid knowledge and understanding of the subject(s) they teach' (Ofsted 2019:10). So, some teachers who engaged with the videos and dialogue may also have felt a determination to also engage in subject CPD due to external pressures such as formal observations or result scrutiny.

As a doctoral researcher and emerging academic, my ideology when developing teachers centres around the aim of bridging the gap between research and practice and ensuring that teachers have practical ideas and strategies that they can take away to use in lessons and expand students' knowledge. This could be labelled as design-based learning (Goodyear 2019) as its pragmatic nature and the channel's goal of solving real world problems of how best to enable students to make progress means it is grounded in both theory and real-world contexts. The approach is fluid and flexible; there is a process of investigation and collaboration between practitioners, where the learning processes are understood within the context of the social media world, where it is shared and created, but also can be envisioned for use in the school.

In order for the channel to have facilitated a long-term change of practice though, there needs to be an opportunity 'for teachers to apply and reflect on the knowledge in collaboration with their peers' (Holmes and Sime 2014:11). Consequently, at key stages in the discussions and during the videos, invitations to join in the discussion were always included, by exemplifying how the viewer had used ideas from the sessions in their teaching, with later re-sharing asking teachers to be reflexive about the impact of the sessions. This element of the collaboration was key, as for teachers to be motivated to engage they needed to believe that it was worth their time and effort, as Kirkwood and Price asserted 'technology itself is not the agent of change: it is the teacher' (2013:336), so those voices of authenticity from the profession were so vital.

Moving forward post-pandemic: a brave new world for CPD?

Now that schools in England have returned to face-to-face teaching and teachers are once again ensconced in the comfort of their collegiate, collaborative departments, has 'CPD Conversations with the Inked Scholar' become redundant? I think not.

Continuous professional development in schools has undergone a transformation in the last 18 months, not only by necessity due to Covid-19 restrictions but also because school leaders are embracing what Mark and Zoe Enser term 'a more radical model of CPD' (2021:11) and giving teachers more autonomy over their own development goals. There will inevitably be some sessions in schools which will still take the traditional structure of an internal or external provider delivering to all staff in the hall, as there are some messages, such as safeguarding or school priorities which need to be disseminated to all staff at once. However, teachers are more frequently being encouraged to take control of their own learning experiences. It is here that the channel allows teachers to have a greater sense of autonomy, through choosing which video may help to address gaps in their subject knowledge and also by choosing their levels of interaction, how they might embed the new knowledge in their work contexts. By being focused on their own learning needs, there is a 'great potential for improving teacher job satisfaction and retention' (Worth and Van den Brande 2020:3).

Therefore, there is a considerable potential for the online learning community of 'CPD Conversations with the Inked Scholar' to continue to help develop teachers' subject knowledge, as it provides opportunities to refresh subject knowledge, while also enabling teachers to belong to wider subject networks and English teacher communities. Moving forward, the links between the channel and professional practice will need to be strengthened, with the launch of an accompanying blog or website where teachers can upload work and school-based examples of the knowledge in action, to share with other practitioners. This addition will help facilitate the vital critical reflections and links between theory and practice which have the potential to make a long lasting change to teachers' pedagogy.

References

Dadds, M. (1997) 'Continuing Professional Development: nurturing the expert within', *British Journal of In-service Education*, 23(1), 31–38.

Daly, C. (2004) 'Trainee English teachers and the struggle for subject knowledge', *Changing English*, 11, 189–204.

Darling-Hammond, L. and Sykes, G. (1999) *Teaching as the Learning Profession: Handbook of Policy and Practice.* San Francisco: Jossey-Bass Education.

Davies, R. and Preston, M. (2006) 'An evaluation of the impact of continuing professional development on personal and professional lives', *Journal of In-service Education*, 28(2), 231–254.

Daw, P. (2000) '"The Gaps I Mean" — Subject Knowledge and the Training of English Teachers', *English in Education*, 34(2), 3–15.

Enser, M. and Enser, Z. (2021) *The CPD Curriculum: Creating conditions for growth*. Carmarthen: Crown House.

Fletcher-Wood, H. and Zuccollo, J. (2020) Evidence review: The effects of high-quality professional development on teachers and students. London: Education Policy Institute.

Goodyear, P. (2019) 'Networked Professional Learning, Design Research and Social Innovation', in A. Littlejohn, J. Jaldemark, E. Vrieling-Teunter and F. Nijland (eds) *Networked Professional Learning: Emerging and Equitable Discourses for Professional Development*. New York: Springer, pp. 239–268.

Gordon, J. (2012) 'More than canons: teacher knowledge and the literary domain of the secondary English curriculum', *Educational Research*, 54(4), 375–390.

Hadar, L. and Brody, D. (2010) 'From isolation to symphonic harmony: Building a professional development community among teacher educators', *Teaching and Teacher Education*, 26(8), 1641–1651.

Hargreaves, D. (1995) 'School culture, school effectiveness and school improvement', *School Effectiveness and School Improvement*, 6(1), 23–46.

Harris, A., Day, C., Goodall, J., Lindsay, G. and Muijs, D. (2006) 'What Difference does it make? Evaluating the impact of continuing professional development in schools', *Scottish Educational Review*, 37, 91–99.

Hodgson, V., McConnell, D. and Dirckinck-Holmfeld, L. (2011) 'The theory, practice and pedagogy of networked learning', in L. Dirckinck-Holmfeld, V. Hodgson and D. McConnell (eds) *Exploring the theory, pedagogy and practice of networked learning*. Dordrecht, The Netherlands: Springer, pp. 291–305.

Holmes, B. and Sime, J. A. (2014) 'Online learning communities for teachers' continuous professional development: an action research study of eTwinning learning events', in: V. Hodgson, M. de Laat, D. McConnell and T. Ryberg (eds) *The design, experience and practice of networked learning. Research in Networked Learning*. New York: Springer, pp. 185–205.

Hoyle, E. (1980) 'Professionalization and deprofessionalization in education', in E. Hoyle and J. Megarry (eds) *World Yearbook of Education, 1980: The Professional Development of Teachers*. London: Kogan, pp. 42–54.

Kennedy K. J. (2003) 'Teaching as an Occupation and Learning Profession', in J. P. Keeves, et al. (eds) *International Handbook of Educational Research in the Asia-Pacific Region*, vol 11. New York: Springer, pp. 867–881.

Kirkwood, A. and Price, L. (2014) 'Using technology for teaching and learning in higher education: A critical review of the role of evidence in informing practice', *Higher Education Research & Development*, 33(3), 549–564.

Murphy, T. and de Paor, C. (2017) 'Teachers' CPD and sectoral interests: Opportunities for convergence and divergence', *Teaching and Teacher Education*, 66, 242–249.

Ofsted (2019) Education inspection framework: Overview of research. London: Ofsted. Available from: www.bit.ly/3vJBVm5.

Stevens, W. D., Kahne, J., and Cooper, L. (2006) *Professional communities and instructional improvement practices: A study of small high schools in Chicago.* Chicago: Consortium on Chicago School Research.

TES (2018) 'Pedagogy Focus: Teaching Styles', *TES* [Online] 3 December. Available from: www.bit.ly/3OGweh9.

Tseng, F. and Kuo, F. (2014) 'A study of social participation and knowledge sharing in the teachers' online professional community of practice', *Computers & Education*, 72, 37–47.

UNESCO (2008) *Education For All By 2015. Will We Make It?* Retrieved from:

Vescio, V., Ross, D. and Adams, A. (2008) 'A review of research on the impact of professional learning communities on teaching practice and student learning', *Teaching and Teacher Education*, 24, 80–91.

Wenger, E. (1998) *Communities of practice: Learning, meaning and identity.* Cambridge: Cambridge University Press.

White, B. (2013) 'A mode of associated teaching: John Dewey and the structural isolation of teachers', in D. J. Flinders, P. B. Uhrmacher and C. M. Moroye (eds) *Curriculum and Teaching Dialogue*, 15(1/2). North Carolina: Information Age Publishing, pp. 37–47.

Worth, J. and Van den Brande, J. (2020) *Teacher autonomy: how does it relate to job satisfaction and retention?* Slough: NFER.

Grassroots professional learning networks

Richard Holme

Overview

The move to online learning in Scotland presented many challenges, but in some ways, Scottish education was well placed to respond. This was due to the presence of a national intranet digital learning platform (also known as Glow) and some forward-thinking local policies, such as free iPads for all learners in Glasgow. Despite these positive factors, many teachers and learners still struggled due to a lack of access to suitable technology or differing local policies. Further barriers included teachers lacking knowledge or experience of digitally enhanced learning and differing approaches required to deliver online pedagogy.

This chapter will consider the role of grassroots CPD/PL groups and informal networks have had and will continue to have, in supporting education post-pandemic. The issue of top-down control (from national and local government or other organisations such as the Regional Improvement Collaboratives and Education Scotland) and newfound autonomy amongst educators will be explored. Furthermore, the tensions between these contradictory influences or approaches will be discussed including lessons learned for teachers, leaders, and administrators. Based on this discussion the chapter will conclude with suggestions of concrete actions for all stakeholders involved in education.

Keywords
Continued professional development and learning (CPDL)

Grassroots professional development
Teacher-led professional development
Online collaboration
Online networks

The seeds of grassroots development

Formal and mandated continued professional development (CPD) has a chequered past. If you speak to teachers and educators about their experiences, most will have a story of a disappointing training session where they learned nothing, felt they had their time wasted, or worse left with a feeling of being patronised by the person leading the session. Possibly this is because of the didactic delivery, as well as lack of control over focus, content, or mode of learning.

On first reading, this might not seem to have much to do with this networked learning in the post-pandemic world, but it shows that before Covid-19 hit teachers and educators were rejecting more one-directional transmissive forms of CPD (Kennedy 2005). This rejection of traditional CPD led to informal groups, or communities, or practice (Wenger 1998) forming. The importance of collaboration, evidence-rich professional dialogue, and embedding professional learning in practice (Cordingley et al 2020) further illustrates how this traditional, transactional form of professional learning is no longer fit for purpose for 21st century education.

Taking advantage of web 2.0 (Merchant 2009) has further facilitated these individuals to form professional learning networks (PLNs) where participants learn with and from each other and incorporates elements of meta-learning (Jackson and Temperley 2007). Despite the obvious problems which the Covid-19 pandemic has caused, against this backdrop informal or grassroots networked professional learning has become available to a far greater number of educators. This chapter will explore these opportunities, and where appropriate draw on the context in Scotland.

History and theory of grassroots professional development and learning

Before exploring and discussing the current situation with grassroots professional learning networks it is useful to understand the history of informal, teacher-led or grassroots professional development and learning. It could be argued that teachers getting together and discussing teaching, and forming fluid informal networks, is probably as old as education itself. If you could travel back in time to a social event involving teachers, such as an end of term celebration in the 1960s or 1970s, it would be inevitable you would hear the teachers talking about education at some point. Furthermore, the idea of informal or self-directed learning is also well established (Rogers 2014), especially in sectors such as adult or lifelong or community education. Rogers (2014) conceptualises this using an iceberg metaphor, drawing a clear distinction between more visible, but less frequent, formal learning (the tip of the iceberg), and non-formal, and informal learning (the hidden submerged bulk of the iceberg); where informal learning includes self-directed, incidental, and even unintentional learning. Within these sub-classifications, Rogers (2014) argues most of the learning takes place unseen or acknowledged. These forms are contrary to the more traditional top-down, individual learning, and are far more likely to incorporate collaborative learning.

The mechanisms for informal learning of teachers have evolved over the last 15 years. One of the earliest recorded examples of teachers getting together to discuss in a slightly more organised way, representing non-formal learning, is the TeachMeet phenomenon. These events owed their origins to the informal 'unconference' phenomenon (Amond 2019) with the first TeachMeet taking place in Scotland back in 2006 (McIntosh 2006; 2016). This initial event involved a small group of teachers getting together to chat about pedagogy and curriculum in an Edinburgh pub. Since then, similar events have sprung up around the world including EdCamps in the US (Swanson 2014) and more recently in the UK BrewEd (Egan-Smith and Finch 2018), which owes much to the TeachMeet phenomenon (Holme 2020). The general approach also has parallels to the unconference movement and the common lack of hierarchy and more democratic ethos appears to be an important factor in encouraging participation (Carpenter 2016). Further research in the EdCamps (Carpenter and Linton 2016) has shown that participants value the sense of collaboration, community, and connectedness. These forms of grassroots events, and their associated networks, have gone global over the last 15 years, pre-Covid-19, but as this form of professional learning has its roots in Scotland it seems apt that Scotland provides the context to explore how educators responded to the pandemic.

The Scottish context

The management and administration of school-age education in Scotland is a devolved matter, and so controlled by the Scottish parliament rather than from Westminster (Bryce and Humes 2008). This means there are some special circumstances that differ from the rest of the UK, including a separate statutory curriculum (known as Curriculum for Excellence, CfE), an independent examination board (Scottish Qualification Authority, SQA), and greater involvement from local authorities or councils. The prevailing political environment is broadly democratic socialist and meaning issues like social justice, addressing inequality and child poverty influence policy making. A recent example of this was Glasgow City Council's decision to provide all pupils with a free iPad (Glasgow City Council 2019).

This combination of national level autonomy and a broadly left of centre political landscape have led to the governing body, Education Scotland, and local authorities pursuing specific initiatives. One of these is the presence of a nationwide intranet platform called Glow, which all Scottish teaching staff and students can access. This resource has received some criticism over the years in staffrooms, on social media, and even from teacher educators, however when lockdown began it gave teachers and learners access to resources (such as the full Microsoft Office 365 suite, including the video conferencing application Teams). One major advantage was that Glow gave teachers access to a ready-made network of colleagues, which simply does not exist in many other countries, including England.

These two examples (the Glow intranet and free iPads in Glasgow) illustrate how, when the Covid-19 pandemic began and teachers moved to home schooling, that in some cases Scottish education was well-prepared. However, in other ways the centralised governmental control, coupled with some local authorities' top-down rules (such as blocking the use of devices being used off council premises) limited some schools and teachers in providing the best opportunity for learners. Therefore, the summary of the situation in Scotland was one of irregularity and a resulting lack of parity amongst teachers and learners. This presented both challenges and opportunities for teachers who were attempting to learn and develop during the pandemic, and access to informal networks were a key part of this.

New networks and best practice during Covid-19

As the Covid-19 pandemic took hold schools began to prepare for teaching during lockdown. Amidst fears of rising death rates, educational leaders scrambled to work out how to continue delivering meaningful education via remote delivery whereas teachers had to rethink the way they viewed teaching. This provided a sudden, real life impetus for teachers to learn. In Scotland, discussion boards and forums, social media and other channels were filled with queries and requests for help. Teacher WhatsApp groups and other private messaging channels pinged to life with questions like: 'how do I login into Zoom/Teams?', 'how do I share my screen?', and 'why isn't my camera/microphone working?' The access to technology, in particular Glow (discussed earlier), gave Scottish teachers the chance to foster, enhance and create their own professional networks. As with Rogers's (2014) conceptualisation of informal learning, the element of collaboration and a departure from individualism featured heavily. The networks of teachers who were learning together developed in an ad hoc, organic manner, with teachers utilising existing contacts and channels and quickly developing new ones.

An interesting observation was that the traditional situation of professional learning custodians and 'who knew what' was disrupted. Teachers with certain knowledge and skill sets more suited to face-to-face teaching now needed help from some of their more tech-savvy colleagues. Observing this it was clear that the way in which educators were helping each other was quite different from the status quo. More formal offerings of professional learning, for example, hosted by local authorities and the governmental agency Education Scotland, faced challenges. Anecdotal reports revealed teachers had difficulties logging into accounts and once online, despite having had access for years, found themselves unfamiliar with how to navigate the Glow intranet, or Google or Teams learning platforms. In many cases, a lack of basic knowledge, and not knowing what they did not know (Luft and Ingham 1961) had a negative impact, with teachers disengaging almost as quickly as they had engaged. However, due to the nature of the pandemic, and the common enemy of the virus, educators from a range of settings and backgrounds offered help and pulled together. In many cases, these networks developed organically, and learning took place incrementally. This collaboration and collegiality further enhanced the formation of informal networks for learning.

In addition to helping those with less technical knowledge, other networks quickly mobilised with schools and other educational establishments setting up groups for those with more advanced understanding. One example was the Microsoft Innovative Educator (MIE) network, which was embraced by teachers in Scotland and beyond, who accessed free training and provided support to each other, and anyone else who needed it, taking advantage of social media, in particular Twitter. Even before the pandemic social media, and specifically Twitter, has been valued by educators and leaders due to its democratic nature (Jefferis 2016) bypassing traditional boundaries and removing hierarchical restrictions on collaboration. Furthermore, those using Twitter have identified the opportunity to grow their professional networks, extending this beyond usual face-to-face staffroom or faculty interactions (Carpenter and Krutka 2014). Teachers who had previously avoided these channels were now accessing and relying on them.

In the current context, and regardless of levels of prior knowledge and expertise, a common factor which encouraged networks to develop appeared to be the positive attitude and personal agency that these individuals displayed. Historically this has been a challenge as interested and engaged teachers have been physically disconnected. This has been even more challenging for those who chose not to participate in social media platforms or channels and so limit their opportunity to foster these networks. The role of attitudinal development in professionalism and professional development and learning has been highlighted by Evans (2014) who suggests this component can be overlooked. This may be, in part, to the difficulty in defining or theorising what attitudinal development may involve. In contrast, practical or behavioural professional development or learning is more obvious.

Closely connected to this attitudinal aspect another key factor, that the online professional networks include, is a feeling of ownership or personal responsibility amongst teachers. The conditions surrounding lockdown and the move to home-based teaching and learning, facilitated by grassroots networks, meant the usual control systems were bypassed. Put simply teachers had no option but to get on and engage in professional learning, without feeling the need to seek permission from the usual power brokers or worry about judgment from peers. The role of teacher agency has been highlighted by Priestley et al (2015), and in turn, the opportunity for agentic professional development is enhanced by collaboration.

Examples of networked online learning during Covid-19

As explored earlier in this chapter, throughout the Covid-19 pandemic opportunities for informal networked professional development learning flourished. Many of these were informal or organic, and often small scale or incremental, whereas others were more structured or organised. One example of this was the formation of a grassroots professional learning community-led by teacher educators at the University of Dundee. This was set up and operated via the Scottish education national intranet Glow. Teachers were invited to join, via personal contacts and through social media, and over 50 educators engaged with the asynchronous content shared by members. Regular remote PLC sessions were then held, using Teams, and a small group of teachers attend these on a regular basis. Anecdotally reported benefits included the support offered by participants to each other. Not only did the teachers benefit but so did the teacher educators, thus providing evidence of a more democratic, less hierarchical network for professional learning.

In addition, nationally, and even internationally organised events, supplemented these more personalised opportunities. These larger scale events included sessions organised by not-for-profit educational support agencies, such as the UK based Teacher Development Trust (TDT), governmental agencies such as Education Scotland, and higher education institutions, including the CollectivED Centre for Mentoring, Coaching & Professional Learning, based in The Carnegie School of Education at Leeds Beckett University. In addition, high profile educators such as Dylan Wiliam and Daniel Willingham contributed by participating in free to access CPD sessions streamed online, publicised through online channels and networks. More informal organisations such as the BrewEd movement took their events online with the first BrewEd Isolation event streamed for free and attended by well over 10,000 people. In each of these examples the participants provided positive feedback reporting the benefits of learning from peers and experts and growing their personal professional networks.

Issues of quality control

Although participants in these sessions regularly reported benefits, this may have been a form of confirmation bias, with those who already appreciated the opportunities looking to justify, even subconsciously, their involvement. Furthermore, research suggests that effective teacher professional development needs to be sustained over time and focused on learner outcomes (Cordingley et al 2015; Timperley et al 2007) and in some ways, the one-off sessions, offered during the pandemic, did not meet these criteria. Instead, many teachers were accessing and engaging in a more ad hoc manner, reaching out for support with very specific queries. However, even when doing so there was still a chance for incidental, and even unintentional learning (Rogers 2014).

A further challenge of deeper learning opportunities, such as the application of educational research, may be overlooked. The importance of enquiry for networked professional learning has been stressed and the relationship between enquiry and professional learning is closely intertwined, with each dependent on the other (Handscomb 2019). In the current case study, at first, there was more of a focus on sharing experiences or interpersonal support. However, as the network and relationships developed, the participants began to value the contribution of others and their expertise and experiences. This included a deeper analysis of teaching informed by research, including innovative approaches to teaching reading and spelling online or remotely leading outdoor learning. The presence of teacher educators, and practitioners allowed both to share their insider's knowledge (Handscomb 2019), so it is important to note this could, potentially, be missing from other, less established, forms of grassroots professional learning networks.

A final criticism that could be levelled at informal or grassroots networked professional development and learning is the lack of quality control. It has been suggested that involvement with professional learning communities will not necessarily result in benefits to the pupil or learner outcomes (DuFour 2007). BrewEd events, for example, allow people to volunteer and present or speak on any topic and the founders stress the importance of people having voices heard, and a lack of hierarchy (Finch 2019). Therefore, like with other new innovations in education informal learning networks cannot be regarded as a 'silver bullet' (Watson 2014). Furthermore, with informal, grassroots networks, those involved may become unaware of limitations within their group or personal connections. This could lead to the network being unable to consider ideas objectively and losing any 'critical edge' with participants: 'left to stew in their own (comfortable, but uncritical) juices' (McArdle and Coutts 2010:210). Therefore, it is essential to balance informal networked learning with intellectual rigour and a clear sense of purpose, interconnected with a sense of mutual engagement or collegiality. As Gore and Rickards (2020:335) identify in their research into teacher CPD: 'When PD is meaningful, intellectually engaging, safe, and collegial, experienced teachers are eager to participate.'

This objective might be more achievable on an individual level, but at a network level due to the greater complexity of those involved, may be more challenging. The final section of this chapter will consider implications for the future.

Moving forward

Those planning to develop networks in this informal way need to be wary of educational leaders, in particular politicians, who may be tempted to jump on the metaphorical bandwagon to push an agenda, based on the latest fad or trend. Any activity or project planned to utilise collaboration and networks needs to be carefully thought through, taking into consideration the specific context. If this is done effectively then these newly developed global networks may encourage teachers and educators to challenge fads or trends and professional learning is instead focused on learning outcomes. More importantly, the leaders who find themselves in this position need to be conscious of their power and their potential to disrupt or damage the informal networks; hence the need to back off and give them space. For policymakers, such as those responsible for teacher professional standards (e.g. the General Teaching Council for Scotland), 'there should also be an explicit acknowledgement of the value of informal or self-directed learning' (Rogers 2014). As local and global informal educational learning networks become more visible and transparent it is harder for ideas, from all perspectives to be ignored.

An area that could be considered, looking forward, is the motivation to engage in professional development and learning cultivating these informal professional learning networks. The motivation to engage in network professional learning during Covid-19 could have been sheer panic or encouraged by the greater visibility of the 'gourmet omnivore' teachers, who enthusiastically consume any opportunity to learn (Joyce and Showers 2002) but regardless of reasons, people did engage in networked professional learning. This may have been further influenced by the unprecedented situation and pressure to act quickly, but the engagement and positivity appeared to be infectious. Therefore, the target for individual teachers and leaders should be *to try and maintain this motivation for networked, informal, and self-directed learning* (Rogers 2014).

The local and global networks for informal or grassroots, professional development and learning have become firmly established in recent years. Therefore, in conclusion, the teachers and educators who inhabit these networks have *a responsibility to each other, and themselves, to keep the collaboration and learning going*. To do this effectively, both formal and informal professional development and learning should 'focus on attitudinal components not just intellectual and behavioural or practical elements' (Evans 2014). They must also consider the importance of the end goal, to improve their students' learning and so any collaborative networks must not lose sight of this ultimate objective. If we all take responsibility for this then the world of networked teacher professional development has the potential to make a sustained positive impact on the attainment of learners and ultimately benefit society on a global level.

References

Amond, M. (2019) Owed to some unconference heroes, magsamondposts [Online] 22 September. Retrieved from: www.bit.ly/3vQJJ5j.

Bryce, T. G. K. and Humes, W. M. (2008) *Scottish education: beyond devolution.* Edinburgh: Edinburgh University Press.

Carpenter, J. P. (2016) 'Unconference professional development: Edcamp participant perceptions and motivations for attendance', *Professional Development in Education*, 42, 78–99.

Carpenter, J. P. and Krutka, D. G. (2014) 'How and Why Educators Use Twitter: A Survey of the Field', *Journal of Research on Technology in Education*, 46, 414–434.

Carpenter, J. P. and Linton, J. N. (2016) 'Edcamp unconferences: Educators' perspectives on an untraditional professional learning experience', *Teaching and Teacher Education*, 57, 97–108.

Cordingley, P., Higgins, S., Greany, T., Buckler, N., Coles-Jordan, D., Crisp, B., Saunders, L. and Coe, R. (2015) *Developing great teaching: lessons from the international reviews into effective professional development*. London: Teacher Development Trust.

Cordingley, P., Higgins, S., Greany, T., Crisp, B., Araviaki, E., Coe, R. and Johns, P. (2020) *Developing Great Leadership of CPDL. CUREE*. University of Durham and University of Nottingham.

Dufour, R. (2007) 'Professional learning communities: A bandwagon, an idea worth considering, or our best hope for high levels of learning?', *Middle School Journal*, 39, 4–8.

Egan-Smith, D. and Finch, E. (2018) 'BrewEd: Pints, pedagogy and the birth of a grassroots movement', *CollectivED* (2). Leeds Beckett University, UK: Carnegie School of Education.

Evans, L. (2014) 'Leadership for professional development and learning: enhancing our understanding of how teachers develop', *Cambridge Journal of Education*, 44(2), 179–198.

Finch, E. (2019) The #BrewEd Charter. *#BrewEd* [Online], 28 September. Retrieved from: www.bit.ly/3kjzu4b.

Glasgow City Council (2019) Thousands of Glasgow pupils to benefit from digital learning strategy – pupil iPad roll out begins Glasgow City Council [Online]. Retrieved from: www.bit.ly/3rXOvgm.

Gore, J. and Rickards, B. (2020) 'Rejuvenating experienced teachers through Quality Teaching Rounds professional development', *Journal of Educational Change*, 22, 335–354.

Handscomb, G. (2019) 'Professional development though enquiry', in Godfrey, D. B. C (ed) *An Ecosystem for Research-Engaged Schools: Reforming Education Through Research*. Abingdon, Oxford: Routledge.

Holme, R. (2020) 'Conceptualising and exploring examples of grassroots teacher professional development', *Teacher Education Advancement Network*, 12, 25–37.

Jackson, D. and Temperley, J. (2007) 'From professional learning community to networked learning community', *Professional learning communities: Divergence, depth and dilemmas*, 45–62.

Jefferis, T. J. (2016) Leading the conversation: the use of Twitter by school leaders for professional development as their careers progress. Doctoral thesis. Birmingham: Department of Education, University of Birmingham.

Joyce, B. R. and Showers, B. (2002) *Student achievement through staff development*. Alexandria, VA: ASCD.

Kennedy, A. (2005) 'Models of continuing professional development: a framework for analysis', *Journal of in-service education*, 31, 235–250.

Luft, J. and Ingham, H. (1961) 'The johari window', *Human Relations Training News*, 5, 6–7.

Mcardle, K. and Coutts, N. (2010) 'Taking teachers' continuous professional development (CPD) beyond reflection: Adding shared sense-making and collaborative engagement for professional renewal', *Studies in Continuing Education*, 32, 201–215.

Mcintosh, E. (2006) TeachMeet06 is open for business, *Ewan McIntosh's edu. blogs.com* [Online] 29 June. Retrieved from: www.bit.ly/3vOZfin.

Mcintosh, E. (2016) Ten years on from the very first unconference for educators: TeachMeet is 10, *Ewan McIntosh's edu.blogs.com* [Online] 21 May. Retrieved from: www.bit.ly/3kmnqPO.

Merchant, G. (2009) 'Web 2.0, new literacies, and the idea of learning through participation', *English Teaching*, 8(3), 107–122.

Priestley, M., Biesta, G. and Robinson, S. (2015) *Teacher agency: An ecological approach*. London: Bloomsbury Publishing.

Rogers, A. (2014) *The base of the iceberg. Informal learning and its impact on formal and non-formal learning*. Toronto: Verlag Barbara Budrich.

Swanson, K. (2014) 'Edcamp: Teachers Take Back Professional Development', *Educational leadership*, 71(8), 36–40.

Timperley, H., Wilson, A., Barrar, H. and Fung, I. (2007) Teacher Professional Learning and Development: Best Evidence Synthesis Iteration (BES). Wellington, New Zealand: Ministry of Education.

Watson, C. (2014) 'Effective professional learning communities? The possibilities for teachers as agents of change in schools', *British Educational Research Journal*, 40(1), 18–29.

Wenger, E. (1998) 'Communities of practice: Learning as a social system', *Systems thinker*, 9(5), 2–3.

Teacher research groups
enhancing teacher professionalism during the pandemic

Daniel Langley

Overview

This chapter explores the positive potential of teacher research groups (TRGs) to enhance teacher professionalism both during and following the Covid-19 pandemic. TRGs are groups of teachers who collaborate in order to learn as a community of practice, either within their own school or wider networks. They read, discuss and attempt to apply research in practice under the auspices of an expert teacher (Firestone et al 2020). My central contention is that the use of TRGs throughout the course of the pandemic provided teachers with opportunities to expand and strengthen the professional learning networks they operate within, thereby increasing their own sense of teacher professionalism.

First, I review a growing body of literature which pinpoints some of the potential benefits of implementing TRGs as a mode of professional learning within secondary schools in the United Kingdom against a wider backdrop of evidence-informed practice. I then elucidate my points with details of how TRGs operated within our secondary school, MAT and networked learning community throughout the Covid-19 pandemic by moving online and traversing physical school boundaries. I then present a conceptual framework for exploring the term 'professionalism', unpacking its changing connotations over time in relation to teachers, teacher professional development and across the sector more widely. I argue that multiple dimensions of teacher professionalism have been variously challenged throughout the pandemic with negative consequences for teachers. However, I suggest that the collaborative learning that has taken place through the networked learning of TRGs during the Covid-19 pandemic has provided teachers with opportunities to enhance their own sense of professionalism, challenging negative discourses and providing a future of new possibilities.

Keywords
Teacher research groups
Professional learning
Professionalism
Covid-19
Communities of practice

The challenge of continuous professional learning

Facilitating opportunities for teachers to engage in continuous professional learning (CPL) activities throughout their careers is a growing priority for those who are concerned with improving educational standards across the UK. An increasing level of literature supports the view that the quality of a teacher and their instruction play the most important role in securing strong outcomes for students (Wiliam 2016; Kennedy 2016; Howard-Jones et al 2020). Whilst multiple effect sizes have been proposed within the literature, one estimation is that the level of student progress secured by students in front of the most effective teachers compared to those in the classes of the least effective teachers differ by some three hundred percent (Slater, Davies and Burgess 2012).

Of particular concern is research conducted by the Sutton Trust (2011) demonstrating that the lack of progress made by the students of less effective teachers is amplified for those from the most disadvantaged backgrounds. Similar disparities have emerged in the wake of the Covid-19, with schools containing high numbers of disadvantaged students less able to adapt effectively to new challenges due to the lack of an agile system of CPL (Wellcome Trust 2021). It is, therefore, my contention that securing and maintaining high quality CPL in secondary schools should form not only a strategic and operational priority, but a moral imperative within the education sector as a whole.

Implementing a useful and impactful programme of CPL consistently across all UK secondary schools faces a series of challenges which are foregrounded by a history of systematic changes, political interventions and the lack of a nationally agreed framework (Creemers et al 2013). Teachers and leaders in the UK looking to external consultants for advice and guidance face one of the least regulated markets of external CPL providers in the OECD (Musset 2010). At the time of writing this chapter, initial teacher training (ITT) programmes face similar uncertainties due to a recent government review that has caused the University of Cambridge and others to consider halting their entire provision of ITT (University of Cambridge 2021). Taken together it is not surprising that teachers and school leaders face a precarious landscape of varied and often inimical wrangling with regards to the most impactful pedagogical practices and the professional learning required to embed them (Sancar et al 2021).

At the heart of these challenges is the epistemological tension regarding who can claim authority with regards to the pedagogical strategies that will have the largest impact on student achievement. One potential solution has been to the shift towards 'evidence-informed practice' (EIP), a movement of teachers and researchers who have sought to strengthen the epistemological basis of real-world decisions in schools through increasing engagement with academic research (Godfrey 2017). The ultimate aim of EIP is to create a body of educational knowledge that can overcome external interventions and settle internal disagreements (Robson and McCartan 2016; Palaiologou et al 2015). In 1996, David Hargreaves brought attention to the credibility enjoyed by medical clinicians working within a profession which had established a working body of knowledge achieving overarching consensus amongst its members and beyond. Medical professionals were able to achieve a consensus of the 'facts' due to the scientific evidence underpinning their claims, which EIP in education seeks to emulate.

One promising solution has been the 'science of learning', a term commonly assigned to the educational insights gained by the invention of neural imaging technology in the field of cognitive neuroscience since the dawn of the millennium (The Royal Society 2011; BERA 2014). Research focused on the structure and function of the brain has introduced scientific methods into an educational sphere which has traditionally relied on techniques from psychology such as observation (Tolmie 2013). This has led many to claim that the revelations of cognitive mechanisms underpinning learning processes can improve the efficacy of teaching practice (Bell and Darlington 2020; Blakemore and Frith 2005). Subsequently, many influential teachers and researchers have cited cognitive neuroscience as the underlying credibility of their preferred pedagogical strategies because they are underpinned by scientific evidence (Sherrington 2017; Wiliam 2018; Hattie 2008). Common examples of such strategies include the processes involved in knowledge acquisition (Hirsch 2016), lesson structure (Allison and Tharby 2018) and retrieval practice (McCrea 2018).

Some research has challenged these optimistic claims by questioning the application of neuroscientific research within teaching practice (Blakemore 2019; Beauchamp and Beauchamp 2013). Moreover, the acceptance of neuroscientific advances by school-based professionals is challenged by the lack of a commonly shared language and the historic division between researchers and practitioners (The Royal Society 2011).

Teacher research groups as professional learning networks

In this chapter, I hope to show that teacher research groups (TRGs) can operate as a component part in the bridge between academic research and teaching practice. Researchers, schools and teachers may understand and articulate their understanding of TRGs in a multitude of ways. For the purpose of this chapter, TRGs are taken to mean: 'any group who engage in collaborative learning with others outside of their everyday community of practice, in order to improve teaching and learning in their school(s) and/ or the school system more widely' (Brown and Portman 2018:1).

Many have argued that collaborative learning activities increase the efficacy of teacher development as a whole (Whitty 2008; Fischer et al 2010; Godfrey 2017; Prenger et al 2020); a view that has been recognised in government publications both under New Labour (DfE 2001) and Conservative governments (DfE 2016). As communities of practice, TRGs seek to meet aims defined by the group members themselves, rather than following the goals of the school or outside influence (Wenger 1998). This extends to the success criteria established by the group, who themselves define what successful practice looks like as opposed to performative criteria assigned externally by diktat (Wenger 2000). Consequently, Willemse et al (2016) identified a number of benefits to teachers when they are empowered to conduct research-based activities with peers, colleagues and those within their wider networking community. Examples include improvements in student attainment, increased research engagement amongst teachers and enhanced mentoring capabilities for trainees who are new to the profession. A growing body of literature has analysed the benefits of TRGs in UK secondary schools and identified positive implications on student attainment (Scott and McNeish 2013), the personal growth of teachers (Greville-Giddings 2020) and an increase in their sense of professional autonomy (Sims et al 2017).

Our school started to implement TRGs as a mode of professional learning within our networked community a year before the Covid-19 pandemic took hold. Small groups of four to eight teachers would form a community of practice with a common goal and a year to complete their engagement with a chosen research area. Some moved beyond the boundaries of the school, collaborating with peers from across multiple schools, seeking to establish professional practice knowledge throughout the network. From March 2020, most TRGs moved online, with peers continuing to collaborate beyond the material boundaries of our school building. Many of the professional networks involved with our TRGs expanded and started to involve members who would not have otherwise joined. This facilitated a wider network of classroom teachers to build shared knowledge and understanding of how to react and respond to the evolving challenges of the pandemic when advice and guidance from the central government was scarce.

In the next section, I want to argue that this created an environment in which the teachers involved were empowered and that their professionalism was enhanced by the opportunity to build collective knowledge about how to respond to a fast-paced and evolving situation.

Recognising teachers as professionals

Teaching is a recent addition to the ranks of the professions when compared to the 'classic professions' of law, medicine and theology, with teachers traditionally perceived as crafts folk or technicians (Crook 2008). The concept of teacher professionalism is multi-faceted and cannot be fully covered here. For the purposes of my argument, I wish to focus on three specific elements that hold particular relevance.

The first is that teachers are professionals because they possess knowledge beyond that of a layperson and it must therefore be acknowledged that this knowledge is distinctive to teachers (Schon 1983; Hargreaves and Goodson 1996; Sachs 2000). The distinctive nature of this knowledge is beyond the domain-specific subject content that may also belong to many individuals in various walks of life and refers to their fundamental knowledge of how to teach. What I mean to say is that the knowledge of pedagogical strategies and how to use them which are employed by those actively working in classrooms is distinctive to them.

Second, similarly to many other professions, teachers must maintain high ethical and moral standards by adhering to the rules defined by their own members (Lunt 2008; Freidson 2001; Koehn 1994). Critically, any transgression of those professional standards is matched with an appropriate sanction, which may include permanent expulsion. For teachers working in UK secondary schools the central code of conduct is the set teachers' standards (DfE 2011) which form the basis of professional behaviours and members who do not follow them may end up the subject of capability measures.

The third dimension of teacher professionalism I wish to explore is *how individual teachers become part of the profession through the construction of a professional identity* (Burke 2008). This sense of self is different from their personal identity and allows them to engage in shared understanding amongst peers and contribute to a large professional body (MacLure 1993). Operating within a wider network of teachers enhances the professional status of each individual because they are empowered to make informed decisions about what takes place in their classroom.

These dimensions of teacher professionalism have often been challenged and undermined by those outside of classroom contexts. For example, Ball (2008) has posited that decisions regarding pedagogy, curriculum and behaviour have been open to various challenges and influences from external agencies since at least the introduction of the 1988 Education Act. The introduction of the act has been seen by some as the threshold moment when the socio-political mechanisms of conservative neoliberalism overtook the control of educational policy (Kumarand Hill 2008). Such challenges have continued and amplified throughout the pandemic with regular interventions made by media outlets, talk show hosts and celebrities, who have sought to erode teacher agency, autonomy and professional status in a way not seen by the traditional professions of law, medicine and theology.

Teacher professionalism and Covid–19

The Covid-19 pandemic created numerous problems within the UK education system. However, it is my belief that the main effects have been felt through the acceleration and worsening of issues that existed long before the pandemic. In spite of such challenging circumstances, teachers continued to work tirelessly throughout both lockdowns to mitigate the detrimental consequences of restricted learning whilst using varying levels of technical support in schools across the country. Impressively, classroom practice was adapted very quickly, both at school and during remote learning episodes, which was guided by the publication of several key sources of guidance (EEF 2020; Lemov 2020).

Despite these rapid responses by members of the teaching profession, the instability caused by the pandemic invited criticism from external commentators including the Department for Education through to celebrities, talk show hosts and other media outlets who were keen to give their own personal views on the best way for teachers to navigate this 'new normal'. Within this pattern of behaviour, teachers received an intense level of scrutiny which resulted in some teachers within our community feeling undermined and unmotivated.

My contention is that our use of TRGs provides an opportunity to challenge the scrutiny received from some quarters and does in fact enhance our professionalism. In light of the Covid-19 crisis, the way that teachers used networked professional learning can enhance our sense of professionalism and increase motivation and enjoyment by exploring the three dimensions of professionalism set out. First, teachers could recognise that they were the individuals who collectively built distinctive knowledge about how to teach both synchronous and asynchronous lessons online. One clear example is how one of our TRGs pooled their experiences of retrieval practice techniques at the start of online lessons to facilitate the smooth entry of students into the digital classroom. This collection of techniques was then shared more widely within and beyond our school to increase the engagement of students, establish routines and strengthen their knowledge. This TRG collaborated to create the necessary knowledge to reinforce and strengthen the pedagogical practice of a wide set of teachers.

Second, teachers within our TRGs have interacted and collaborated during the pandemic with a reimagined code of conduct which they themselves have co-constructed. For example, when our TRGs collaborated with colleagues from different schools they created a list of ten professional expectations about how those meetings should operate, the manner in which ideas should be shared and the mutual respect that should be given to those who were sharing within a digital space. This list was distributed before the start of meetings and reinforced the boundaries of ethical practice in the online space for all those involved without the need for external intervention.

Finally, a renewed sense of individual and collective professional identity can now be established amongst teachers as the collaborative successes of individuals and the larger professional body become apparent. It is teachers who have operated within small, networked communities to create the learning conditions in which they were able to support each other and thrive. One clear example is how history teachers with one TRG connected with colleagues from other schools during online meetings to review the sequence of their curriculum and the techniques used to deliver each topic. It was satisfying to learn that the connections have remained strong beyond the periods of remote learning and continue to operate whilst children physically attend school. The irony is that without the pandemic these connections may have taken years to form or perhaps never have formed at all.

Moving forward

I would argue that TRGs have enhanced the professionalism of our teachers both during and following the Covid-19 pandemic and could provide a positive alternative to the high stakes accountability measures currently endured by schools in the UK in the future. TRGs can provide a beneficial model of professional learning for the future by using online meetings to engage a greater number of teachers with academic research informed by evidence. TRGs in our school first moved online at the start of the pandemic, but most have continued to meet online due to the greater number of potential connections they have made both locally and nationally. As members of these professional learning networks, our teachers have been able to construct distinctive knowledge of how to teach online and in school with physical distancing measures in place. Some have gone on to present these approaches at conferences, through blogs and publications, supporting and enhancing their sense of professional agency. TRGs have facilitated this process and reinforced their sense of professionalism by locating the source of knowledge within the teachers themselves.

The increased willingness of colleagues to collaborate online without the need to physically attend a professional learning course has accelerated the pace of development amongst our staff and helped to forge connections that may have taken years under pre-pandemic circumstances. Teachers who participated in our TRGs provided feedback noting that they felt supported by colleagues and were able to tailor their learning to localised concerns and provide the best possible learning opportunities for the students they see in their classrooms every single day. This work was completed within a new code of conduct that all members of the online TRG adhered to.

The most satisfying experience for me was learning of one colleague who had been considering retirement but had then decided to stay on in the profession and seek promotion. After discussing the ideas presented in this chapter, he told me that his sense of achievement throughout the pandemic had made him realise that he still had much to give to the education sector and to his students. He found his value in the fact that he had collaboratively redesigned the entire maths curriculum to suit online learning. The true potential of TRGs is the ability to empower teachers with professional agency by making them the co-constructors of knowledge within a renewed code of conduct and an enhanced sense of professional self.

TRGs can play an important role in educational recovery by supporting teachers and enhancing their professionalism rather than relying on high stakes accountability measures. I would argue that providing a rich and stable curriculum to help all students and particularly the most disadvantaged following the pandemic must be our highest priority. It is my firm belief that TRGs can play a vital role in this recovery.

References

Allison, S. and Tharby, A. (2015) *Making Every Lesson Count.* Carmarthen: Crown House Publishing.

Ball, S. (2008) 'Performativity, privatisation, professionals and the state', in B. Cunningham (ed) *Exploring professionalism.* London: University College London, Institute of Education Press, pp. 50–72.

Beauchamp, C. and Beauchamp, M. C. (2013) 'Boundary as bridge: An analysis of educational neuroscience literature from a boundary perspective', *Educational psychology review,* 25(1), 47–67.

Bell, D. and Darlington, H. (2020) 'So what does it mean in the classroom?', in M. Thomas, D. Mareschal and I. Dumontheil (eds) *Educational neuroscience: Development across the lifespan.* Abingdon, Oxford: Routledge.

Blakemore, S. J. (2019) *Inventing Ourselves.* London: Penguin.

Blakemore, S. J. and Frith, U. (2005) *The learning brain: Lesson for education.* Oxford: Blackwell.

British Educational Research Association (2014) *Research and the teaching profession.* Retrieved from: www.bit.ly/38wNLb2.

Brown, C. and Poortman, C. L. (2018) *Networks for Learning; Effective Collaboration for teacher, school and system improvement.* Abingdon, Oxford: Routledge.

Burke, P. (2008) 'The challenges of widening participation for professional identities and practices', in B. Cunningham (ed) *Exploring professionalism.* London: University College London, Institute of Education Press, pp. 121–143.

Creemers, B., Kyriakides, L. and Antoniou, P. (2013) *Teacher professional development for improving the quality of teaching.* Dordrecht: Springer Netherlands.

Crook, D. (2008) 'Some historical perspectives on professionalism', in B. Cunningham (ed) *Exploring professionalism.* London: University College London, Institute of Education Press, pp. 10–28.

Department for Education and Skills (2001) *Learning and Teaching: a strategy for professional development.* London: Department for Education and Skills.

Department for Education (2011) *Teachers' standards.* Retrieved from: www.bit.ly/3vICqg8.

Department for Education (2016) *Educational excellence everywhere.* Retrieved from: www.bit.ly/3MFCggy.

Education Endowment Foundation (2020) *Remote learning rapid evidence assessment*. Retrieved from: www.bit.ly/3MBigLJ.

Firestone, A., Cruz, R. and Rodl, J. (2020) 'Teacher study groups: an integrative literature synthesis', *Review of Educational Research*, 90(5), 675–709.

Fischer, K., Goswami, U. and Geake, J. (2010) 'The future of educational neuroscience', *Mind, Brain and Education*, 4(2), 68–80.

Freidson, E. (2001) *Professionalism: The third logic*. Cambridge: Polity Press.

Godfrey, D. (2017) 'What is the proposed role of research evidence in England's self-improving school system?', *Oxford Review of Education*, 43(4), 433–446.

Greville-Giddings, B. (2020) 'Journal clubs: Promoting a career-long culture of research engagement', *Impact* (9), 30–36.

Hargreaves, D. (1996) 'Teaching as a research-based profession: possibilities and prospects', *British Educational Research Journal*, (23), 141–161.

Hargreaves, A. and Goodson, I. (eds) (1996) *Teachers' professional lives*. London: Falmer Press.

Hirsch, E. D. (2016) *Why Knowledge Matters*. Cambridge, MA: Harvard University Press.

Hattie, J. (2008) *Invisible learning*. Abingdon, Oxford: Routledge.

Howard-Jones, P. A., Jay, T. and Galeano, L. (2020) 'Professional development on the science of learning and teachers' performative thinking – a pilot study', *Mind, Brain and Education*, 14(3), 267–278.

Kennedy, M. (2016) 'How does professional development improve teaching?', *Review of Educational Research*, 86(4), 945–980.

Koehn, D. (1994) *The ground of professional ethics*. Abingdon, Oxford: Routledge.

Kumar, R. and Hill, D. (2008) *Global neoliberalism and education and its consequences*. Abingdon, Oxford: Routledge.

Lemov, D. (2020) *Teaching in the online classroom*. San Francisco: Jossey-Bass.

Lunt, I. (2008) 'Ethical issues in professional life', in B. Cunningham (ed) *Exploring professionalism*. London: University College London, Institute of Education Press, pp. 73–98.

MacLure, M. (1993) 'Arguing for yourself: Identity as an organising principle in teachers' jobs and lives', *British Educational Research Journal*, 19(4), 311–323.

McCrea, P. (2018) *Memorable teaching*. CreateSpace Independent Publishing Platform.

Musset, P. (2010) *Initial teacher education and continuing training Policies in a Comparative Perspective: Current Practices in OECD Countries and a Literature Review on Potential Effects.* Paris: OECD Publishing.

Palaiologou, I., Needham, D. and Male, T. (2015) *Doing research in education: theory and practice.* London: Sage.

Prenger, R., Poortman, C. L. and Handelzalts, A. (2020) 'Professional learning networks: From teacher learning to school improvement?', *Journal of Educational Change*, (22), 13–22.

Robson, C. and McCartan, K. (2016) *Real-world research.* (4th ed). West Sussex: John Wiley.

Sachs, J. (2000) 'The activist professional', *Journal of Educational Change*, (1), 77–95.

Sancar, R., Atal, D. and Deryakulu, D. (2021) 'A new framework for teachers' professional development', *Teaching and Teacher Education*, (101), 1–12.

Schon, D. (1983) The reflective practitioner: How professionals think in action. Basic Books: New York.

Scott, S. and McNeish, D. (2013) *School leadership evidence review: Using research evidence to support school improvement.* London: Department for Education.

Sherrington, T. (2017) *The Learning Rainforest.* Woodbridge: John Catt.

Sims, S., Moss, G. and Marshall, E. (2017) 'Teacher journal clubs: How do they work and can they increase evidence-based practice?', *Impact*, (1), 72–75.

Slater, H., Davies, N. and Burgess, S. (2012) 'Do teachers matter? Measuring the variation in teacher effectiveness in England', *Oxford Bulletin of Economics and Statistics*, 74(5), 629–645.

Sullivan, W., Colby, A., Wegner, J.W., Bond, L. and Shulman, L. (2007) *Educating lawyers: preparation for the professional of law.* Stanford, CA: Carnegie Foundation.

The Sutton Trust (2011) *Improving the impact of teachers on pupil achievement in the UK - Interim findings.* London: Sutton Trust.

The Royal Society (2011) *Brain waves module 2: Neuroscience: implications for training and lifelong learning.* London: The Royal Society.

Tolmie, A. (2013) 'Research methods in educational psychology', in D. Mareschal, B. Butterworth and A. Tolmie (eds) *Educational neuroscience.* West Sussex: Wiley Blackwell, pp. 110–134.

University of Cambridge (2021) 'Statement on the UK government initial teacher training review report', *University of Cambridge* [Online] 6 July. Retrieved from: www.bit.ly/3y0krnZ.

Wellcome Trust (2021) *Quality assurance of teachers' continuing professional development: Design, development and pilot of a CPD quality assurance system*. London: Wellcome Trust. Retrieved from: www.bit.ly/3xWHosf.

Wenger, E. (1998) *Communities of practice: learning, meaning, and identity*. Cambridge: Cambridge University Press.

Whitty, G. (2008) 'Changing modes of teacher professionalism: traditional, managerial, collaborative and democratic', in B. Cunningham (ed) *Exploring professionalism*. London: University College London, Institute of Education Press, pp. 28–49.

Wiliam, D. (2016) *Leadership for teacher learning: Creating a culture where all teachers improve so that all students succeed*. West Palm Beach, FL: Learning Science International.

Wiliam, D. (2018) *Creating the schools our children need*. West Palm Beach, FL: Learning Science International.

Willemse, M., Boei, F. and Pillen, M. (2016) 'Fostering teacher educators' professional development on practice-based research through communities of inquiry', *Vocations and Learning*, (9), 85–110.

Networking inside and out
using student voice to improve professional practice

Marcella McCarthy

Overview

When we talk about networking and good practice, the conversation more often turns to ways in which teachers can help and support each other, and student voice as an active force can be ignored. Student voice is well established as a principle of educational improvement, but too often its implementation is less than systematic. Too few students feel that they have a voice in school, and the range of interest that they are allowed to represent is narrow. Traditional student councils tend to focus on micro-managing issues such as the quality of canteen food rather than opening out larger ideas of political and social justice. Yet we know that students are vitally concerned with these global issues, and in the wider world, it is often young people who are driving change.

During the recent educational restrictions caused by the Covid-19 pandemic, staff at the Royal Latin School (RLS) changed our ways of working, and as a result, realised that we were virtually ignoring an unexpected network of expertise that was under our noses – our students. Over lockdown, we learned to listen more closely, created opportunities for a more developed student voice, and have now, post-lockdown, made a conscious effort to use this neglected 'internal network' of student voice so as to fuel significant curriculum and pastoral changes in school.

Keywords
Student voice
Curriculum

BLM
PSHE
Online learning
Sexual harassment

Student voice and the dangers of tokenism

The idea of student voice is embedded in recent educational philosophy. In the UK, the 2002 Education Act foregrounded the idea that schools should consult with their pupils, and Ofsted soon latched onto this, asking schools preparing for inspection in 2005 to ascertain 'What are the views of learners, and how do you know?' Since 2014, indeed, government advice from the Department for Education has stated schools are obliged 'to provide opportunities for pupils to be consulted on matters affecting them or contribute to decision-making in the school'.

What does this look like in real life? The questions that Ofsted highlight in their 'Pupil Voice' questionnaire are dismayingly bland: options to rate for accuracy include 'I enjoy school', 'Teachers help me to do my best', 'My teachers give me work that challenges me', and 'I enjoy learning at this school'. Questions about bullying are confined to asking if bullying is dealt with well by staff and if students feel safe. Throughout, there is very little sense that students themselves might take a more active role in the school or might promote change. Rather than showing that students are 'consulted on matters affecting them' or 'contribute to decision-making', such questions seem to imply that they are people who are 'done to', well or badly, not people who are active agents.

This kind of passivity is reflected elsewhere. Student councils are now the norm in many schools; yet their focus is often as uninspiring as the Ofsted questions, and it is rare that they are consulted at a strategic level or seen as a vehicle for 'authentic pupil voice that has bite' (Handscomb 2014). They are often seen by students themselves as not worth bothering with because they have no impact, and research suggests that they can also be unrepresentative, with self-selecting representatives who are few in number, especially in larger schools (Keogh and Whyte 2005). The student council at the Royal Latin School (RLS) was no exception. Meetings were not very frequent – perhaps once a long term – and lasted less than an hour, over lunchtime. Attendance was less than 20 on average, from a school of 1350 pupils, and typical discussions centred around the quality of canteen food. Students complained that they didn't often see the results of what they had discussed, and there was a strong sense that it was a missed opportunity and a very quiet voice.

We knew that our students were interested in larger issues because we already had a very active and influential environmental group 'Green Touch'. We were discussing ways of bringing this energy into student council with our student leadership team when the pandemic struck, and school shut down for most students. Among the practicalities of organising online learning while supporting the most vulnerable, our student council moved online, and we thought that student voice might become a lower priority for a while. How wrong we were!

What changed following lockdown

Our only previous experience of lockdown was an exercise requiring students to hide from an imagined intruder, but as UK schools closed for months at a time, and exams were cancelled, innovation and creativity took off. Initially over-cautious, we created lesson materials that students could access online, but not 'live' lessons. Safeguarding concerns meant we were anxious about protocol, and staff expertise was still developing. However, students are confident and comfortable in an online environment. When we surveyed students about teaching, they had plenty of suggestions. By the time the second lockdown came, their feedback meant that we had seriously raised our game. Online lessons became the norm, and our teachers – only recently introduced to Chromebooks and cloud-based infrastructure – became confident in looking for new ways to teach, sharing expertise with each other.

This reminded us how important it was for us to listen to our students. They were patient with our lack of technical expertise, but they wanted to know that we were hearing what they had to say, and responding to their input. Relationships in school are relatively easy to maintain when you may see an individual student several times a day in passing. Suddenly our time was scheduled, and, except for our most vulnerable students and those whose parents were key workers, we were seeing students only on-screen. We wanted to engage with them, and we wanted to tap into the things that were important to them. Online systems became our route to improving student voice.

In recent years, we have seen an explosion of activism from children determined that their voices should be heard. From the climate-change campaigners inspired to school strike by Greta Thunberg, through to the young people protesting that 'Black Lives Matter', those who joined in silent vigils for Sarah Everard, or who wrote testimony on the 'Everyone's Invited' website, young people have stepped forward to say that the adult world, and adult presuppositions, aren't working. Schools cannot and should not stay apart from this energetic drive for change. The nature of the Ofsted 'pupil voice' questionnaire, and the discussions we had in our student council before lockdown seem to be a long way away from the kind of questions that really occupy young people now.

Responding to 'Black Lives Matter'

Big things happened in the world over lockdown. The murder of George Floyd in May 2020 was an example of something that affected students deeply. Had we been in school, we might have had assemblies about it, or discussed it in form time: teachers would have been in charge. As it was, we watched while momentum built in an anti-racist movement that it was clear would have huge implications for schools, and felt helpless.

Networking with students online saved us. A group of former and current students got together to share experiences, and, crucially, shared them with us, the staff, as well, helping us to formulate an initial response. We formed a virtual working party using a Google classroom, where students and staff could share ideas, reading, blogs, articles, and film recommendations, frankly sharing our concerns about the dangers of the school, like all schools, having an implicitly racist culture. We spoke via video call to both current students and former students, and learned about the micro-aggressions that they had experienced both in a school context and in wider society. We came up with a strategic plan moving forwards and built it into our School Development Plan.

We learned a lot of things from the virtual working party, including that the well-meaning assumptions of our teaching staff were often wrong; that showing certain films or teaching certain books had caused students' distress; that it really mattered if you got names wrong, or avoided using them because you were uncertain about pronunciation; that commenting on a hairstyle could cause agonies of self-consciousness. We heard about the child who was the only black student in their primary school, and had still not had their name remembered by staff; we found out about students whose parents had advised them not to call out racism in case it interfered with how they were seen by others; we discovered the discomfort of students who found themselves glanced at by peers in class every time there was a reference to a black person in a text. We found out about a bully in the lunch queue that no one had reported because they were too embarrassed to repeat the racist jibe.

What we also learned was that there is no one-size-fits all cure for some issues. Young BAME people were wary about representing a whole group when they were all too aware of how diverse their own experiences could be. As a result of what we had heard, when we returned to school in January 2021 for an INSET day, the students from the working party created a video presentation for all staff, which shared their experiences, and explained why anti-racism was a school priority. Talking about how they felt when someone mispronounced their name, misidentified them, or mixed them up with another student, made staff wince but produced some amazingly positive responses, and changed all our practice for the better. Staff feedback described it as 'outstanding', 'thought-provoking, insightful and helpful' and said 'it has made me think hard about how I teach'.

Student voice networking bringing about change

One of the points raised by the working party was that even if Steinbeck was trying to highlight the wrongs of oppression, the use of the 'n' word in *Of Mice and Men* could not be seen as innocent. Having discovered this, the English department created their own network working party with students to discuss their teaching and decide whether *Of Mice and Men* was still a viable text. This became a project focused on curriculum design; the teacher leading it polled a large number of students to find out their thoughts and ideas about race and identity, and then took things further with a smaller discussion group of volunteers. For the first time, perhaps, these students were being given the opportunity to have a real impact on what was taught in their curriculum, and decide what should be taught to younger students.

Interestingly, student voice proved to open out the debate in unexpected ways, as we made new network connections across year groups and teaching groups through our working parties. This meant that students who might not normally have discussed issues with each other drew in different ideas to the debate in the safe space provided. In a context where such students are in a minority, through networking, they got to share their experience of being taught a text in a way that might not otherwise have happened across classes. For example, the school had considered stopping teaching *Of Mice and Men*, but they discovered that this was not what all BAME students wanted. They also found that the impact on students went beyond the ways in which any specific text was taught. Students reported feeling awkward when race was mentioned or foregrounded in a text because others in the class looked to them so as to check their reaction. They suggested that Year 9 was too late to have their first experience of a text which mentioned race and that the school should seek to investigate new and more diverse texts to teach at Key Stage 3. They also highlighted the teaching of one member of staff whom they felt had taught *Of Mice and Men* in an especially sensitive and knowledgeable way, starting off by foregrounding issues of race and taking time to discuss this and inform all students before plunging into the novel. This last insight was especially helpful for staff development; now all teachers in the department use this strategy and have developed their teaching as a result.

As a result of this working party, the Key Stage 3 curriculum for English has changed in our school. It has made us rethink our sequencing and the breadth of our curriculum in terms of cultural capital. In Year 7, students are now introduced to more diverse literature, and initial feedback has been overwhelmingly positive. Surveying students studying *Tender Earth* by Sita Brahmachari, for example, only one student out of 84 surveyed said that they hadn't enjoyed the lessons, and 93% suggested they would be happy to have more lessons about authors from diverse backgrounds, with over 70% actively asking for this. Even those who did not especially want further lessons of this type commented 'I felt more connected to the other people in my class' or 'I felt my beliefs and heritage were more understood and respected afterwards'. Interestingly, the one child who said that they hadn't enjoyed the lesson, also said that they didn't feel that they had a cultural heritage or any beliefs that they wanted to share with others. The department's work on this area continues.

'Everyone's Invited'

The experience of working with students on recognising and addressing racism, made us realise what an untapped source of power our students were when it came to curriculum development. Returning to school after the first lockdown, we realised that if we were sincere about empowering students to be future leaders, then we were going to have to face up to some potentially uncomfortable responses. In other words, 'as soon as we touch upon the question of participation we have to entertain and work with issues of power, of oppression, of gender' (Reason 1994).

It was clear that our current structures were not supporting students to share their experiences with us. When the 'Everyone's Invited' website went live, in common with many other schools, our safeguarding team searched through it to see if we could find any references to our school. We found one, which alleged an out-of-school assault by students from a local university some years previously. The student concerned had not felt able to report this assault to staff at either institution. As a result, we put in place an anonymous reporting mechanism, which brought forward a group of girls who told us about specific issues that they had experienced, up to and including sexual assault in school. This group developed into the basis of our networking action about peer-on-peer abuse.

Again, the idea of a network cut across the divides of year groups, friendship groups and form groups and enabled serious discussion at a level we had not seen before. Initial social media contact between a small group of students was developed into a survey, owned and run by students, where girls were invited to contribute their experiences anonymously in the knowledge that this would be shared with staff in school. This social media context seemed to allow greater openness. So when the girls who had taken ownership of this initial network met with us to discuss what had emerged, we found that we had a great deal of testimony to work with, including incidents that girls had thought would be deemed 'trivial' or ones where they were worried that they would be judged for initial flirting online with someone who then pushed boundaries. Finding out that others of different ages had shared similar experiences meant that some young women felt more able to disclose details of what had happened to them without the cloak of anonymity, enabling us to take crucial safeguarding actions and connect up incidents and investigate them.

The new relationships and sex education curriculum, statutory from 2020, made a good starting point for reform. Using the initial reflections of this small group of girls, we drew in more students and asked them about what they thought should change. As a result of this work, we put in place extra training for all staff about peer-on-peer sexual abuse. We highlighted how 'banter' was a gateway towards serious sexual crime; how stereotyping and nicknaming, casual uninvited touches in passing or comments on clothing could push boundaries about what was appropriate and tolerated until girls felt as though they could not speak up without seeming to be 'spoilsports' or humourless. We had already revised our uniform policy so that it was gender-neutral, but, listening to how it made students feel, we now advised staff that it would no longer be appropriate to comment on the length of girls' skirts as long as they were complying with the uniform rules.

If pupil voice is truly representative, then schools are empowered by 'a community of participants engaged in the common endeavour of learning' (Flutter and Rudduck 2004). We knew there was potentially an iceberg of experience beneath the issues we knew about, and we wanted to learn more. We needed to find different ways in which our students could talk openly about what needed to change in school and a forum in which we could pick up issues so as to be strategic rather than reactive. It was time for our student council to be transformed.

'LATIN Learning'

One criticism frequently levelled at high-performing schools such as RLS is that they are 'exam factories', and we consciously try to defeat this stereotype through our teaching and learning philosophy, 'Latin Learning', which derives from Deborah Eyre's system of 'High Performance Learning' (Eyre 2016). 'LATIN', in 'Latin Learning', stands for leadership, aspiration, teamwork, innovation, and nurturing. Each of these elements is designed to remind us that education is not simply knowledge-based in a narrowly academic sense, but should develop a moral compass and sense of enrichment and enjoyment in learning. It focuses on developing real-world life skills that will enable children to thrive not just in the sheltered environment of school, but in work and university. It highlights that leadership might consist of taking a step back and letting others thrive, and that mental health is as important as aspiration.

In the UK, child mental health has never been more vulnerable. A recent study showed that the percentage of children identified as having a probable mental disorder had increased from 10.8% in 2017 to 16% (NHS 2020).

Lockdown has exacerbated the internal strains on families, with domestic violence increasing, and financial strains sometimes exacerbating relationship issues, while at the same time support has become harder to find. The crisis of the Pandemic has often been compared to the rigours of World War 2, and this reflects our experience; it was easy for academic work in school to seem trivial in comparison with the horrible totals of deaths and hospitalisations on the evening news. Giving young people a voice is one of the things that can build their resilience and recovery from trauma (Lind 2007). More and more we saw an emerging sense that students felt that they needed to talk about what was important to them, and we had to listen to this.

To capture the vibrant student voices that had emerged over lockdown, student council has now been radically changed. Using the model of a school governing body, it now has five subcommittees, named after our LATIN qualities. Each form group thus has five representatives, immediately multiplying student voice. Year groups meet first as a unit in each committee but then meet with older years to exchange ideas before the subcommittees take proposals to full council. Experienced sixth formers chair these meetings, with a structured system of shared agendas and minutes, all shared on the student council Google classroom. Instead of once a term, meetings are every couple of weeks.

Using this system, we have 25 representatives from each year group giving active feedback about the issues that they find really important. The first set of meetings gave us invaluable input at a strategic level on issues such as the redesign of our curriculum for Personal Social Health and Economic Education (PSHE). Students were asking for more input on the issues that were most important and relevant to them, and we were able to communicate what we were already doing about this and get a live critique on our future planning. Now, for example, we have sixth form students working with staff to deliver sessions on sensitive issues. Student feedback suggests that they have far greater credibility than staff when talking about matters such as the dangers of alcohol and drugs as there is a sense, as one younger student put it 'that they might actually have been to parties'!

There is a tangible sense of excitement in the meetings. Occasionally, the canteen is still discussed, but now larger issues dominate: how to create a stronger and more enabling culture; how best to celebrate diversity in school; how to transform the future curriculum; how to teach about relationships. Each group has the opportunity to run assemblies, hold charity events, speak to the senior leadership of the school, and be the agent of meaningful change. The council has never been so popular, and with the visible evidence of the impact of student voice, more and more students are asking to join working parties, to collaborate with teachers in developing new ways of learning about what vitally concerns them. Student council has grown from under 20 students to over a hundred – and it's still growing. The online classroom that supports council means that no one who wants to contribute is turned away. Working with students has led to a stronger focus on student wellbeing and engagement that we plan to build into our positive permanent changes at school in a post-pandemic world.

Moving forward

Although there is a great deal written about student voice, relatively little of this reflects on how it is changed because of the huge difference made by online learning, and online input. Google forms and documents transformed the way in which we were able to communicate with students – with a single email, we could send a questionnaire to a whole year group or department. More research needs to be done on how the online experience – and the online input to our student knowledge base about the issues which most concern them – affects student voice.

Going forwards, we would like to link up with other student networks, and share experiences. Looking back, we would have these pieces of advice about the challenges:

1. Look at your power dynamics

Experts such as David Hargreaves rank learner voice on a level with curriculum development as a 'gateway' for bringing about positive change in education. But this only works properly when students become 'allies' and active partners rather than subjects. (Walker and Logan 2008). One of the greatest barriers to student voice is the tendency for students to believe that they won't be listened to because of the existing power dynamics of school.

2. Widen participation

The more students we listened to, the better our input became. You may need to have a lot of dialogue to find out the subtle detail that will make a difference. The loudest voices aren't always the most representative. Online forms, anonymous surveys, and classroom discussions are highly effective at gathering opinions from quieter voices.

3. Take time to set up structures that will work
The challenge for networking effectively with students is that it has to be highly structured. Organising the new student council, and organising the groups that preceded and inspired it, has taken a great deal of work, from considering timings of meetings to working out how agendas are communicated. Template agendas and sharing documents through Google were invaluable for us in sharing ideas.

4. Educate your students in the use of their voice
Although students need to be able to express themselves freely, they also need to be equipped to engage in effective dialogue and listen to each other. Students may need to be shown how to run a meeting, how to assess conflict in a discussion, and how to debate appropriately and knowledgeably. Give time for this.

5. Forget your preconceptions
Listen openly to students and you will be astonished. We thought we could predict what they would say about some issues, and we were absolutely wrong. Really listening to student voice is as important as facilitating it in the first place; acting on it is the next step.

References

Eyre, D. (2016) *High Performance Learning: How to become a world class school.* Abingdon, Oxford: Routledge.

Flutter, J. and Rudduck, J. (2004) *Consulting Young People: What's in it for schools?* Abingdon, Oxford: Routledge Falmer.

Groundwater-Smith, S. and Mockler, N. (2015) 'From Data Source to Co-Researchers? Tracing the Shift from "Student Voice" to Student-Teacher Partnerships in Educational Action Research', *Educational Action Research*, 24(2), 159–176.

Handscomb, G. (2014) Pupil *Researchers and Pupil Power – token or authentic.* Inaugural Professorship lecture given at University College London by Graham Handscomb, Dean and Professor of Education, The College of Teachers.

Keogh, A. F. and Whyte, J. (2005) 'Second Level Student Councils in Ireland: A Study Of Enablers, Barriers And Supports', report by The Children's Research Centre, Trinity College, on behalf of the National Children's Office. Dublin: Stationery Office.

Lind, C. (2007) 'The power of adolescent voices: co-researchers in mental health promotion', *Educational Action Research*, 15(3), 371–383.

National Health Service (2020) Mental Health of Children and Young People in England, 2020: Wave 1 follow up to the 2017 survey. Retrieved from: www.bit.ly/3rVQG40.

Walker, L. and Logan, A (2008) *A review of learner voice initiatives across the UK's education sectors*. London: National Foundation for Educational Research.

Professional learning in adult education

crucial roles and future actions of networks and networking

Sandy Youmans, Lorraine Godden
and Hanne Nielsen Hamlin

Overview

Adult education (AE) provides flexible programs and supports to help adults meet a variety of educational goals including, language training, high school diploma completion, accessing post-secondary education, career transitions, and employment skills training. Typically, AE learners include vulnerable and transient populations that may not have experienced success in the traditional school system (e.g. due to learning disabilities, mental health challenges, addictions, difficult home life). The majority of academic credit AE programs are delivered by school boards across Ontario, Canada. Most school board stakeholders are unaware of the type of AE programs offered by their board or the impact they have on their community; as a result, AE is often not included in school board strategic planning. Additionally, AE administrators, teachers, and instructors tend to lack specialised training in how to teach adults or support adults with diverse needs, and subsequently rely on formal and informal networking as their main professional development activity. During the Covid-19 pandemic, AE programs in Ontario suddenly transitioned to remote learning in the spring of 2020. This unique situation provided an opportunity to investigate the difficulties faced by AE educators during the pandemic, and the role of their professional networks in mitigating these challenges. This chapter outlines these challenges and highlights successes experienced by AE teachers and administrators as a result of networking through two key organisations during the pandemic. The chapter concludes by summarising the importance of networks in AE and ideas for further strengthening networks.

Keywords
Adult learners
Adult and continuing education
Professional networks

Adult education: a neglected but vital area

Adult education provides flexible programs and supports to help adults meet a variety of educational goals such as language training, high school diploma completion, course upgrading to access post-secondary education, retraining for a new career, and employment skills training. Typically, AE learner cohorts include vulnerable and transient populations that may not have experienced success in the traditional school system because of challenges they experienced in their youth (e.g. learning disabilities, mental health challenges, addictions, difficult home life). With this in mind, AE provides adults with an opportunity to achieve success where it was previously unobtainable. Indeed, many adults who participate in AE describe it as a transformational experience because it enables them to achieve lifelong goals of high school completion and post-secondary participation (Youmans et al 2017). In addition, refugees and immigrants often join AE for language training or to re-do their school credentials in the Canadian system, so they can actively participate in society and achieve their educational and employment goals.

Despite the transformational nature of AE, it has not historically been prioritised in the Ontario (and Canadian) educational system. For example, the *Ontario Learns: Strengthening Our Adult Education System report* (released in 2005) begins with the acknowledgement of widespread agreement from multiple stakeholders that 'Ontario lacks a cohesive adult education system' (Ontario Ministry of Education 2005). The majority of the for-credit adult education programs are delivered by school boards across the province. Most school board administrators, trustees, and staff are unaware of the type of AE programs offered by their board or the impact they have on their community; as a result, AE is often not included in school board strategic planning (Youmans et al 2017). Additionally, adult education administrators, teachers, and instructors tend to lack specialised training in how to teach adults or support adults with diverse needs. Subsequently, teachers within AE rely on formal and informal networking as their main professional development activity.

Networking infrastructure

The Ontario Association of Adult and Continuing Education School Board Administrators (CESBA) is a provincial, non-profit professional association established over 20 years ago to represent, advocate for, and support AE program staff working in about 60 school boards across Ontario. Part of CESBA's mandate is to raise awareness about the value of AE and build capacity in its members through the exchange of knowledge and resource development, which it does through a series of formal networking events. Fundamentally, CESBA is a provincial organisation that provides professional development opportunities for AE staff that are not otherwise available through individual school boards.

In an attempt to improve Ontario's adult education system, the Ontario Ministry of Education developed and funded the Adult Education Strategy (AES) from 2016 to 2019. Six regional partnerships and one French language partnership were formed, with the intention that each partnership would work collaboratively within a network to achieve the four AES mandates:

1. Regionally coordinated access to flexible delivery of AE programs and/or services (e.g. e-learning or hybrid delivery programs) that best meet adult learner needs.

2. Access to coordinated information, intake, assessment, and referrals at school boards to ensure learners are directed to the program or service that best meets their needs.

3. Regionally coordinated access to consistent Prior Learning Assessment and Recognition (PLAR) for mature students working towards a high school diploma.

4. Regional guidance, career counselling and pathway planning for mature students working towards a high school diploma or seeking prerequisites for post-secondary education.

One notable AES regional partnership was the Eastern Regional Partnership for Adult Education (ERPAE), which had the support of the Eastern Ontario Staff Development Network, and was strategically led by a coordinator with experience as an AE administrator. The partnership also benefitted from having two researchers to document its work (see eosdn.on.ca/initiatives/adult-education-strategy). The ERPAE implemented the AES with the following activities:

- an environmental scan of AE programs in the eastern region and the development of a regional strategic plan (Year 1);
- capacity building of its members by learning from each other and from other professionals in the field (Year 2); and
- piloting innovative AE projects in relation to the four AES mandates (with the addition of a fifth mandate about positioning AE to raise awareness about it and its value) to support the success of adult learners (Year 3).

Over the course of the strategy, the partnership members developed a strong network with AE staff from other school boards in their region and strengthened teamwork and growth within their own individual boards (Youmans and Godden 2022). During the Covid-19 pandemic, adult education programs in Ontario suddenly transitioned to remote learning in the spring of 2020. This chapter outlines the challenges experienced by AE staff during remote learning and how CESBA and the ERPAE responded to them. It also describes the successes experienced by AE teachers and administrators as a result of this networking during the pandemic. The chapter concludes with ideas for strengthening the CESBA and ERPAE networks and of a summary about the importance of networks in the field of adult education.

Professional challenges faced by AE teachers and administrators during the pandemic

The Covid-19 pandemic certainly created a challenging context with respect to the delivery of programming for adult learners in Ontario.

As Ontario schools transitioned 'instantly' to remote learning, teachers in AE were required to make a significant shift to their teaching that impacted many adult learners across the province. This unprecedented situation provided an opportunity to investigate the difficulties faced by AE educators during the pandemic and the role of their professional networks in mitigating these challenges.

Godden and Youmans (2022) asked AE teachers (including instructors and guidance counsellors) and administrators to identify challenges they faced during the pandemic via an online survey. In total, 27 teachers and 11 administrators participated in the study. Surveys included closed-ended questions and open-response questions about how AE programs responded during the Covid-19 pandemic. Quantitative data analysis was conducted on closed-ended survey responses using Microsoft Excel and open-ended responses were coded using thematic qualitative analysis.

A significant challenge reported by teachers was the adjustment to online teaching (similar to findings by König et al 2020). For example, AE teachers had difficulty finding high-quality digital resources suitable for teaching adults, despite comparable online teaching resources being available in the K-12 sector. In addition, given that adult learners experienced competing priorities and distractions when doing online schooling from home, teachers found themselves re-teaching concepts and spending more one-on-one time with individual students to ensure learners had understood all of the course material. Increased amounts of instructional time on the part of AE teachers made it hard for them to support their own children's learning, especially during lockdown periods. Subsequently, teachers indicated that finding a healthy work/life balance during the pandemic was a struggle (e.g. Davis et al 2021). Further predominant challenges reported by teachers related to the lack of face-to-face communication they normally experienced, including a lack of regular targeted communication from school leaders, and sadness at not being able to interact with students like they would during in-person learning.

For school administrators, the biggest problem they encountered was insufficient technology equipment to ensure that adult learners' needs could participate in online learning (e.g. Martínez Martínez and Tudela Sancho 2020). Also important was the additional support that needed to be directed towards supporting teachers and staff in making adjustments to working practices for the online environment. A further significant challenge for school administrators was interpreting and implementing ministry Covid-19 guidelines and balancing this demanding role with providing necessary support to their staff, teachers and learners.

How professional AE networks responded to the needs of AE staff during the pandemic

A major strength of CESBA is that it has a full-time team of six employees that are responsive to the needs of its AE staff members. During the pandemic, it recognised that its members required training and support to successfully navigate the transition to online learning. Consequently, CESBA (2021) undertook the following activities during the 2020/2021 school year:

- Hosted their first virtual conference with over 20 workshops that were attended by nearly 350 members.
- Revamped their website to include a library with over 300 resources. The use of the website increased significantly over the previous year, with 13,492 users (+48%) 20,056 (+36%) sessions and 50,329 page views (+32%).
- Organised a three-part Lunch and Learn series – Connecting in Challenging Times. The three sessions offered were: get started with virtual teaching, support your staff during challenging times, and mental health supports for students and staff.
- Hosted nine well-attended regional meetings throughout the school year for the north, east, central and west regions to connect with their colleagues, hear from government representatives and meet in small, sector-specific groups (Credit/PLAR/Guidance, ESL/FSL/LINC, LBS, IL, PSW, Francophone).
- Commissioned a research study about how AE staff transitioned to remote learning during the pandemic.

Although the Eastern Regional Partnership for Adult Education no longer has a full-time paid coordinator, the Executive Director of the Eastern Ontario Staff Development Network (EOSDN) connected with the partnership's school board members to determine their interest in participating in the CESBA study about how AE staff transitioned to remote learning during the pandemic. All eight school boards with AE programs agreed to take part. Their participation resulted in a regional report (The CESBA Adult and Continuing Education Study: A Report for the Eastern Regional Partnership for Adult Education) and a tip sheet for supporting adult learners with online learning called 'How Can We Support Adult Learner Success During Remote Learning?'

Successes experienced by AE staff during the pandemic as a result of professional networks

AE staff (including teachers and school administrators) shared how they were able to respond to the challenges of the pandemic through the networks they had built during their participation in the AES strategy, and through the support of CESBA and the ERPAE. The online resources and the lunch and learn sessions provided throughout the pandemic by CESBA were reported as valuable in:

- helping teachers make the adjustment to online teaching;
- sourcing resources relevant to adult learners, and
- helping to mitigate the sense of isolation that teachers felt.

Many teachers explained how during the pandemic they missed the hallway conversations with colleagues, and the informal form of support that these offered. Attending the online lunch and learns was described as an important space for colleagues to come together, share their ideas, and support each other.

For school administrators, the pandemic made new demands on their time by trying to find appropriate technological equipment for adult learners to minimise disruption to their learning, and the time needed to interpret what the government guidelines aimed at regular schools would mean for the adult high schools. Balancing these obligations with the necessary support that was needed by their staff and teachers proved to be challenging. However, participating in the AES provided positive mitigation for administrators. For example, during the three-year period of the strategy, ERPAE administrators had the opportunity to work closely with their staff in new and innovative ways. These shared experiences developed and nurtured relationships and trust within each participating district school board. Subsequently, when the team was placed under the stress of the pandemic, it was an easier process to come together to form responsive planning and strategising. The previous relationship building that took place within the ERPAE, the regular meetings and events facilitated by CESBA, and the resources that were available to educators from their activity within these networks provided much-needed support through the challenging period of the pandemic.

Moving forward: strengthening professional AE networks

Given the lack of training and sense of isolation that many adult education staff experience in their profession, which was even more pronounced during the pandemic, strengthening professional AE networks is critical. A major benefit of CEBSA is that it is a provincial organisation with dedicated full-time employees that focuses on advocating for AE staff and offering opportunities for professional development that are often lacking in the field. From 2016 to 2019, the AES provided an unprecedented chance for regional partnerships to engage in collaborative action-oriented professional learning. In fact, the Eastern Regional Partnership for Adult Education developed a model called the Coalition Model for Professional Development (CMfPD) during their implementation of the AES. The three main elements of this model were:

- a collaborative structure in which members from different school boards worked together;
- a culture of care in which all AE staff (e.g. teachers, administrators, guidance counsellors, administrative secretaries, instructors) were valued and supported, and
- continuous learning that led to actionable outcomes (Youmans and Godden 2022).

This model resulted in notable growth for ERPAE members which included: greater collaboration within the regional network, increased capacity as AE professionals, and the planning of innovative practices to support positive change for AE learners. Moreover, some members said that it was the best professional development experience they ever had. We believe that this success in a regional setting could be scaled up and applied at the provincial level by CESBA. For this to happen,

CESBA would need to work with their membership and the regional partnerships to establish a clear mandate and strategic plan for the next five years. In line with this, it would be great to renew the mandates of the regional AE partnerships, which have unique needs based on their geographic areas; this would ensure the work begun during the AES is not lost and would enable new regional work to be shared among the province. Ultimately, the CMfPD could enable professional networks to move to a deeper level of advocacy through an action-oriented coalition.

Our work with adult education in Ontario, before and during the pandemic, revealed a number of promising practices for developing and strengthening the entire field through expanded networks. For some organisations, the first place to start is to mobilise their own staff through a shared action research project. In action research, stakeholders work together to identify an area that needs improvement, consider possible solutions to the problem (by reviewing research literature), select a solution to implement, and collect and analyse data to evaluate the effectiveness of the solution (Thiollent 211). A relevant action research question worth exploring in AE is, 'How do we strengthen online learning practices to support adult learner success and prepare for future disruptions?' Other organisations and individuals may be interested in establishing or joining existing in-person networks. In addition, there is the possibility of working collaboratively across regions, provinces, and nations to improve adult education through online communities of practice. For such communities to be successful, we suggest they include dedicated leaders, opportunities for members to build relationships, and are guided by action-oriented goals. Lastly, online professional development in adult education, like virtual conferences and lunch and learns, makes the opportunity to network more accessible, efficient, and affordable. As the value of AE is increasingly recognised by governments, we hope to see National (and International) Centres of Excellence in Adult Education that provide quality networking opportunities and online learning commons with beneficial resources available for educators and adult learners.

References

CESBA (2021) CESBA Annual report 2020–2021. Retrieved from: www.bit. ly/37XbwZU.

Davis, C. R., Grooms, J., Ortega, A., Rubalcaba, J. A.-A. and Vargas, E. (2021) 'Distance learning and parental mental health during Covid-19', *Educational Researcher*, 50(1), 61–64.

König, J., Jäger-Biela, D. J. and Glutsch, N. (2020) 'Adapting to online teaching during covid-19 school closure: Teacher education and teacher competence effects among early career teachers in Germany', *European Journal of Teacher Education*, 43(4), 608–622.

Martínez Martínez, J. M. and Tudela Sancho, A. (2020) 'Interactions between virtual spaces and schools: A collective case study', *Future Internet*, 12(12), 217–227.

Ontario Ministry of Education (2005) *Ontario learns: Strengthening our adult education system*. Retrieved from www.bit.ly/38wah3Y.

Thiollent, M. (2011) 'Action research and participatory research: An overview', *International Journal of Action Research*, 7(2), 160–174.

Youmans, S., Godden, L. and Hummell, F. (2017) *An environmental scan of adult and continuing education in the eastern Ontario region*. Kingston, ON: The Eastern Regional Partnership for Adult Education.

Youmans, A. and Godden, L. (2022) The coalition model for professional development. *Teachers and Teaching*.

Concluding reflection:

What next for professional learning networks?

Collaborative caldrons

Graham Handscomb and Chris Brown

As the chapters in this book illustrate, the genie has been let out of the bottle for professional learning networks (PLNs). They are no longer the preserve of the few enthusiasts, initiated and sustained by, albeit well-intentioned, leaders. The clarion call message that resonates throughout is that PLNs have the greatest potency when bubbling up from practitioner ideas, activities and concerns, and when they are teacher or participant-led. From this central tenant, a number of significant things follow. Prominent among these is a radical shift in the understanding of the purpose, focus and leadership of such networks, and with this a reassessment of the nature of professional learning. So, we contend that the focus and outputs of PLNs should be directed by what matters to teachers and should be something that addresses their concerns. PLN participants should also have the freedom to leverage and share what emerges from networks. As such, the sustainability of the power of networks is likely to come from the following:

- An acceptance by educational leaders that the aim of professional learning networks may often shift from their traditional foci of being solely concentrated on pedagogy or performance-related outcomes.
- Leaders ceding control in certain domains of responsibility.
- A reframing of the role of the school leader from that of agenda setter to that of facilitator and provider of support.
- New understanding as to the role of participants that moves beyond mere engagement to incorporate responsibility to sustain, develop and replenish networks.

- Similarly, rather than simply being pliant, willing members of networks, participants need to be seen as – and empowered to be – agents of change.
- Embracing the dynamic nature of networks; understanding that in order to flourish they need to be responsive, agile and iterative, and even short-lived – remaining organic, supple and re-shaping/ reconfiguring according to participants' needs.

The implications for the leadership and facilitation of networks are profound. Traditional network leader modes like 'initiator', 'convenor', and 'gatekeeper' fall away and are replaced by coach, mentor, and catalyst ... and someone who can provide access to the types of resources that might foster success. Such resources might include the provision of time; impact measurement tools (where appropriate); signposting to new partners across a range of spheres; and, fostering communication within and between networks, etc. This reimagining of the contribution of those hitherto in formal leadership positions in turn highlights new professional development needs. So, for instance, we need to know more about effective network facilitators: who should they be; where should they be based; what knowledge and skills do they require; and, how should they be resourced?

The recasting of network participants in the way anticipated also has significant implications. What kind of skills and competencies do PLN participants as agents of change need? Amongst other things this is likely to include:

- the confidence to engage;
- the disposition to collaborate and operate collegially;
- the ability to challenge, question or provide feedback in ways that are respectful, supporting and empowering;
- the ability to engage maturely with challenge;
- the aptitudes and dispositions to be a change agent;
- the temperament to adopt an ethical student-led outlook;
- be able to exercise critical thinking skills; and
- being evidence literate.

Much of the rich testimony provided in this book highlighted how this kind of participant networking spontaneously emerged during the pandemic experience, particularly via online engagement. However, these accounts also make clear that the pandemic environment proved to be simply the circumstantial opportunity for a movement that was already underway. Both key features – participant-led networking and virtual engagement – had been nascent within professional communities for some time. Now that they have been given the momentum of the Covid years, now they have begun to become an embedded feature of network engagement and learning there's no going back! However, it would be a blinkered outlook if we viewed the future development of professional learning networks to be more of the same as experienced during lockdown and recovery.

During these times, practitioners were beginning to connect not just locally but wider afield and there is the potential for this to expand exponentially. With the emergence of virtual and augmented realities (often referred to as the 'metaverse') PLNs now offer the possibilities of engaging across the globe and doing so in an egalitarian way. Here what matters is more about our ideas than our status or position in the hierarchy. We see the end result in international communities of practice in which educators of all types of standing, hailing from both the global south and north, can come together, engage and learn. The added advantage is the environmental benefit of not travelling! So what is emerging is a genuinely brave new world where networks create spaces which enrich people's sense of identity, where ideas rather than status have leverage, and the nature of the profession is fashioned by its participant members.

Such a world populated by these empowered professional learning networks presents challenging questions at the door of school leadership, education governance and government itself! Indeed, our chapter contributors call upon governments and policymakers to embrace networks not just to help in implementing their reform agendas but also to regard networks themselves as crucial change agents and key means to achieving school improvement. Rather than being perceived as comfortable collaborative clubs for like-minded localised professionals, we suggest networks should be seen as a cauldron of ideas, a formative test bed for development and facilitating learning for the benefit of the whole system. We look forward to this bold new future.

Index

A

adult and continuing education, 315–324

academies, 31–34

accountability, 30, 33, 61, 63, 70

agency, 40, 62, 67, 83, 100, 121, 251–254, 258

arts, 22, 193–197, 206, 215

assessment, 98, 138, 215, 317

autonomy, 19, 29–33

B

BAME, 307–308

best practice, 32, 130, 171, 180, 185–189, 281

Big Education, 71, 127–149

Black Lives Matter, 306–307

Brown

Chris Brown, 17, 223, 226, 292

C

Canada, 158, 315–324

catalysing, 84–85

Centre for the Use of Research and Evidence (CUREE), 146

CESBA, 317–323

Church of England Foundation for Educational Leadership, 76

citizenship, 78

coaching, 21, 65, 75–77, 84, 104–106

coastal schools, 78

collaboration, 17, 19

collaborative learning, 22, 70, 115, 279, 292

collegiality, 21, 46, 250, 256, 263, 292

community of practice, 233

comparative and international studies, 44

complexity, 68, 204, 220, 224, 227–228

convening, 75, 84

Covid-19, 44, 56, 60, 65, 70, 76, 169, 175, 183, 204, 219, 241, 241, 255–258, 261, 274 creativity, 92, 95–96, 106, 193, 199, 304

culture, 46–48, 52, 60, 65, 100, 130, 170, 179, 182, 188, 197, 214, 237, 268, 322

D

Danielson
Charlotte Danielson, 93–95

DfE
Department for Education, 32, 292, 294, 304

digital communication 19–20, 54

diversity, 19, 21, 39, 106, 111, 164, 219, 227, 263

Drake
Gavin Drake, 100

Durham Commission for Creativity, 193

E

Early Career Framework, 85, 205, 214, 266

early career teachers, 203–204, 209, 216, 266

ecologies of practice, 203, 207–208, 214

economies of performance, 203, 205, 207, 209, 215

ecosystems, 184, 220–221

Europe, 155, 158, 212

evidenced-based learning, 61

G

Gilbert
Christine Gilbert, 18–19, 70, 181

global networking, 249

Glow, 277, 280, 283

grassroots, 12, 20, 72, 155, 164, 224, 241, 277–279, 282–284

H

Handscomb
Graham Handscomb, 18–19, 184, 221–223, 243, 284, 304

Hargreaves
David Hargreaves, 34, 185

Harvard Business School, 174

Hattie
John Hattie, 91, 98, 292

Hopkins
David Hopkins, 28–30, 34, 37, 97, 240

I

ICEE
International Centre for Educational Enhancement, 96, 103, 106

ICSEI
International Congress for School Effectiveness and Improvement, 37

improvement, 17, 253, 293, 303, 323, 329

initial teacher education, 204, 208

information technology (IT), 113

Inked Scholar, 265, 269, 274

instructional core, 104–105

instructional rounds, 101, 107

intersubjectivity, 250, 254

J

Jackson

David Jackson, 239, 278

joint practice development, 78, 179–180, 184, 189

K

Krutka

Daniel Krutka, 195, 282

Kunskapsskolan, 9, 103–104, 106

L

Laboratory Schools, 92, 106

LATIN learning, 310–312

leadership, 20, 23, 32, 34, 36–39, 44, 63, 75, 77, 81, 83, 112, 128, 144, 151, 162, 176, 181, 183, 188, 224–227, 234, 243, 250, 253, 257, 260, 305, 310, 327–329

learning ecosystem, 220

lockdown, 59, 64–65, 71

M

MATs

multi-academy trusts, 31, 96, 103, 169, 187, 189

mentoring, 172, 174–176, 293

music, 193–199

mutuality, 18

N

NCSL

National College for School Leadership, 35

networks, 27–28

network facilitators, 75–77, 328

networking, 9, 17, 20–22, 27–30, 34, 38–41, 69–70, 75, 79, 93, 103, 119, 160, 169, 171–174, 188, 203, 248, 250, 292, 306, 312, 314, 317–318, 328

networking principles, 78–80

NLCs

Network Learning Communities, 35

NLS

Networked Learning System, 243

O

OECD, 22, 28–29, 43, 50–56

Ofsted, 33, 70, 105, 185, 215, 272, 304, 306

online networks, 200, 251, 263, 278

P

pandemic, 21–23, 44, 56, 60, 64–67, 69, 75–77, 81–84, 91–92, 95, 100, 112–114, 124, 151, 160, 169–172, 175, 188, 195, 203–206, 209, 214, 215, 222, 229, 241, 250, 255, 261, 267, 273, 280, 283, 289, 293, 296, 305, 312, 315, 318, 321

partnerships, 27, 33, 63, 67–71, 78, 108, 180, 226, 317, 322

peer review, 20, 59–71, 78, 96, 131, 180, 185–187

personalisation, 22, 96, 103, 121

personal learning spaces, 111, 118

PISA, 29, 33–34, 36

policy, 28–35, 40, 44, 79, 95–97, 114, 193, 204, 226, 238, 260, 266, 280, 294, 310

problem solving, 54, 65, 92, 225

professional development and learning, 20, 277–279, 282, 284–286

professional identity, 121, 203, 207–210, 216, 237, 257, 269, 294, 296

professional knowledge, 17, 36, 116, 207

professional learning networks, 19–22, 28, 40, 54, 180–182, 187, 194, 200, 206, 213, 220, 223–224, 228, 278, 284, 292, 296, 327

professionalism, 22, 33, 47, 55, 100, 208, 282, 292, 294–297

Q

quality control, 284

R

ResearchEd, 197

resilience, 60, 64, 86, 92, 175, 311

rural schools, 75–79, 81, 234, 236

S

SAIL schools, 103–105

Schleicher
    Andreas Schleicher, 29, 45

school climate, 44, 46–47

schooling, 39, 41, 78, 96, 100, 130, 280, 319

school to school support, 63, 180

Scotland, 233–247, 277–288

self-efficacy, 18, 22, 43, 175, 240

self-review, 62

SIAMS inspection, 82

SISS
    self-improving school-led system, 31–33

small schools, 78–79

specialist leaders of education, 31

SPP
    Schools partnership programme, 61–64, 71

student learning, 30, 36, 39, 44–45, 121, 123, 221

student voice, 303–313

subject knowledge, 183, 214, 265, 268, 270–274

Sweden, 99, 103–105

system reform, 27

systemic change, 164

T

TALIS, 43, 50–56

teaching and learning, 32, 39, 43, 97–98

teacher agency, 66, 282, 295

teacher identity, 22, 203, 207–211, 216–216, 266

teacher job satisfaction, 274

teacher mentor, 115

teacher-led networks, 197

teacher-led professional development, 278

teacher motivation, 53

teacher research, 22, 204, 289, 292

teacher retention, 55

teacher social capital, 234, 236

Teaching school alliance, 31, 81

teaching domains, 94

Temperley
    Julie Temperley, 35–37

Theatre in Education, 203–207, 212, 216–216

top down verses bottom up approaches, 18–21

trainee teachers, 113–114, 208

TRGs

teacher research groups, 289, 296–297

U

unconcious bias, 163

Unleashing Greatness, 37, 39, 96–99, 101

V

virtual communities, 266

virtual staffroom, 265, 269

vulnerable students, 219–231

W

wellbeing, 18, 22

Wenger
    Étienne Wenger, 233–238, 241, 269, 278, 292–293

WomenEd, 151–165

Y

YouTube, 22, 162, 265, 269, 270–271